Economies and Cultures

Economies and Cultures

Foundations of
Economic Anthropology

Richard R. Wilk
Indiana University

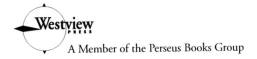

A Member of the Perseus Books Group

For Bob

Illustrations courtesy of William F. Pyburn

Published in 1996 in the United States of America by Westview Press, 5500 Central Avenue, Boulder, Colorado 80301-2877, and in the United Kingdom by Westview Press, 12 Hid's Copse Road, Cumnor Hill, Oxford OX2 9JJ.

Library of Congress Cataloging-in-Publication Data
Wilk, Richard R.
  Economies and cultures : foundations of economic anthropology /
Richard R. Wilk.
    p. cm.
  Includes bibliographical references and index.
  ISBN 0-8133-2059-3 (hc) —ISBN 0-8133-2058-5 (pb)
  1. Economic anthropology. I. Title.
GN448.W55 1996
306.3—dc20   96-30367
                                                  CIP

Printed and bound in Great Britain by
Marston Book Services Limited, Oxford

20 19 18 17 16 15 14 13

Contents

Illustrations and Figures

Illustrations

Figures

Preface: Becoming
an Economic Anthropologist

When I began graduate school at the University of Arizona in 1974, I was set on becoming an archaeologist, and my major goal in life was to run my own excavation of an ancient Mayan city. But the graduate adviser at Arizona thought that my training was much too narrow; as an undergraduate at New York University I had taken many archaeology and physical anthropology courses but had managed to evade almost all cultural anthropology and linguistics. Arizona emphasized balanced training in all four fields of anthropology, so my first two years of graduate school were devoted almost entirely to making up for my deficiencies, starting me down a path from which I never returned.

I was fortunate to have some excellent and inspired teachers who gradually seduced me away from my romance with the ancient Maya. Eventually, I got over my fear of cultural anthropology, and in my third year I dared to take a notoriously difficult seminar with Robert Netting on cultural ecology. The course drew me in and involved me in a study of household organization, population pressure, and economic change that eventually turned into a dissertation topic and resulted in a year and one-half of fieldwork with Kekchi Maya communities in Belize (a country in Central America) and the start of a career.

Three years later, I was still looking for a permanent job teaching anthropology and was sitting in a hotel room facing a hostile group of professors, who had already interviewed a couple of dozen candidates that day. They were tired and made no effort to be nice; the first question was, "So what kind of anthropologist are you? How do you label yourself?"

I don't *like* to label myself. I felt that my real strength as a scholar was just that I didn't fit into any category and did all kinds of different work—but I needed the job, so I gave it a try. I groped for the right mixture of telling the truth and fitting the job description: "I guess I'm kind of a cultural ecologist," I said. "I'm interested in kinship and social organization and also economic development. I've started to do some applied work on agriculture and livestock, and I'm still doing some ethnoarchaeology." Their faces were falling, and I started to tell them about my interests in ideology and the politics of the past, but the eldest and grayest of the group cut me right off. "Oh, I see," he said, putting my application on a large and messy pile on the table and, starting to rise toward the door for the next candidate, "You're really an economic anthropologist."

I went away feeling like I been accused of some kind of deviant behavior, labeled and stereotyped and thrown onto the reject pile. And I blamed myself for not playing it the right way, since even though I had told the truth about my interests, I knew I was *not* an economic anthropologist. In graduate school I had taken a course called "Economic Anthropology," and I hadn't liked it very much. The text used was Harold Schneider's *Economic Man.* The first half of the course was an accelerated version of "Economics 101," and the rest of the semester was spent in endless arguments about what the economy was and whether people in other cultures could be studied using economic tools and concepts. Some of those arguments were interesting, but they no longer excited many anthropologists by the time I took the course.

As it was presented to me in the 1970s, economic anthropology revolved around a debate over the essential nature of human beings: Are they rational maximizers, cold calculators who build cultures as tools to satisfy their material needs and desires? Or are people guided by their cultural values, seeking moral goodness and the kinship of others instead of direct material gain? I could see what people were arguing over, but it was not a debate I could get passionate about. Both positions seemed limited and partial, as if they were answers to the wrong question. And other anthropologists seemed to think so too, since the debates had mostly fizzled out and cultural anthropology was moving in other directions, leaving economic anthropology behind. Or so I thought.

My views didn't start to change for some time after the interview in which I was accused of "really" being an economic anthropologist. By that time I had also acquired a label as an "applied anthropologist," having spent a year consulting for a government agency on development projects in Belize. Then, unexpectedly, I was invited to give a poster presentation in 1983 on my research on Kekchi household organization at a meeting of the Society for Economic Anthropology (SEA), a small group that had formed in 1981, mostly through the efforts of Harold Schneider. And at those meetings in Iowa City, I began to think that maybe I *was* an economic anthropologist after all. What I found in the SEA were people who shared most of my eclectic interests—the pursuit of a freewheeling and open-minded mixture of archaeology and cultural anthropology, applied anthropology, and "pure" theory, thoroughly engaged with the real problems of today's world. They brought the different parts of anthropology together instead of dividing them or tearing them apart. There was real debate and engagement with the issues of modern anthropology, but people were civil with each other and seemed more interested in solving problems and explaining things than in putting each other down or showing off how sophisticated they were. There seemed to be room in this group for someone like me, someone interested in people because they are both rational *and* cultural, because they pursue both money *and* morality.

At about that time, my own research was moving away from agricultural change and more toward issues of consumption. I was becoming more interested in why people want things than in how they make them. In my research I had seen that social changes were often driven along by a rising "standard of living"; people's tastes changed, and what were once luxuries became necessities. Few anthropologists were studying these issues—and almost all of them were economic anthropologists. I gradually became more comfortable with the label, even though I had never taught a course on the subject. This was soon to change.

Harold Schneider, who had done so much to establish economic anthropology as a coherent field, to give it an identity, and to build its theory, died unexpectedly and prematurely in 1987. I was fortunate to be hired to fill the vacancy he left at Indiana University, where I quickly found myself institutionalized as "the economic anthropologist" on campus, advising his students and teaching his classes.[1] I felt like an impostor for quite a while, as I waited for someone to discover that I was not a *real* economic anthropologist. What got me over that feeling was the experience of teaching economic anthropology for the first time. I found it exciting and challenging, and a series of extremely bright and critical groups of students have driven me to think through and reexamine many issues that had confused or bored me when I took economic anthropology myself as a graduate student. And the course I teach today bears almost no relationship to what I was taught in 1975. This is partially because so much more research has been done since then—there are so many new books and resources. But the course is also different because the whole definition of economic anthropology has changed in twenty years; today the field is broader, more diffuse, less dogmatic, more creative and eclectic, perhaps less confident, but much more engaged with the problems of the world.

The Aims and Scope of This Book

The actual number of people who call themselves economic anthropologists has not grown very much in the last decade (the Society for Economic Anthropology counts only about four hundred members). But if we define economic anthropology broadly (more on this later), there has been tremendous growth in the number of people *doing* economic anthropology. Applied anthropology—in academia, business, government, and development—has grown enormously, and much of this is really applied economic anthropology. Anthropology has stopped hiding its head in the world of the "primitive," in isolated villages and marginal tribes, and has cast its eye upon every institution and crevasse of modern life, from gold mining in central Brazil to prostitution in Los Angeles. And since so much of what ties the modern world together is economic activity, a lot of this recent boom in ethnography is also economic anthropology, even if the authors don't identify themselves as belonging to the tribe. The past ten years have seen a wonderful flowering of topics that were once neglected or ignored; from the anthropology of the workplace to the anthropology of space colonies and possible alien cultures. Anthropology is rising to the challenge of global and regional cultural and economic integration, addressing issues that range from free trade and political struggles for ethnic territory to the spread of Hollywood films and satellite television to every tiny village and backwater on the planet.

Other trends in academia during the past twenty years have also expanded the scope of economic anthropology. These include the growth of interdisciplinary, multidisciplinary, and "crossover" studies. Once upon a time, we anthropologists seemed to spend a great deal of our time building fences to separate our discipline from others—finding all the ways that anthropologists were *not* economists or psychologists or (perish the thought!) sociologists. We don't seem to put so much energy into this any more. In fact, faced with the tremendous complexity of the modern world and the increasingly specialized technical skills and knowledge of other disciplines, we often find good reasons to interact with researchers who are interested in the same issues and topics but who were trained in another field. Anthropologists cross a lot of disciplinary boundaries these days and often find themselves welcomed in territory they once thought was hostile. In the last few years I have been to conferences in consumer research, cultural studies, history, development studies, political science, and law. Despite language differences, I have come back with a great deal that has enriched my anthropological work.

The softening of disciplinary boundaries has led to the emergence of a whole series of "halfway" subdisciplines that are meant to combine the strengths of two or more disciplines to focus on common issues or on problems that do not fit neatly into the nineteenth century intellectual landscape provided by conventional fields of study. These include gender studies, human ecology, economic philosophy, ethnohistory, socioeconomics, political economy, ethnoarchaeology, and sociobiology, among many others. Geographical area studies are another place where scholars from many disciplines come together and broaden each others' perspectives and knowledge.

The result of all this boundary breaking is sometimes frightening or at least exhausting. There is so much to read, and so much to know just in anthropology that the idea of reading in all these other disciplines sometimes seems too great a burden. On my own campus, I follow my economic interests through affiliations and seminars in cultural studies, women's studies, the population institute, workshops in political theory and economic history, economics, African studies, Latin American studies, comparative literature, journalism, media studies, and a host of other areas.

For a textbook like this, the state of the field presents both marvelous opportunities and difficult choices. Many new and exciting publications provide wonderful sources and examples to use in a textbook. Economic anthropology has expanded in many directions, providing an abundance of material and ideas on almost every conceivable topic.

This abundance and diversity is like the Central American rain forest where I did my field research. It is rich and sustaining, offering almost everything needed for life. But it can also be confusing and dense, and it is easy to lose your bearings and get lost. The riotous flowering of economic anthropology provides a real challenge for the gardening author who wants to fit everything into a small and digestible package.

This diversity proves to be a problem every time I teach economic anthropology. How do I choose what belongs in a short semester, and how do I tell what is "really" economic anthropology? When I asked colleagues what topics belong in an economic anthropology textbook, everyone gave me a different list of "essentials" and suggested a different group of important case studies, and I agreed with all of their recommendations! But if I followed all their suggestions, I would have years of reading and would then write twenty chapters and five hundred pages.

The alternative to writing such an encyclopedia of economic anthropology is to search, instead, for the core of the discipline, for the threads that tie all the diverse elements together. Instead of trying to cover all the possible topics that can be included in economic anthropology, I have designed this book as a "core" reading, a source to be used with supplemental readings, books, and ethnographies. The goal of this book is to focus on the problems and ideas—the shared history of ideas—that makes economic anthropology a distinct subfield. I expect that readers will end up taking their own direction from this starting place, and I hope to provide a kind of theoretical guidebook that will help them along their own particular journeys. In the last chapter, I suggest some of the important and intriguing areas that are now of most interest to practicing economic anthropologists, and the Appendix includes a list of monographs and ethnographies in economic anthropology that my own students have found useful in finding supplementary readings relevant to their interests. In each chapter, there are also suggestions for further reading on the topics I cover, as well as many references to current research.

A good deal of the current work I refer to is *applied* anthropology. I point readers in this direction because I believe strongly that the proof of the pudding is in the eating; the best test of good ideas is to put them to practical use in the world and see if they work. A lot of the most exciting and intellectually important economic anthropology these days is explicitly applied, and many of the best economic anthropologists have enthusiastically stepped out of the staid halls of universities into the "trenches," where they put ideas into action. I also use applied examples because of my own moral commitment to anthropology as a discipline that can make a positive difference in the world, that can help to solve some of the serious problems that plague so many. That was what originally drew me to anthropology back in the idealistic 1960s!

Why Go Back over Old Ground?

Every generation of students seems to reinvent anthropology, rejecting the work of previous generations and forging a new set of goals. I remember, as a graduate student, feeling weighed down by all the intellectual baggage of anthropological history and theory. I hated beginning each course with what I felt was a dry recitation of ancient ideas, what one of my teachers used to call an "ode to the ancestors." But here I am, writing a book based mostly on the writings of long-dead philosophers. What happened?

Simply put, I began to realize that many of the problems I was having defining economic anthropology, trying to find the common threads and the deep controversies that give the field an identity, required reevaluating the roots of the enterprise. Weak foundations make for shaky houses. A lot of current confusion has its origin in old and unsettled problems; as the field changes, we need to constantly rethink our assumptions, most of which are passed down consciously or unconsciously from previous generations (or adopted from current popular culture—but that is another story). My solution has been to reorganize and rethink the past debates along new lines that are suited to the anthropology of the 1990s.

This recasting of old debates is particularly important, I believe, at this time. Economic anthropology was forged and acquired an identity in a setting where the fundamental issues in anthropology centered around a split between *mentalist* and *materialist* theories of human behavior. One side cast humanity as a tool-using animal and perceived of culture as a means of adaptation; the other saw humans as symbol-using creatures and viewed culture as a means of expression and a system of meaning. For much of the past forty years, anthropologists have tended to line up on one side or the other. Economic anthropology was firmly established within the materialist camp, but even economic anthropologists were divided, with some focused more on the economy as material and rational and others interested in the social and spiritual aspects of economic behavior.

But now a good deal of anthropology is moving onward from this discussion and is trying to find middle ground. Of course, some people want to continue arguing one extreme or the other, but the really exciting topical and theoretical trends in anthropology these days seem to have shifted to territory that is more complex and interesting.[2] Most economic anthropologists can no longer be easily classified as mentalists or materialists and seem quite willing to accept the importance of *both* thoughts and actions, symbols and tools, rituals and systems of land tenure. Even economists themselves seem less sure of their materialism; many have broken away to form the Society for the Advancement of Socioeconomics, the International Association for Feminist Economics, and a host of other diverse organizations that tend to be more friendly to an anthropological approach. In 1993, a Nobel Prize in economics was awarded to an economic historian (Douglass North), whose major interest is social institutions.

There is still a good deal of controversy and debate in economic anthropology. As discussed in Chapter 1, economic anthropologists continue their essential and deep-seated disagreement about human nature and motivation, which affects their choices of what to study, how to do research, and what kinds of solutions are possible to human problems. I find that most arguments can be lumped into three groups, depending on whether economic anthropologists see human beings as essentially social, moral, or self-interested beings. After reviewing the history of economic anthropology, I find the same tripartite scheme makes good sense of the arguments and debates that shaped the discipline. I will show how different assumptions about human nature have led to diverging (and often mutually hostile) models of "the economy." I use this as a vehicle for writing a partial intellectual history of economic anthropology (and its relationship with economics) that concentrates on content instead of personalities.

Finally, this historical approach provides something that I have been unable to find in any article, speech, book, or ethnography, something my students beg for and my colleagues argue about—and that is a clear and concise definition of economic anthropology. There is no simple, one-line definition of the field that distinguishes economic anthropology from all other kinds of anthropology or social science. The field is too diverse, and it overlaps too many other groups and disciplines. This book defines economic anthropology as the part of the discipline that debates issues of *human nature* that relate directly to the decisions of daily life and making a living. The important thing to remember is that economic anthropology is not limited or defined by boundaries or by a list of topics or ancestors. It is instead an enterprise held together by *disagreements* and often passionate debate about how we explain human behavior.

Acknowledgments

There are so many individuals who have knowingly or unknowingly, directly or indirectly, contributed to this book, that I cannot thank even a fraction of them. Dean Birkenkamp at Westview Press provided an initial impetus and much thoughtful feedback during the process. Anne Pyburn, my wife, friend, and colleague, discussed every single concept and decision with me as I went along, provided many important ideas and insights, and supported me emotionally and financially during the unpaid semester that I took in order to get the writing done. I no longer really know where her ideas stop and my own begin.

I owe a tremendous debt, also, to the many people who have taught me practical lessons about the economy and about economic anthropology. I have found great masters and teachers in many places, from markets in Ghana to the villages of Belize. The members of the Society for Economic Anthropology provided me with a sense of intellectual belonging, and many have contributed substantially to my understanding of the field, especially James Acheson, Bob Hunt, and Peggy Barlett.

Karen Kessel was an able graduate assistant and helped me with some of the research for two chapters of this book. After I finished a first draft in fall 1994, I used it as a text in teaching my economic anthropology class at Indiana University (E420). The twenty-one graduate and undergraduate members of that class started out as guinea pigs but ended as colleagues and collaborators. They made a huge contribution to shaping the final version of the book you now hold in your hands. They each wrote frank and detailed comments and critiques of every chapter, and as smart students always do, they found every weakness and made many good suggestions. Their research and reading during the semester has enriched this text in many ways. They were the toughest editorial board I have ever worked with and deserve credit as coauthors of many sections of the book. The class members were Aixa Ansorena, Nathalie Arnold, Elizabeth Babcock, Melissa Bauer, Emily Brouwer, Geoff Childs, Eileen Cooper, Fabio De Castro, Gary Garufi, Stacey Hann, Karen Jewell, Karen Korn, Adam Krugel, Alisa MacNeille, Kevin Meskill, Krista Miller, Mary Pirkl, Toddy Reid, Jason Sabo, Mike Strezewski, and Julie Zimmer. Drafts of the manuscript and proposals for the book were also read by several anonymous reviewers, all of whom provided insightful comments and suggestions that were extremely useful in making revisions.

The single most important person in my intellectual life, and the friend who guided me from uncertain studenthood into being a professional anthropologist, was Robert M. Netting. He provided a model of intellectual integrity, and he showed me over and over again how anthropology can make a difference in the world. More important, he never lost his sense of humor or his kindness and grace, and he never stopped caring about the people he wrote about.

In fall 1994, Bob Netting read the first draft of this book and wrote his typically meticulous and funny comments in the margins. We talked over some of the chapters, and we were going to get to the rest, when he was suddenly diagnosed with cancer. At the end of two months, like snow falling on water, he was gone. This book is dedicated to his memory and his legacy.

Richard R. Wilk

Notes

1. Although I never met Schneider, he still has a kind of ghostly presence at Indiana University. As I have developed my own courses and theories and have worked with my own students, I often wonder what he would have thought. From his writing, I can be pretty sure he would have violently disagreed with most of what comes out of my mouth and would have been appalled that I was his successor at Indiana. Nevertheless, this book has benefited a great deal from a kind of "silent dialogue" with his ghost.

2. I think a great deal of the impetus to move anthropology beyond a preoccupation with mentalism and materialism has come from the gradual digestion of the ideas of theoreticians like Pierre Bourdieu, Michel Foucault, Maurice Godelier, and Mary Douglas. But an equally important source has been the practical, no-nonsense kind of analysis of social and economic problems pioneered by people like Audrey Richards and Polly Hill, which treats theory as a tool rather than as an end in itself.

1 ⁓

Economic Anthropology: An Undisciplined Discipline

We do not see things the way they are; we see them the way *we* are.

—Chinese fortune cookie found by David Pilbeam,
cited by Roger Lewin, *Bones of Contention*

Science is built up of facts, as a house is built of stones; but an accumulation of facts is no more a science than a heap of stones is a house.

—Jules Henri Poincaré, *Science and Hypothesis*

Controversy and Social Science

Textbooks often present anthropology as a cumulative collaboration, as a complete whole that has sprung from its history as naturally as apples falling from trees. Most professional social scientists know that this is not how things work at all. Anthropology, like the other social sciences, is in a state of constant change and fermentation, and our definitions of relevant facts, our preoccupations, and our questions and answers change all the time.

If that is so, why do we present our field in such a static way in our textbooks? I suspect it is partially out of fear of losing credibility and authority. Students might drop our classes if we admitted how provisional our knowledge is, how contentious the divisions and differences between us, how changeable "the facts" are from generation to generation. Students, we think,

Academic Strife

want facts and truth, not challenges, contention, and the soft, shifting ground of advanced theory.

When we simplify our field in textbooks, we may also be acting with the normal shortsightedness of the present moment, with the idea that what we know now is so much better than what we used to know that it will surely last, instead of being overturned by the next generation. And we textbook writers may also be acting as gatekeepers—keeping the behind-the-scenes action secret, as a way of keeping the tribe together and excluding outsiders. Becoming an anthropologist means learning the sacred history, the names, factions, and fights.

At this particular time in anthropology, issues of relativism, objectivity, and authority are the center of attention, often presented under the banner of "postmodernism." Is anthropology just another way that the Western societies impose their worldview on other people? Is objectivity an outmoded and dangerous concept? At one relativist extreme, *all* knowledge is relative and provisional, and science is just another culture-bound worldview. Some of my more relativist colleagues who take this position no longer believe textbooks are useful, relevant, or practical. Texts, they think, just organize the current culture-bound point of view and make it *seem* authoritative.

I don't agree. I recognize that science, especially social science, is a political and social construction and that, as the fortune-cookie wisdom cited above says, social science often tells us as much about our own society as it tells us about the world. Anthropologists have criticized themselves and each other a lot lately for serving colonialism, for imposing their own cultural and gender categories on others, and for a host of other sins.[1] But I am not willing to throw the baby out with the bathwater and abandon any idea of empirical knowledge or scientific progress just because we find the quest to be imperfect or tainted with politics. Social science is always a mixture of objective and subjective, of ideology and truth, a blend of both power and knowledge. In practice, the two kinds of work depend on each other; without political and cultural context, knowledge is just a useless collection of unrelated and boring facts (Poincaré's pile of stones). But without empirical facts as a check and reference, the political or cultural discourse goes nowhere and remains just rhetoric.

If objective and subjective are two parts of a whole, there can really be no justification for presenting them in isolation when we teach anthropology. The debates, arguments, factions, and fights are the context that give meaning to "the facts." Controversy is not an aberration in science; it is the substance of it. And economic anthropology is a good example, since the field emerged only through debate and often heated disagreement, the polite academic equivalent of a barroom brawl. If the fight between formalists and substantivists had never broken out, economic anthropology would barely exist on the academic map.

Hindsight gives us the luxury of looking back on a fight and judging all the moves. This can be an exercise in arrogance if the only goal is to feel superior to the players. Here, instead, our objective is to build on and move beyond the debate and to make sure we do not repeat the same errors. If the formalist-substantivist debate was the defining moment of economic anthropology, and the ending of the debate caused something of an identity crisis. Revitalizing the discipline means finding the elements of this debate that are worth carrying forward to another level and onward to a new generation of scholarship.

The Formalist-Substantivist Debate

In later chapters I will delve into the early history of economic anthropology and economic philosophy. Here, we will start in the 1960s, with the goal of showing how the *formalist-substantivist debate*, once the centerpiece of economic anthropology, has now become an obstacle instead of an inspiration.

The field needs to move beyond the debate and ask more sophisticated questions. But before we move onward, we have to be clear on what was being debated, what was at stake, and why the arguments petered out instead of continuing to generate excitement and new research.

Up until the 1950s, economic anthropology was primarily descriptive, couched in a generally social-structural theoretical framework that concentrated on finding out how each culture made a living. Economic anthropologists argued with economists because they saw them as being ethnocentric and narrow, ignorant of the importance of culture in shaping economic behavior. They thought economists should pay more attention to anthropology and to the diversity of economic systems in the world.

Economists, in the meantime, mostly ignored anthropology and went on with the business of advising politicians on how to run the world economy. But then some turncoat economists started to attack the discipline from within, using arguments very similar to those of anthropology. For a time, economists and economic anthropologists engaged in real debate, and economic anthropologists wrote about almost nothing besides their relationship with the larger and more powerful discipline. Other anthropologists paid close attention, and for the first time, the discipline as a whole listened to economic anthropologists.

Like most academic quarrels, the formalist-substantivist debate was sometimes personal and political; it built some careers and tore down others.[2] Some anthropologists are still well known to their colleagues only because of their role in it. Most important, the struggle created a common community. Many anthropologists have seen how exchange and gift giving can create community and interpersonal relationships. Paradoxically, fighting and conflict can often lead to the same end; opponents and enemies are locked together as surely and often as closely as friends and allies. Economic anthropology as a subdiscipline was at least partially created by the formalist-substantivist debate; to this day, this is the part of economic anthropology that most other anthropologists, economists, and sociologists know about, the part that appears in introductory anthropology textbooks.

Some indication of how dramatic this event was for the field can be found in H. T. Van Der Pas's bibliography of economic anthropology, which was published just as the debate was ending in 1973. From 1940–1950, an average of only four major articles and books were published in economic anthropology per year in the whole world! (Of course at that time much less anthropology was published than today.) From 1951 to 1956, the average went up to only ten per year. But in 1957, with the publication of Karl Polanyi's *Trade and Market in the Early Empires,* the debate started, and the number jumped to twenty-seven. As Figure 1.1 shows, the number continued to rise, though after 1971 most publications were no longer concerned with the formalist-substantivist debate. The peak year was 1964, with fifty-five publications.

The Opening Battles

The first rumblings of the formalist-substantivist debate can be heard in Bronislaw Malinowski's critique of Western economics in his studies of the economy of the Trobriand Islands, off the east coast of New Guinea. The ongoing debate over whether Western economic tools can be used for the study of "primitive" economies was renewed, with more force, during a published exchange between the anthropologist Melville Herskovitz and the economist Frank Knight in 1941.[3] Half a century later, it is clear that both parties had some valid points; the anthropologist said that other cultures need to be understood on their own terms, and the economist argued that we need to build general models of all human behavior in all cultures. It is equally clear that neither party understood the other's science, assumptions, or language and that they were mostly arguing past each other, from a sense of deep conviction that their's was the only right way. One also detects that the participants took a certain pleasure in the combat, like rams butting heads during the rutting season. The rest of the formalist-substantivist debate was carried out in much the same combative and righteous spirit.

The fundamental positions within the formalist-substantivist debate were already established, then, by the early 1950s. They are a variation on a much older debate about the differences among human groups. A *relativist* argues that cultures are so different from one another, especially primitives from moderns, that they cannot be understood with the tools of Western science, tools that are fundamentally modern. A *universalist* says, on the contrary, that all human experience is fundamentally the same and can be understood using

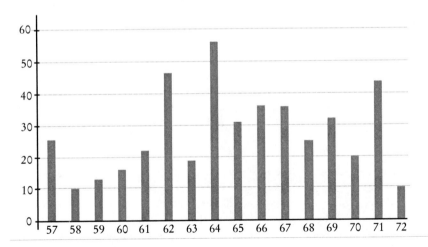

FIGURE 1.1 Publications in Economic Anthropology

objective tools that are universal. To the universalist, science is not bound by a single culture and therefore can make general comparative statements.

Here we have a classic *reflexive* debate; we argue about the nature of the "other," about how to understand different cultures, but we are also reflecting on our own "modern," "Western" science. In the process of defining the mysterious other, we define ourselves. For some of the combatants in the debate, the goal is to learn about the "real" nature of other societies. But for many, the more powerful and emotional issues are their own culture, work, and identities. The reflexive stakes are high; who will define that most powerful idea, *science*? Who will have the authority to speak about the world and guide policy? And at a philosophical and moral level, how much can we empathize and share with people from whom we are separated by language, distance, culture, and even time? How universal is human experience? The only way to understand the passion and conviction raised by the formalist-substantivist debate is to see behind it to the reflexive, political, and moral issues it raised.

The Substantive Position

Karl Polanyi was an economic historian, whose book *The Great Transformation*, published in 1944, traced the development of modern market capitalism from earlier systems, with great nostalgia for the past. He predicted the imminent "breakdown of our civilization" (1944, 3–5). In his view, modern capitalism had elevated profits and the market over society and human values, turning everything into a commodity to be bought and sold. He thought that economics developed along with market capitalism as its servant and is merely a part of the system that helps keep capitalism going by making it seem natural.[4]

In his later work, Polanyi went further back in time to look at earlier empires to try to understand other ways, besides market capitalism, that civilizations had built their economies. When this work was published along with other studies of nonmarket systems in an edited volume called *Trade and Market in the Early Empires* in 1957, anthropologists had to pay attention. Here was a group of economists and historians challenging the economic establishment from what sounded like an inherently anthropological point of view.

One of Polanyi's papers in *Trade and Market,* entitled "The Economy as Instituted Process," defined two meanings of the word "economic": *formal,* meaning the study of rational decisionmaking, and *substantive,* meaning the material acts of making a living. Polanyi then said that only in the historical development of the modern West have the two come to have the same meaning, for only in modern capitalism is the economic system (substantive) fused with rational economic logic (formal) that maximizes individual self-interest. Only capitalism institutionalizes formal principles in this way, through the medium of the marketplace and the flow of money. In precapitalist cultures, all kinds of economic activities take place, but not within the framework and values of formal rational economic logic, the characteristics of the competitive marketplace.

In modern capitalism, Polanyi said, the economy is *embedded* (in the sense of "submerged in," or "part of") in the institution of the marketplace. In the economic systems of other cultures, however, the economy is embedded in other social institutions and operates on different principles from the market. In some cultures the economy may be part of kinship relations, whereas in other places religious institutions may organize the economy. Other economies, Polanyi observed, are not built on the market and are therefore not built on the logic of choice. Without markets, formal economics has no meaning. To study these other societies we need other principles, and these will depend on how the substantive economy of making a living is organized in each place. Polanyi concluded that economics should therefore seek to find out how the economy is embedded in the matrix of different societies. This "substantivist" economics should look first at nonmarket economic institutions (for example, temples and tribute), and second, at the processes that hold the social and the economic together in different settings. Polanyi's followers in economics came to be called "institutionalists" for this reason.

Polanyi suggested, through his historical and cross-cultural studies, that there are three major ways that societies integrate the economy into society—modern formal economics only studies the third and is unable to comprehend the first two, because they have different logics. The types are *reciprocity, redistribution,* and *exchange.* Reciprocity is a general kind of helping and sharing based on a mutual sense of obligation and identity. People help each other because they have cultural and social relationships; they belong to the same family or clan. Redistribution is a system with a central authority of some sort, a priest, temple, or chief who collects from everyone and redistributes different things back. For example, some people give grain to the temple and receive cloth in return, whereas others give cloth and receive grain, while the temple uses some of both for rituals and to maintain the temple for the greater good. Exchange is calculated trade, which comes in several varieties, according to Polanyi. Modern market exchange using money and bargaining to set prices is a very special case that only recently became central to the European economy. Polanyi thought that different combinations of these three kinds of economic logic were found in all societies, but in each society one of them was dominant.

This substantivist model is profoundly relativist; it says that the economy is based on entirely different logical principles in different societies. Therefore, the tools for understanding capitalism are as useless for studying the ancient Aztecs as a flint knife would be for fixing a jet engine. Each system has to be understood on its own terms. And Polanyi's substantivism leaps instantly from relativism to evolutionism. He is not simply defining types but is showing how those types form a historical series in which one develops into another, implying that reciprocity is the simplest and exchange the most complex.

Like most cultural evolutionary models, Polanyi's can be used to order all societies from the simple ("primitive") to the complex ("modern") and depicts modern society as a radical break from the past.[5] In other societies that preceded capitalism, money, and markets, people did not always make choices, nor did they act out of self-interest. They had no "motive to gain." Because people make moral or social choices, the formal modern economics, which is based on unlimited wants and scarce means, cannot apply. And because of their environments and low technology, primitive people really don't have many choices to make.

> A Trobriand Islander learns and follows the rules of *economy* in his society almost like an American learns and follows the rules of *language* in his. . . . In primitive economies, the constraints on individual choice of material goods and economic activities are extreme, and are dictated not only by social obligation but also by primitive technology and by physical environment. There is simply no equivalent to the range of choices of goods and activities in industrial capitalism which makes meaningful such economic concepts as "maximizing" and "economizing." (Dalton 1969, 67)

In other words, "primitive" people follow customs and social rules, and when they do make choices, they are rarely thinking about immediate self-interest. In the balance, the most prominent substantivists like Polanyi and the economist-turned-anthropologist George Dalton, tend toward what can be called *social economics.* They are interested in economic *institutions,* the social groups that carry out production, exchange, and consumption, and they assume that people generally follow the rules of these institutions. Polanyi and Dalton's human beings are conformists. Social systems therefore change because of their large-scale dynamics, not through individual behavior, decisions, strategies, or choices. Their unit of analysis is the society as a whole, not the individual or family.

In fact, there is also not much room for what anthropologists call "culture" in Polanyi's substantivism. Everything is social structure, groups, and institutions rather than systems of symbols, meaning, or customs. Nevertheless, many anthropologists have found sweet music in substantivism, for it has offered their discipline an means of understanding past as well as future processes of development. George Dalton and Marshall Sahlins were early voices for substantivism in anthropology, with the former most interested in development and economic change (1971), and the latter writing on the classification and evolution of "stone-age" economies (1960, 1965, 1972).

The Formalists Strike Back

In the early 1960s, there was a powerful movement in social science promoting more rigorous and "scientific" theorizing and methods. Like their Enlightenment ancestors, many wanted to remodel anthropology and sociology to resemble something more like particle physics, with formal hypotheses (and null hypotheses), experiments, mathematical modeling, and universal laws that could predict future events. Fieldwork, it was felt, should be designed to test these laws, rather than to explore a particular case. For anthropologists with these goals, economics may have been imperfect, but it was a lot closer to science than the kinds of descriptive and unsystematic ramblings that they were used to in so many ethnographies. The substantivists seemed to be pushing things backward, not forward, threatening to shape economic anthropology into a descriptive field of the humanities like history instead of into a "modern" comparative, rule-generating science. (Archaeologist Kent Flannery would later taunt these anthropologists with being the "Gee Whiz, Mr. Science" school.)

There was also, at the same time, a brewing dissatisfaction among anthropologists with using the concept of *culture* to explain *everything*. What about the role of individuals? Focusing on politics and rapid cultural change, anthropologists like Frederik Barth were arguing that people did not simply follow the rules of their culture but, as individuals, took a hand in shaping it (1959, 1963, 1967). These anthropologists saw innovation, creativity, conflict, and logical reasoning instead of passive "sticking to tradition" when they went to the field.

It should therefore not be a surprise that in the years after Polanyi's manifesto, the substantivists came under a barrage of criticism and attack by anthropologists who adopted Polanyi's label and called themselves formalists. They wanted to look outside of anthropology for models of rational choice. Robbins Burling, Harold Schneider, Edward LeClair, Frank Cancian, and Scott Cook were prominent in the first wave of formalist reaction. Instead of detailing each contribution, I will aggregate their many propositions into a short list of points they mostly agreed upon.[6]

1. The substantivists got their microeconomics wrong; they do not understand that "maximizing" (as used by economists) does not require money or markets. Anything, like love or security, can be maximized.
2. The substantivists were romantics engaged in wishful thinking, not realists.

3. Formal methods work in noncapitalist societies because all societies have rational behavior, scarce ends and means. Formal tools may have to be adapted and improved but should not be discarded.
4. Substantivists are *inductive* butterfly collectors, who try to generalize from observation, instead of using *deduction* to explain each instance as an example of a general law of human behavior. Deduction is better.
5. Polanyi got his history wrong; markets, exchange, and trade are found in many early empires and "primitive" cultures. And anyway, most of the societies in the world are now involved in a cash economy, so substantivism is no longer relevant.

The formalists moved attention away from economic *institutions,* and their classification and evolution, toward economic *behavior,* specifically focusing on decisionmaking and choice. They made their case with a lot of clever argument and logical gymnastics, but they also set out to demonstrate that classic tools of economics could be useful in a series of case studies. They analyzed everything from marriage markets among Australian aborigines to the trade feasts of the Pomo in California. They expanded their range of formal analytical techniques into game theory, linear programming, and decision trees (see Plattner 1975 for examples). Unfortunately, their enthusiasm for formal tools was not always matched by their skills; some economists (Mayhew 1980) thought the formalists needed remedial economics classes in order to correct their terms and definitions!

The formalists certainly demonstrated that economics *could be* applied to noncapitalist economies. They wanted to demystify non-Western economic behavior, to show that people really are rational. This was a critical message to get across to government officials and policymakers, who had (and many still have) a tendency to dismiss the behavior of the poor or of ethnic minorities as "irrational," sunk in tradition, or just plain stupid. Formalists preached that there was reason and rationality behind a lot of behavior that seemed strange to outsiders; you just had to understand more about the environment people lived in so that you could see what their resources and constraints were. Then you would view their behavior as really quite logical and understandable, even by the strict rules of Western economics. The problem was not with Western economic science but with ignorance about the real circumstances that framed people's lives.

The formalists were also very successful in poking holes in Polanyi's historical classifications of economies, pointing out, for example, that market exchange was common in medieval Europe long before the Industrial Revolution (and that noncash relationships remain important in so-called modern economies). And many contemporary anthropologists, particularly those working on problems of development and social change, have freely adopted the formal analytical methods and ideas as part of their ethnographic work. But does this mean the formalists won the debate? Not really. Instead, after some substantivist counterattacks, the debate fizzled out. In 1973, Richard Salisbury declared it over and found only "postmortem spasms." It ended with a whimper instead of a bang because the parties were for the most part arguing past each other, and they avoided the most fundamental issues.

Postmortem

The strongest formalist proposition was that the economic rationality of the maximizing individual was to be found in all societies, in all kinds of behavior. The strongest substantivist position was that the economy is a type of human activity, embedded in different social institutions in different kinds of societies. If we look at these premises carefully, we see that *they are not mutually exclusive.* They do not negate each other; both could be true. Furthermore, both could be wrong, and they could be wrong in a much larger number of ways than either side recognizes. For example, there are many alternatives to the formalist rationality hypothesis, including these (some of which were pointed out by substantivists):

1. People are irrational or nonrational, and other kinds of rationality can be defined besides that based on maximizing.
2. Economic rationality is only found in some kinds of behavior or among certain social subgroups.
3. Economic rationality as defined by economists is meaningless, circular, or vague, because it can never be proven.
4. Economic rationality is only found in some kinds of societies.

Equally, there are many alternatives to the substantivist idea that the economy is always embedded in other social institutions:

1. The economy is an autonomous subsector of society—it is not embedded at all.
2. Society is embedded in the economy, not the other way around.
3. The economy is only partially embedded in social institutions.
4. The economy is embedded in every single society in a different way, so there are no "types."
5. The economy is not a sector of society or a type of behavior at all—it is instead pervasive in all human activity.

Thus, even on their main propositions, the two camps only considered a narrow range of options in challenging each other's basic positions. But how could formalists and substantivists fail to engage each other, when they were

trying so hard to do so? Part of the problem was their starting points; substantivists compared societies, whereas formalists compared individuals. The
substantivists argued down from social structure to individual behavior,
whereas the formalists worked up from individual choice to the dynamics of
economic systems as a whole. On one side, you can certainly contend that
society sets the rules of the game and that we really have few and limited
choices to make in our lives. On the other side, you can equally well assert
that society itself is created from the patterned actions and decisions of individuals, so that people themselves change society through their choices.

If we pay close attention, we see that the formalists and substantivists are
caught in the same intellectual dances that run very deeply in the Western
philosophical tradition from the time of the Enlightenment. These are questions about rationality, truth, reason, and progress. Do we learn truth from
observation of nature (Francis Bacon, 1561–1626) or from using our intellectual abilities to reason through logic (René Descartes, 1596–1650)? Does society advance through rational discovery and decisionmaking (Auguste
Comte, 1798–1857)?[7]

The modern scholars say they are arguing analytical anthropology, but
they are also taking classic philosophical positions about ontology (the nature of being), organized around polarities like *free will versus determinism,
rationalism versus romanticism,* and *selfishness versus altruism.* They are debating human nature! That is where their passion and anger comes from. But
they are starting from sets of assumptions about human nature rather than
testing those assumptions. And this is why the debate goes nowhere; it is the
academic version of an argument between a Buddhist and a Catholic about
the nature of God. Shouting ultimate beliefs at each other is not likely to
convince anyone to convert.

Despite these problems, there are still two reasons the formalist-substantivist debate continues to deserve some attention. The first reason is that the
debate itself resonates with themes that seem quite universal in human affairs. *Many* societies have debates about selfishness and altruism, about the
ability of individual humans to change their lives or society as a whole, and
about the relative merits of logical thought and intuitive understanding or
emotion. The formalist-substantivist debate touched some very deep, important, and universal human issues.

Second, during this debate, anthropologists finally began to ask wider
questions about social change and evolution and to ask how the economy re-
lates to other classic objects of anthropological study like kinship and ritual.
The debate raised important subsidiary questions outside the main arena,
and in the end these have had a more lasting impact on the field. The
sideshow included questions like these: Are humans always rational? How
can rationality be defined? How can you tell if someone is acting out of self-
interest? Is the difference between modern and primitive economies one of

degree or of kind? Are there universal laws applicable to all societies? And, is the economy always embedded in social structure?

The Winner?

Did anyone really win the debate? When I asked economists on a feminist economics E-mail discussion group (femecon-l), everyone who answered thought that the substantivists had won. I am not so sure. If we judge the winners to be the ones with the most influence on later work, I think we have to call it a draw. Substantivists, particularly Marshall Sahlins, have had the most effect on sociocultural anthropology in general; his developments of Polanyi's types of reciprocity and types of economy have become part of the general vocabulary of anthropology, particularly in archaeology. The idea that economic activities are deeply embedded and submerged in all kinds of institutions, from kinship to football teams, has become quite commonplace and accepted (see Granovetter 1985 for discussion). Even so, applied, ecological, and demographic anthropologists have enthusiastically embraced many of the tools and ideas of formalism. Many anthropologists accept that some kinds of economic analysis based on assumptions of rationality and least effort are useful for understanding noncapitalist and non-Western societies. Just as economists are coming to understand that there are different kinds of capitalism, that Japanese businesses work differently from American or Turkish ones, so anthropologists are recognizing that economizing can take place in many settings besides the floor of a stock market. More important, the idea that human choices and decisions *do* shape the future and that people are *not* culturally programmed robots is now fundamentally accepted by most anthropologists (e.g., Comaroff 1985; Giddens 1979).

In some sense, then, both sides won by making their points heard. But in an ultimate sense, neither side won since nobody really addressed the more fundamental assumptions being made about human nature. And historically, economic anthropology itself quickly left the debate behind. Although a few scholars still try to recapture the excitement and keep the old arguments going, since the beginning of the 1970s, issues raised by Marxism have taken center stage in the discipline. As we will see in Chapter 4, the Marxian focus is on systems of production and the pursuit of power by social groups, an approach that is neither purely formalist nor substantivist.

Economic Anthropology After the Great Debate

The formalist-substantivist debate was largely philosophical and academic; it happened at a time when the vast majority of anthropologists were employed teaching anthropology in university departments in the United States and Great Britain. By the early 1970s, however, the discipline was completely transformed by the decline in university employment and the flood of anthropologists into applied positions in government agencies, foundations, and various kinds of social action and social service organizations. Theoretical concerns quickly shifted from the contemplation and analysis of precolonial or colonial-era societies—the "untouched"—to the analysis of the vast majority of the world's population that is part of nation-states. By the 1970s, there was almost nowhere left on the planet where people remained separated from radio, Western goods, and national politics. Everywhere, people were striving to overcome poverty and faced problems of overpopulation, health, resource depletion, political strife, and social turmoil. Economic anthropologists were among the first to recognize this challenge and change their thinking, their methods, and their goals.

How have anthropologists met the challenge? Economic anthropology after the great debate diversified rapidly in a number of directions. I will detail some of these trends in the remainder of this chapter, although at first there may seem to be so many tangents that you may question whether something called economic anthropology really exists anymore. I think it does, and I aim to show that there are still core issues, though not the ones that obsessed the formalists and substantivists. The rest of this book is devoted to finding the common threads that tie this diversity together, in order to recapture some of the unity of purpose that appears to have been lost after the great debate subsided.

Neo-Marxism

While studying African peoples in the 1960s and 1970s, French Marxists laid much of the theoretical groundwork for an engagement with problems of real social and economic change. In his 1972 article *From Reproduction to Production*, Claude Meillassoux argues convincingly that if the goal is to better understand general processes of economic change, neither formalism nor substantivism will do; it takes something else—Marxism. Marx, he says, came up with the idea that economic systems are always embedded in social formations and that these formations fall into an evolutionary range of "types" called modes of production, and Marx did this long before Polanyi. Like the substantivists, Marx also thought that modern economics is basically ethnocentric, a way of looking at the world determined by the capitalist system in which economists live. *Homo economicus* (the rational human being of economic theory) is a product of history. Classical economics provides only an illusion that people are free to make choices in a "free market," whereas in reality, as Marx says, "everywhere they are in chains."

All the same, Meillassoux thought that Marxism provides an alternative set of formal principles for understanding all economies (see Chapter 4), with its focus on modes of production and its assumption that dominant and powerful groups will pursue their own class interests. Marx provides an alternative formalism based on class interest instead of individual choice. Marx's alternative contradicts a lot of modern microeconomics because it does not assume that people are free actors in an open marketplace.

But Marxian anthropology did more than synthesize theoretical debate. It changed the topical focus of the field so that all economic anthropology began to pay more attention to the ways different groups of people, traditionally considered isolated, are linked together through colonialism and trade, by the violence of power and exploitation. Instead of seeing societies as static "cases," frozen in time like museum displays, Marxists talked about dynamism, change, and struggle, thinking about how one kind of system could change into another (Friedman 1975, Godelier 1977). Although there was a lot of endless reanalysis of Marx's sacred texts, the Marxists also focused their attention on peasants, small-scale industry, social stratification, land tenure, state intervention in markets, and a multitude of other issues that were directly relevant to economic and social policy.[8]

Feminism

Feminist anthropology poses a similar set of challenges for economic anthropology. Modern neoclassical economics builds its whole analysis on a strict separation of the public sphere of production and business from the private, domestic realm of household consumption. Both the family and the state are defined by modern economics as "not the economy" (Waller and Jennings 1991, 487). Feminists have argued that economics is a powerful part of a modern patriarchy that tends to define women out of positions of power and control. Feminist scholars point out ways that modern economics takes nineteenth-century Western cultural norms about gender (women stay at home, men work) and turns them into, supposedly, *universal scientific law.*[9] (Here I am using the anthropological definition of *gender* as particular *social and cultural* distinctions that are associated with, but far from being the same thing as, *sexual* biological differences.)

Until the seventeenth century, the economy was not thought of as a separate entity but was instead considered a component of the basic economic unit of society, the *household.* From before the time of Aristotle, household management *was* economics; philosophers taught that the wealth of a society flowed entirely from properly managed households. Even the word "economics" is derived from the Greek word *oikos,* meaning house. Both the Greek philosophers and the Christian theologians of the Renaissance taught that the economy, like the family, was a partnership of men, women, and children under the firm leadership of a patriarch.

Only in the early years of the eighteenth century did things change, when a notion of "the economy" separate from the household or estate came into being. With the growth of trade and industry, more and more wealth was being generated outside the household. To some, this was a disruption of the natural order, and the market came to represent the beginning of the breakdown of the orderly and prosperous household economy. But for others, especially British moral philosophers, the emergence of the market signaled the division of society for the first time into separate spheres of "public" and "private."

At this point, ideas about gender were changing in Europe, and an ideology was emerging that assigned women to the domestic realm and excluded them from public life to a degree not previously known. At the same time, economics was completely redefined. It was no longer the art of household management but rather the science of industry, trade, and public power. Economics became the concern of the state, of global politics and warfare, not the household or family. And *all* of the areas covered by economics were in the male domain; economics redefined what women did as "domestic" and therefore not economic.

Anthropologists have long known that many cultures divide their world into halves; good and evil, light and dark, mind and body, for example. These divisions do not describe what people actually do, but they reveal how people think about themselves and the world. This is how cultural dualisms have power; they push us into thinking in particular ways, they define order, they help us organize experience and ignore things that don't fit. They serve some people's interests and make it hard for the disadvantaged to understand the source of their problems, because the dualisms make their suffering seem "natural" (see Rosaldo 1980a). They can therefore serve very oppressive purposes.

When we look at dualism in Western culture, we find that many of these dualisms mirror a basic division between public and private, which is deeply gendered, as in the following list (from Jennings 1993, 121):

> public : private
> economy : family
> man : woman
> rational : emotional
> mind : body
> historical : natural
> objective : subjective
> science : humanities
> economics : sociology
> competitive : nurturant
> independent : dependent

The point is that economics has systematically defined itself as an enterprise concerned with male-gendered activities. It has defined the things women do, largely, as noneconomic. Production took place in factories; the work people did in their houses was increasingly defined as something else, as housework, reproduction, or consumption.

This classification has not been consciously designed as a means to oppress or torment women; instead, it is a process that reflects a broader cultural dualism. It is one way Western culture has divided up the world. This dualism still runs so deeply in our ideas about the economy that it seems quite "natural" much of the time. For example, most economists persist in arguing against including housework in the measurement of the gross national product (GNP)! In the 1990s, if a parent takes the day off and stays home to take care of a sick child, this is not counted as part of GNP, whereas if a parent pays a nephew to stay with the child, it does count. The reasons that work in the house is not considered "real work" are deeply cultural and historical; they are not based on objective scientific fact.

The feminist critique of microeconomics therefore goes much further than that made by Polanyi and the substantivists. Polanyi thought microeconomics was only a useful tool for understanding modern capitalist economies dominated by business and especially markets. Feminists, along with many Marxists, say that microeconomics is not even a good tool for understanding modern capitalism because it is part of the very ideology that makes capitalism work. Furthermore, the modern economy is *not* entirely dominated by the market, as Polanyi thought. Households and other kinds of nonmarket relationships, like friendship, kinship, religion, and class, remain of central economic importance, even in the world of the Home Shopping Network and ATMs (automatic teller machines). The Western economy should therefore be seen as being just as deeply embedded in social (gendered) relations as is the Trobriand or Tlingit economy. The feminist critique also demands that we look closely at the links between gender, power, and the economy. Culturally based gender differences, not the "fair market" for labor, dictate that women so often receive a lower wage for the same work as men in the United States.

Feminists have begun to shift the topical focus of economic anthropology to reflect their theoretical critique. This means an explicit rejection of the division between the *domestic* and the *economic*. The household has become a central unit for feminist economics because it is very often a place where economic relations have been neglected and even concealed. In the household, large-scale changes in the economy have a direct effect on gender roles, on fertility and population growth, and on the kinds and amounts of work that people do.

For most of the world today, the household is really the center of the economy, because most jobs do not pay enough for a family to live on. Thus, the household is where people mix and pool all kinds of income from wages, crafts, farming, and small businesses; it is the place where the economic and the social interact every day, when food must come out of the pot. Many are looking at the relationship between women's wage labor and their domestic lives, at all the parts of the world where women are putting together computers in factories or sewing shirts. Such books as Diane Wolf's *Factory Daughters* (1992) on Java and Jenny White's *Money Makes Us Relatives* (1992) on Turkey show us just how artificial and useless (even harmful) the division between *economic* and *domestic* can be in the real world. Work relations *are* social relations; in Turkey, we cannot separate the knitting industry from the system of kinship and marriage. In Java, the family, farm, village, and factory are tightly linked into a single system. The goal of much of this work is to find out how exploitation, inequality, and injustice continue or are intensified when previously isolated societies become linked to global markets and multinational corporations and to explore how government policies and actions affect daily life and economic survival.[10]

Ecological Anthropology

Ecological anthropology overlaps considerably with economic anthropology, and at times they appear indistinguishable, especially in the work of archaeologists.[11] These two subdisciplines have a very different academic genealogy, however, for the most important ancestor of modern ecological anthropology was the cultural ecology of Julian Steward (1955) and the energy-oriented evolutionary anthropology of Leslie White (see Netting 1965, 1977, for history of ecological anthropology).

Steward and White followed the tradition of Franz Boas in taking as their central problem the variation in social organization among different cultural groups. They sought order and reason that would explain why there was such variety in systems of kinship, leadership, and settlement among the world's peoples. They both thought the key was to be found in the ways that people made a living, in their *subsistence system.* Borrowing the idea of *adaptation* from evolutionary biology Steward was most direct in asserting that the way people got their food from the natural environment had a direct shaping effect on their social life and customs (e.g., Murphy and Steward 1956). A key concept was the notion of an *ecosystem,* a complex web of relationships that bound human groups in complex ways to other species and to aspects of the natural physical environment. Like natural ecologists, cultural ecologists have tended to be interested in the dynamics of systems—in other words, in the properties that make them stable or unstable.

Of course, as soon as you start to look at the way any human group makes a living, you find that people do not just produce or gather food and resources for themselves. They are constantly trading and exchanging back and forth; you can't understand how people survive without also looking at how they store, trade, and barter, at the accumulation of surplus and the investment of time and resources in objects like houses, irrigation canals, and pyramids. These are the classic domains of economic anthropology. Therefore, any complete cultural ecology that traces all the connections between people and their natural environment has to include economic connections.

This means that ecological anthropology must always consider economics in the *substantive* sense of "economic activities." But there is no necessity for ecological anthropology to adopt the *formal* elements of economic rationality and economic methods. Instead, most ecological anthropologists have borrowed their theory and methods from fields like systems theory, demography, and biological ecology. They are interested in the rationality of systems, not individuals. In the classic studies of ecological anthropology, like Roy Rappoport's *Pigs for the Ancestors* (1968), the cultural system of rules, customs, and groups makes sense as a whole and achieves a balance with the natural world, but it does this without the participants' knowledge. They are not aware that their system of warfare regulates population density, and they don't need to know. Their individual choices and decisions play no particular part in the system. Classical ecological anthropology was therefore a kind of substantivist economic anthropology that rejected formalism.

All this changed during the 1980s when cultural ecologists began to study dynamic systems of cultural change instead of people who were imagined to be isolated and unaffected by the outside world. When you are working among a group of people who are rapidly changing their way of life and their natural environment, you are forced to look more directly at the choices that people are making. This leads some ecological anthropologists to look more closely at how people perceive and understand their natural environment (e.g., Ingold 1992). It has led others to explore formal methods for modeling human decisionmaking, including *optimal foraging strategy*, a concept originally developed in ecology to understand how the distribution of food affected birds' search strategies and social organization. Others are borrowing techniques and ideas from economics, locational geography, and general systems theory. This convergence is well represented in a recent collection, *Risk and Uncertainty in Tribal and Peasant Economies* (1990), which includes both economic and ecological anthropologists. As Elizabeth Cashdan points out in her introduction to this book, however, there is still a serious difference between the two groups when it comes to a very central issue: What is it that people are trying to maximize when they make choices? Ecologists (and sociobiologists for that matter) think people generally maximize "fitness," meaning their chances of making a genetic contribution to the next generation. Economists focus instead on maximizing "utility," which, as we shall see in Chapter 3, often translates as "immediate satisfaction." The convergence of economic and ecological anthropology is therefore stuck on yet another difficult philosophical issue of human nature and the human condition.

Development Anthropology

Economic anthropology became more engaged with development problems during the 1970s and 1980s, as it became a more applied field and more economic anthropologists took work with development agencies. Many began to turn their attention to the economic and especially to the agricultural problems faced in the developing world. Some of this work was inspired by Cold War tensions, which brought issues of economic philosophy to center stage. One Kennedy-era philosophy for fighting Soviet domination and world communism was to promote equitable development in impoverished countries, so that they would remain aligned with the West instead of turning to Marxist revolution and socialism. During the initial optimism of the Peace Corps, Food for Peace (which gave surplus food to poor countries), and the Green Revolution (which introduced new high-yielding crops and agricultural chemicals), some anthropologists thought they could be most helpful by using anthropological knowledge to make these programs go more smoothly. Development just needed a helping hand from people who knew the local culture and language (see, for example, Foster 1969, Mead 1955, Spicer 1952).

The Vietnam War disillusioned many anthropologists, who began to see that anthropological knowledge could also be misused to the detriment of the poor and powerless and that government policies aimed at helping people sometimes led to their destruction. During the 1970s, many economic anthropologists began to question the assumptions of development theory and went out into the field to see how various projects and programs were actually working and affecting people's lives. Dependency theory (see Chapter 4) sparked a new appraisal of how political interests often warped development policies to help the rich instead of the poor. Particularly important work was done on the Green Revolution, which promised to increase food production but often ended up driving poor farmers off the land into teeming urban shantytowns.[12]

Applied economic anthropologists have largely continued the formalist program of showing that the problems of poverty are not caused by "illogical," "irrational," or even culturally biased behavior on the part of the poor. Instead, they have shown that poor people often do amazingly creative things with their few resources and work long and hard. Economic anthropology has focused attention on the government agencies, tax systems, unfair policies, and corruption that often drives rain forest destruction, the drug trade, urban squalor, mass migration, and the growth of black markets and underground economies.

But development anthropology also faces a serious philosophical contradiction; it often presents a very inconsistent view of human nature. On the one hand, development anthropologists celebrate the ability of people to make rational and creative choices, to face adversity and overcome it. On the other hand (and often on the same page), people are often portrayed as hapless victims who are not responsible for their own actions because they have been brainwashed, dominated, pushed around, or torn from their cultural roots. These two ideas about human nature coexist, but we rarely ask why people are sometimes one way and sometimes the other. This waffling and ambivalence between people as *agents* or *victims* arises because some very basic questions about human nature remain unasked and unanswered.

Peasant Studies

All the themes I have raised in discussing Marxism, gender, ecology, and development converge on the issue of defining and understanding the largest single group of people on the planet—peasants. For this reason, the study of peasants generated perhaps the most controversy in economic anthropology during the 1970s and 1980s.[13] In Chapters 4 and 5, we will see why peasants are such crucially difficult people for economic theorists. Part of the problem for economic anthropologists has been to figure out what kind of category peasants belong in: Do they have their own culture and economy or are they always part of larger systems? Are they a separate mode of production or are they really just a special kind of farmworker in peripheral capitalism? Are they a permanent part of the landscape or do they emerge only in a transitional stage between feudalism and capitalism? Do they always polarize into rich landholders and the landless poor, or do peasants have ways of leveling their wealth differences and keeping the rich under control (see Shanin 1990; Netting 1993)?

A tremendous amount of work on peasants has circled around the work of the early twentieth-century Russian economist, A. V. Chayanov.[14] Chayanov thought that the peasant household has its own logic, which can be understood with formal mathematical analysis but on terms very different from those of a capitalist farm. Peasants, he said, are always balancing the drudgery of work against the return, and they have few desires beyond food and security. This is why they cultivate enough land to feed their family, but no more. When their family has small children, they work harder to feed them, and when the children grow up and start to work, each person in the household works less. The peasant household is therefore a distinctive institution that shapes the economic logic of peasant farming (sounds substantivist, doesn't it?).

Chayanov attracted so much attention because he offered a formalist solution to a substantivist problem. He used economic curves of demand and production to demonstrate why Russian peasants act so differently from midwestern American corn farmers. His solution, however, does not address the underlying issue of *why* peasants want less and are satisfied with feeding their families and no more. The issue remains whether peasants are really culturally different from fully commercial farmers, and if so, why? Is their economic behavior a product of their culture or vice versa?

This theme comes out clearly in another major controversy in peasant studies, one that was reflected in two important books on Southeast Asian farmers, James Scott's *The Moral Economy of the Peasant* (1976) and the reply to it, Samuel Popkin's *The Rational Peasant* (1979).[15] In his study of twentieth-century farming, Scott argues that capitalist farming, pushed by the colonial powers, was an attack on a preexisting village-based subsistence tradition. The capitalist agricultural system, based on export commodities like rice and rubber and on commoditization of land and labor, hurt the peasant economy. The peasant mode of production was based on reciprocity within the village, sharing and communal management of important resources, and cooperative labor. It was encoded in moral norms—the obligation of reciprocity, the right to subsistence, and a just price for goods. The peasant system is therefore based on moral order and on an economic logic that operates at the level of the community, not the individual. Peasants' relationships with landlords and feudal aristocrats had always formed a moral system of mutual obligation, in which the mighty repaid loyalty with protection and assistance in hard times. The conservatism and risk-averse behavior shown by peasants is a long-term survival tool that has been handed down from antiquity as part of peasant culture.

In this moral economy, peasant villages are mostly homogeneous, bound in traditional ties to landlords and rulers. Peasants do not usually innovate, and they have submerged individual well-being in the larger good of the village in order to survive as a community. The peasants saw capitalist farming and the colonial intrusion of the French and Japanese as attempts to break down and destroy their moral order, and they sometimes rebelled but more often resisted passively. Their religious cults and self-help movements, as well as the roots of communism, were grounded in the moral world of the peasantry.

Popkin, by contrast, employs the historical approach more deeply. He argues that the moral, corporate, cooperative peasant community found in Vietnam and so many other parts of the world is not, in fact, a precondition of capitalism. It is instead a *creation* of feudalism and capitalism that has been turned into a myth that justifies state intervention. The peasant community is a rational response to heavy taxes and a government system that denied farmers the right to own individual property. The state therefore *created* the peasant village as a means of administration and extraction.

Popkin says that these communities are riven with strife and conflict and have profound economic inequalities; the putative cooperative and leveling mechanisms imposed by the state often perpetuate privilege instead of removing it. He sees the peasantry not as a morally constituted group that is

Moral Peasant

culturally distinct, but as a political group that is motivated by class identification and class interest. Whereas Scott finds that the peasants' behavior is grounded in their culture and moral universe, Popkin finds that the same behavior is explained by the political economy—the structure of power, property, and privilege that forces peasants to behave in certain ways in order to survive.

The two studies carry very different messages for the future; Scott's peasants have to change and give up some of their culture if they are to enter the "modern" world of markets, whereas Popkin's peasants are already fully modern in their behavior and thinking—all they need is the opportunity, the power, and the resources. Give them a fair deal, and they will become highly productive market-oriented farmers. They only act like peasants because they are oppressed.

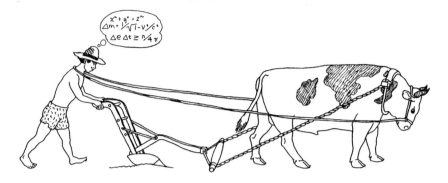

Rational Peasant

On historical grounds, Popkin's work is more satisfying and convincing. He makes a good case that the so-called peasantry is not some kind of remnant of primitive times but is instead a creation of colonial capitalism. But does it follow that he is right about human motivations? That mutual interest, rather than moral identity, holds peasant villages together? This is a much harder question, one that is never properly resolved.

Conclusion?

Confronted with the problem of peasants, we are forced to return to the issues of economic philosophy and human nature. Once again the work remains fundamentally incomplete because it starts out by assuming the answers to the most important questions! To some extent, Scott and Popkin are arguing issues of faith in human nature, debating a point that cannot be settled by any amount of historical research, hard facts, and persuasive argument about Vietnamese peasants. Does this mean we have no hope of ever answering those questions? Each of the topics that economic anthropologists are concerned with seems to come back to these fundamental problems. In the next chapter, I propose that there is indeed a way to resolve them, but first the questions have to be posed clearly and unambiguously.

Notes

1. James Peacock's *The Anthropological Lens* (1986) is a clear and sensitive introduction to the issues of reflexivity and the status of knowledge in anthropology. For a more polemical statement of the relativist position, read Renato Rosaldo's *Culture and Truth* (1993).

2. The basic sources on the formalist-substantivist debate are collected in LeClair and Schneider's reader *Economic Anthropology* (1968), though the authors are hardly impartial. Some of the acrimony and anger generated by the debate can be found in the letters responding to George Dalton's substantivist manifesto in *Current Anthro-*

pology in 1969. Scott Cook's formalist proclamations, published in 1966 and 1969, are equally polemical, and show how the debate was linked with much wider issues of social science, history, and philosophy. Both Cook (1973) and Godelier (1972, 1988) provide excellent retrospectives on the debate, from Marxist points of view. A more recent discussion from a substantivist point of view is provided by Isaac (1993).

3. See Schneider (1974, chap. 2) for a discussion of this debate. Their argument quickly sidetracked on the issue of whether science should be *inductive* (generating rules from observation) or *deductive* (generating rules through logic). These philosophy-of-science issues arose again later in the formalist-substantivist debate, mainly as debating tools whereby opponents could accuse each other of being unscientific or unrealistic.

4. The work of Polanyi has been most thoroughly discussed and analyzed in anthropology in two eclectic and interesting books by Rhoda Halperin (1988, 1994).

5. In general, when I use the words "primitive" and "modern" in this book, they are in quotes because I do not think they have a legitimate use in anthropology any more. Labeling societies in this way tends to obscure more than it reveals and contributes to the mistaken idea that non-Western peoples are somehow simpler or that they represent earlier stages of human development. Elsewhere I have written a great deal about why these assumptions are untrue and why the use of these terms should be discouraged (Wilk 1991). Polanyi strongly denied that his types were in any way an evolutionary sequence, since in most actual cases different types of economic integration coexist. Nevertheless, reciprocity is said to characterize "savage" society; redistribution, the Oriental empires; and exchange, the recent West. The Polanyi school is well summarized by Dalton and Köcke (1983) and is defended by Halperin (1994).

6. For this discussion I have depended on the original classic sources, including Burling (1962), Cancian (1966), LeClair (1962), and Cook (1966). Some discussion of early formalism can also be found in Firth (1967) and Prattis (1973, 1978). Prattis also edited a collection in 1973 with some excellent early formalist essays. Mayhew provides a very nice, concise critique of the formalists from an economist's perspective (1980).

7. This discussion of philosophical origins draws on Rocha (n.d.) and Nisbet (1966).

8. Littlefield and Gates (1991) give a good sampling of contemporary Marxist interests in anthropology, and their bibliography can be used to trace the field through the 1970s and 1980s. Hart (1983) also provides a superb survey of Marxist economic anthropology. The original writings of French Marxist anthropologists like Rey, Godelier, and Meillassoux can be rough going, especially when they are poorly translated into English. I find Terray (1972) is by far the clearest French Marxist.

9. Waller and Jennings (1991) give a short and concise summary of recent feminist rethinking of economics and history. Other good sources are Ferber and Nelson (1993), another paper by Nelson (1992), and the new journal *Feminist Economics*. These arguments about economics as a system of power are closely related to the concerns and conclusions of Michel Foucault, in his persuasive study of the origins of social science (1970). Part of this section is based on an unpublished paper by Marion Gray (1994), which is a chapter of a forthcoming book. It also draws on William Booth's fascinating book about the household economy (1993) and a paper by Rebel (1991). For more on the economy as a household, see also Gudeman and Rivera (1990) and Wilk (1989).

10. In addition to White and Wolf, other good studies of gender, households, and labor include Aihwa Ong (1987), Deere (1990), Salaff (1981), Margery Wolf (1986), Beneria and Roldan (1987), Cohen (1988), Folbre (1994), Goodnow and Bowes (1994), Greenhalgh (1994), and papers collected in Redclift and Mingione (1985), Oppong (1983), Dwyer and Bruce (1988), Rothstein and Blim (1991), and Wilk (1989).

11. Halperin (1989) discusses the difference between economic and ecological anthropology at some length with the aim of reuniting them, a problem that Cook (1973) also considered important.

12. Arndt (1987), Carol Smith (1983), and Black (1991) summarize recent development theories. A good anthropological critique of development is given by Hobart (1993), and there are numerous texts and case studies in applied and development anthropology.

13. Halperin and Dow (1977) have edited a good collection on economic anthropology of peasants, and Eric Wolf (1966) is still a basic source. A more recent bibliography can be found in Trouillot (1988), an excellent synoptic review of peasant issues in Cancian (1989), and good critiques in Roseberry (1989). Some of the most important papers appeared in the *Peasant Studies Newsletter* and the *Journal of Peasant Studies*.

14. The Chayanov literature is huge and seems to grow without end. Chayanov's popularity in anthropology can be traced to Sahlins's use of his work in *Stone Age Economics* (1972). Durrenberger edited a collection of papers on Chayanov in 1984 that is quite useful, and there are more recent discussions in Netting (1993), Ellis (1988), Donham (1990, chap. 1) and Chibnik (1987). A very detailed attempt to apply Chayanov's models to a series of communities is found in Durrenberger and Tannenbaum (1990).

15. The debate about the moral and rational nature of peasants is very clearly discussed by Bernal (1994).

2

Economics and the Problem of Human Nature

We shall see that classical economics came into being as an answer to a problem which had been challenging some of the best minds in moral philosophy ... the relationship between self-interest and the public welfare.

—**Milton Myers,** *The Soul of Modern Economic Man*

The First Law of Economists: For every economist, there exists an equal and opposite economist. The Second Law of Economists: They're both wrong.

—**Jennifer Olmstead, "Economics Jokes"**

As we have seen, controversy in economic anthropology has revolved around the problem of defining "economic" behavior and "the economy" as an objective set of activities and objects. In this chapter, I will dig down through these debates and disagreements to expose the most basic "bedrock" positions. I will suggest that neither the formalist-substantivist debate nor the later theoretical trends in the discipline have asked the right questions. At the end of the chapter, I propose what I see as a better set of questions. In Chapters 3, 4, and 5, I then take up these questions and trace the answers that can be found to them in the existing writing on economics in various social sciences. Several of my students have compared my strategy to an "interrogation," where I strap a series of scholars into a chair, turn on some bright harsh lights, and force them to answer my own questions.

In this process, I try to be sympathetic to the point of view of each scholar and his or her approach, but sometimes I play the devil's advocate. The point is to cut through the incidental or superfluous material, to reject the unproductive and fruitless issues, to find the gold that is often hidden beneath and within. In the process you will see that economic anthropology has some serious problems and misconceptions, but my goal is not to bury it. Instead I hope to convince you that it is definitely worth saving—especially when it asks the right questions.

Defining the Economy

To begin, let's go back to the formalist-substantivist debate and look at the way the participants defined their object of study and their goals. The terms *formal* and *substantive* represent two ways of defining the term *economic* (here I follow Polanyi's [1957] definitions).

"Formal" as we have seen, refers to a kind of logic, a way that people make choices. The "substantive" pertains to the *substance* of the economy, the daily transactions of producing, exchanging, storing, and consuming that form so much of human existence. This definition of the economy was used by early ethnographers when they went off to write complete descriptions of exotic cultures. It was really just a convenient and arbitrary category for lumping together particular kinds of behavior, for the sake of describing and comparing them. A wonderful illustration of the substantive definition of the economy can be found in Daryll Forde's *Habitat, Economy, and Society*, first written in 1934 but reprinted well into the 1960s. The book groups societies according to the ways they make a living, classifying them into economic types like "food gatherers," "cultivators," and "pastoral nomads."

Forde discusses a society in each chapter, methodically describing in great detail where the people live, key aspects of their natural environment, how they get their food, the tools they use, and their crafts, social organization, and types of exchange, including gift giving and trade. At the end of the book, there is a summary section explaining that cultures that share a particular economic type have other features in common. Forde makes some sensible arguments for linking a natural environment (e.g., hot desert) with a particular kind of economy (gathering and foraging), which leads to characteristic social and cultural configurations (simple technology, small mobile bands).

It is important to remember that many anthropologists and other social scientists still use the word *economic* in this substantive way to refer to a category of observable human behavior. When you find a chapter entitled "the economy" in the average ethnography, you can be quite sure of what you will find. The problem with this practice is the need to clearly demarcate what is part of the economy and what belongs in some other category, like religion. Another problem arises when it turns out that the people themselves conceive of their economy in very different ways. They may consider some kinds of exchange to be religious (giving alms to the poor, for example) instead of economic.

Some subdisciplines of anthropology divide things up in very different ways. A cultural ecologist, for example, may see the actual process of gathering or producing food as part of the "subsistence system" and might argue that "the economy" consists only of the system of trade. Some archaeologists have argued for a science of "material culture" that includes *all* human interactions with material objects, which would include some parts of the economy (trading objects) but not others (exchanging ideas or labor) (Schiffer 1976).

Still, many cultural anthropologists would be happy with a simple substantive definition of the economy as "production, exchange, and consumption"; and this is what appears in the average introductory anthropology textbook. But the closer we look at these terms, the less concrete they become and the more difficult it is to find a dividing line that is not arbitrary. We know that when I sell you a horse, this is an economic exchange. Most people would have no problem calling it an economic exchange if I traded you the horse for the right to cut some trees from your yard. But what if I traded you the horse for your sister's hand in marriage? Or if I gave you the horse because I loved you? Or traded you a kiss for a promise? Where does the economic end and something else begin?

If sociocultural anthropology had remained a straightforward descriptive and comparative science, devoted to producing holistic ethnographies of all the world's peoples, these problems would not be crippling. Economic anthropology would simply be the sum of all those descriptive chapters called "the economy," along with a taxonomy created by classifying all the economies into types.

But of course, sociocultural anthropologists are no longer content just to document and describe. They want to ask deeper, more complicated, and difficult questions. Anthropologists want to explain, to reason, to compare and contrast, and ultimately to understand *why* there is so much variability in human lifestyles, so many paths of change. They want to enter other cultures and understand why people behave the way they do from an insider's point of view. At the same time, they are also looking for *human universals,* the constants that tie all cultures together and unify the experience of all human beings. And this quest has driven anthropology into knots of controversy, into a fundamental debate about the most basic characteristics of human beings. Sometimes it seems that anthropologists are tied together more by what they *disagree* about than what they all know, to the point that they cannot even agree on whether the field is a science or a humanity. For these reasons, a simple substantive definition of the economy as a set of practices no longer works very well. What are the options?

Formal Economics: An Alternative?

The analysis of gender and the definition of the economy helps us recognize that a substantive definition of the economy will always be deeply patterned by our own culture and therefore has to be at least partially arbitrary. How can we ever try to define the economy without imposing our own cultural prejudice, ethnocentrism, or sexism upon the world? How can we compare the economies of different cultures and at the same time recognize that each unique group of people defines the economy in a different way?

These are just the kinds of questions that drove anthropologists to seek another definition of "economic," one that would describe a kind of *logic* rather than a kind of behavior. The formalists believed that a substantive definition of the economy was always going to be arbitrary and relative, that beneath acts and behavior that we recognize as economic, there lies something much more fundamental—a way of thinking. The most common formal definition of the economy finds that crucial nugget in some basic common and universal principles of human thought. Conventionally, particular kinds of rationality, calculation, and goal-seeking thought are considered economic—and not contemplative, philosophical, or empathic thought. The most formal of all models is found in the subdiscipline of microeconomics, where the economic is rigorously defined as rational decisions that maximize utility (more on this in Chapter 3). Many microeconomists believe that the formal principles of economics are universal and natural, just like the first law of thermodynamics or the Pythagorean theorem.

I argue instead that a formal definition of the economy is just as arbitrary as a substantive one. Why should some kinds of logic be included as economic and other kinds excluded? A formalist finds it easy to model my choice between planting corn and soybeans as an economic one, a balance of risks, costs, and benefits. Some formalists, like recent Nobel Prize–winner Gary Becker, believe we can find formal models for marriage, for voting, and even for joining the army to die for one's country. The key element that makes a kind of decision formally "economic" is that it is a *choice to allocate scarce resources to different possible ends.*[1]

But do all important decisions boil down to a choice between alternatives? What makes choice a special kind of logic and the only kind worth considering as "economic?" Some important kinds of logic are used for deciding what kinds of causes lead to what kinds of effects. For example, I might decide that if I threaten you, you will back down instead of fighting. Aesthetic judgments are another kind of choice that is very common, but they are rarely seen directly as economic. When I see a new painting in a gallery, I am learning something, thinking about my experience, trying to be in touch with my intuition and feelings and to reach some conclusion. Another logical process is *classification*, where I decide, for example, that a new CD belongs in the bin labeled "heavy metal" instead of "rock." The question is, why should decisions about what to buy with limited money or how to get the best price for what I sell be called "economic," when other decisions are not?

A Workable Definition

In this section I am not particularly interested in setting boundaries around economic anthropology or defining the economy too precisely. I would prefer to use the words "economy" and "economic" as imperfect and provisional terms and to retain both their formal and substantive meanings. At times, it is useful to think about the economy as a group of activities, objects, relationships, and institutions that can be separated from other aspects of cultural life and that can be compared with each other from culture to culture. At other times, it is useful to think of "economic" behavior as a way of thinking that may be present in *any* arena of culture. Substantively, then, every culture has "an economy," and formally, all people engage in some form of "economic" behavior and thought at various times and places (see Figure 2.1).

Substantively, the core of the economy can be seen as the classic circuit of production → exchange → consumption, but these often seem to be arbitrary and ethnocentric categories. I find a broader and more useful substantive definition of the economy to be *the relationships between human beings and the*

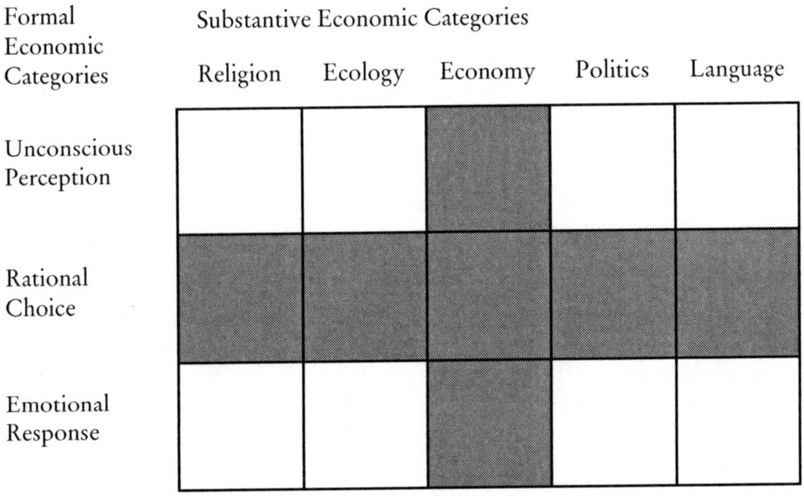

Formal Economic Categories	Substantive Economic Categories				
	Religion	Ecology	Economy	Politics	Language
Unconscious Perception			▓		
Rational Choice	▓	▓	▓	▓	▓
Emotional Response			▓		

FIGURE 2.1 A grid of theories. Economics can be defined either formally as a kind of thought, or substantively as one of a number of kinds of social activity. This figure shows how the dimensions intersect.

human-produced world of objects, ideas, and images. Although ecological anthropology can be thought of as human relationships with the natural environment, in economic anthropology we are interested in the things people
themselves create, that is, artifacts. But some of the most important artifacts
are not material objects but are, like songs, still valuable. This definition focuses on relationships, not on artifacts themselves. The economy is not just a
material world. It is the portion of the world where human beings are tied to
each other through their relationships with things they have created.

Formally, we can define economic thought and behavior as simply choice
and decisionmaking. This definition drops the economist's insistence on
choices involving scarce goods and defined ends. Instead, it broadens the object of study to include all the different ways that people acquire values, desires, and needs and all the ways they set about fulfilling them. Conventional
economics tends to ignore values—it assumes that people have them but says
nothing about where they come from. The truly distinctive contribution of
recent economic anthropology is that it restores values to a position on center stage. Economic anthropology asks *why* people want things, not just
how they set about to satisfy those wants.

If economics is defined as the study of choice and decisionmaking, that
should not blind us to the realities of power and to the fact that many people
today are systematically denied choices. It certainly seems cruel and ironic to
discuss the "economic choices" of people living at the very margins of survival, clinging to a tiny corner of sidewalk and a begging bowl on the streets
of Calcutta. Yet these people remain enmeshed in an economic world. For
this reason, the study of economic behavior must extend into the political,
into the ways people influence each other and acquire power. The boundary
between the economic and the political is hard to define in any way that
makes sense, as we will see in Chapter 4. Now, let's turn to the issues of academic boundaries in more detail.

Defining Economic Anthropology

One of the easiest ways to define something, when we are not sure of its limits, is to determine what it is *not.* I have already started to define economic
anthropology in opposition to that "other" discipline called economics.
Economic anthropology emerged as a separate subdiscipline of anthropology mostly because it picked a fight with its bigger, stronger, and more afflu-
ent neighbor, economics. In fact, this provides a very convenient way of
defining economic anthropology. It is the *part of anthropology that engages
in dialogue with the discipline of economics.*

When Bronislaw Malinowski went to study the Trobriand Islanders in
1915, one of his goals was to find people who were thoroughly unlike the
civilized Europeans of his time. His critique of European culture targeted

what he saw as modern materialism, the obsession with money and possessions. He also aimed at European selfish individualism. On one side, he
placed a European "economic man," who constantly pursued self-interest
and money, who made all his choices solely on the basis of efficiency and his
own satisfaction. On the other side were the Trobrianders, portrayed in his
famous *Argonauts of the Western Pacific* as motivated instead by "a very
complex set of traditional forces, duties and obligations, beliefs in magic, social ambitions and vanities" (1961, 62).

Malinowski argued that because the Trobrianders were so different from
westerners, the tools and concepts of Western economics were useless in understanding the Trobriand Island economy: The Trobriand Islanders simply
thought differently. Conventional Western economics was an ethnocentric
tool by which Europeans could understand themselves but not others.

In making this argument, Malinowski was putting himself very much in
the mainstream of early twentieth-century anthropology. He was arguing for
relativism, the practice of understanding and judging each culture according
to its own standards, instead of using a universal yardstick (in this case, economics). For Malinowski, radically different cultures were a useful stick with
which to beat the dominant Western tradition he belonged to and about
which he had very mixed feelings (Malinowski 1967). Perhaps most laudably,
Malinowski wanted to affirm that human beings were not *naturally* selfish,
that all people had a capacity for harmony, altruism, and unselfishness. It was
modern Western society that brought out the selfishness in people. What
made Malinowski especially furious was that modern Western economists
claimed exactly the opposite, saying that "primitive economic man" was naturally selfish and savage, incapable of sharing or giving (1961, 58–60).

Malinowski threw down the gauntlet, challenging economics and staking
out a claim for anthropology as a broader and more global science. This difficult, challenging, and ambivalent relationship with economics remains part
of economic anthropology. Many anthropologists continue to see economics
as their main enemy, as a dismal science intent on reducing the wonderfully
complex human being to a "need-driven utility seeker maneuvering for advantage within the context of material possibilities and normative constraints" (Geertz 1984, 516).

Some of the reasons for our hostility are obvious. Western culture has elevated economics far above other social sciences. Economists are on TV every
day. They speak an exclusive language, they predict the future, and they oc-
cupy positions of high authority—in other words, they are the high priests
of our culture. Of all the social sciences, economics makes the strongest
claims to being a "real" science like physics. Economists use complex mathematics and aim to find natural laws. They have tremendous power: They
make the predictions that determine the interest rates of our credit cards and
their advice shapes the everyday lives of hundreds of millions of people.

In comparison, economic anthropologists sit on the sidelines, not even accorded the status of second-string junior varsity players in the affairs of the world. Thus, one of our major tasks must be to answer the question: If we are so smart, why aren't we being listened to? Perhaps one reason is that we have not engaged enough in dialogue with academic economics. We have spent far too much effort preaching economics to anthropologists, rather than preaching anthropology to economists.

There are other good reasons for the continuing hostility—often compounded by mutual ignorance—between anthropologists and economists. The two disciplines begin from very different assumptions and ideas about the essential nature of human beings. A lot of the surface differences in tools, techniques, and language are a logical product of these underlying disagreements. To understand economic anthropology better, we need to dig deeper and ask some questions about human nature. In the process, we may be able to settle on some definitions of the economy and economic behavior that transcend the terms of formalism and substantivism and move the discipline into a more equal dialogue with economics itself. Then we would have a more secure position of our own to offer, instead of merely arguing that we are right because economics is wrong.

Redefining Economic Anthropology

Writing a textbook means providing some theoretical structure that is based on the positions people have adopted on major issues. But in reading the history of economic anthropology, I have usually found myself torn between opposing sides in most of the major arguments and debates. I usually find some truth in both sides, even when the authors are arguing that their positions are completely different and they have nothing in common. For this reason, I have been unable to structure this book along the conventional lines of debate, presenting each position and its counterargument. I simply don't believe that the positions most people have staked out have clearly expressed their underlying assumptions and disagreements. This suggests to me that we need to dig deeper.

I suggest that we can divide different theoretical camps in economic anthropology into three different groups, each of which represents a different idea about fundamental human nature. I call these ideas *assumptions* because they are where people start their analysis; these are like the axioms of geometry, which are themselves unprovable. Once we accept them, we can reason from them to the solutions of all kinds of problems, but our work does not set out to prove or challenge them.[2]

The real heat and argument in economic anthropology comes from underlying disagreement over these starting assumptions. Once you recognize where someone is starting, you can better understand why they have chosen particular topics to study, what methods they use, and the kinds of answers they seek. I will use this scheme to organize my discussion of the history of economic anthropology in the next three chapters. As a way of tracing the history and content of economic anthropology, I find this approach makes much more sense than using the categories of formalism and substantivism (though I am sure readers will find affinities between my three assumptions and the ideas of formalists and substantivists).

The Question of Human Nature

Economics began, in Europe, as the study of moral philosophy. Like Christianity itself, economics asked questions about human nature: Are we conceived in original sin or born innocent? Does evil come from within or without? As economic philosophy emerged as separate from theology, those philosophers phrased the question differently. They asked instead, Are human beings self-interested or altruistic? Are people naturally prone to place their own needs above others, to take what they want at the expense of others? If so, they have to be coerced or forced into working together for the common good (this was Thomas Hobbes's position). Or is there an inherent moral sense in people that leads them to naturally care for and work with each other? If so, they need no coercion or government pressure to get them to cooperate.

Thus, economics asks a fundamental question about the origins of selfishness and altruism. Everyone can see that in real life people sometimes act selfishly and at other times appear to put others' interests above their own. The question is *why*. Is one response due to the "natural" state of man and the other caused by something artificial? Early moral philosophers like Hobbes (1588–1679) and Jean-Jacques Rousseau (1712–1778) were deeply interested in so-called primitive people for exactly this reason; they figured that primitive people represented a natural state. So when Hobbes said that savages' lives were "solitary, poore, nasty, brutish, and short," he was arguing that the only solution was a firm government hand that would enforce cooperation and peace. Similarly, Rousseau's depiction of the "noble savage," living naturally in a state of peace and prosperity, was an argument against the need for the coercive nation-state, since harmony came naturally. It is no coincidence that this sort of philosophy emerged at the time when the European states were becoming more and more powerful, global, and bureaucratic.

Economics, in the hands of Adam Smith and the later theorists of the nineteenth century, followed Hobbes instead of Rousseau, in accepting that human beings *are* essentially selfish. When they cooperate or help each other, it is because of "enlightened self-interest." People use their reasoning powers and may find it in their own *self-interest* to work with others.

Groups and institutions (including governments) encourage corruption, avarice, and inefficiency, precisely because they are not based on individual self-interest (see McGraw 1992).

But other social philosophers never accepted this premise, beginning a disagreement that is partly responsible for the emergence of sociology as a field distinct from economics. Sociology, in the hands of Auguste Comte and Emile Durkheim, assumed that human beings are naturally social animals. Humans cooperate and sacrifice, social philosophers said, because it is part of our *social nature,* not because we selfishly calculate the results of our actions. People often think and feel like unique individuals who are making their own decisions, but when taken in large numbers, people fall into groups. They are willing to fight and die for their families, clans, tribes, and nations.

Differences of opinion developed among sociologists, however, on the exact means by which human beings maintained their solidarity and altruism toward one another. Some, like Emile Durkheim (1858–1917), stressed the encompassing nature of social groups. They thought that people were kept in line by group pressure, by their desire to conform, and by their fear of the consequences. But other sociologists, like Max Weber (1864–1920), thought that the individual's moral imagination had much more of an effect than social pressure. All people, said Weber, learn a set of moral precepts as they grow up in a particular setting and religion. And their ability to be social, to cooperate altruistically, is a product of that moral imprint. Anthropologists, with their notion of culture as a system of learned and shared behavior, have tended to draw on both Durkheim and Weber.

Three Ways to Answer

In this short and simplified intellectual history, there are three very different models of human behavior and decisionmaking. I do not think the modern social sciences have gone far beyond these three models in finding explanations for human behavior; I call them the *self-interested,* the *moral,* and the *social.*

The Self-Interested Model.   This is the basis for the dominant approach in *microeconomics,* the part of economics that is concerned with individual behavior. The self-interested rational individual, or "economic man," has been a feature of social science since the Enlightenment (Mansbridge 1990). The self-interested individual appears in countless folktales and proverbs; a common theme is that selfishness is "natural" and that civilization struggles constantly to tame the natural beast. Modern economics has softened the harshness of selfishness by emphasizing that the self-interested individual is not necessarily maximizing *material* gains. Instead, that person is maximizing an internal *utility* that may include love, security, and many other things. Thus, a self-interested individual may appear to be doing things unselfishly for other people, when in fact the person is still doing it for his or her own satisfaction. (For example, a person may give money to charity, but only because doing so produces a good feeling.)

A weaker form of this assumption is that people do have other motives besides self-interest but that they always think of themselves *first.* ("Look out for number one.") Although many anthropologists have trouble with the idea that self-interest is the fundamental human motivation, this "softer" selfishness is basic in a great deal of anthropological functionalism, including much of ecological and economic anthropology. The key element that distinguishes all approaches based on self-interest is that the individual is taken as the basic unit of analysis.

The Social Model. A social theory of human nature focuses on the way people form groups and exercise power. This forms the basis for approaches often labeled *political economy.* The social person identifies with a group and is motivated by the interests of the collectivity—the household, clan, social class, and so on—sacrificing for the greater good. This kind of theory assumes that people are "joiners." They want to belong to something, and once they do, they give up some of their autonomy and take on the group's interests as their own. Understanding their behavior therefore requires that we study *norms* (shared group beliefs) and the solidarity and continuity of the *group,* rather than individual self-interest. As mentioned earlier, Emile Durkheim, the French sociologist, is often associated with this concept of human beings. However, Durkheim did not think humans were *naturally* social; he argued that religion was the human institution that taught people to be social, that led them to place the interest of the group above the self through the use of common symbols. A more fundamentally biologically social model appears in E. O. Wilson's famous book *Sociobiology* (1980), in which he has proposed that humans have genetically evolved to be social through natural selection.

Social human beings appear and reappear in anthropological writing. In 1947, Robert Redfield proposed a "folk society" in which people identified so strongly with their clans and villages that they could not even imagine how their own interests could be different from group interests. More recently, in *The Gender of the Gift* (1988), Marilyn Strathern has argued that in many Melanesian societies, there is not even a notion of the person as a separate self. Indeed, women are thought of as extensions of kin groups, and the idea that they could make independent decisions is unthinkable.

In the strongest form of a social theory of human behavior, real individual human motives do not exist. People may *think* they are making their own decisions and following their own desires, but this is no more than an illusion of self-will allowed by society. Weaker social theories of behavior would allow people different degrees of autonomy and individuality. From Durkheim onward, many social scientists have thought that the most important difference between "modern" and "primitive" societies was that only in modern times has the individual emerged from the group.

The Moral Model.   A moral model of human behavior looks mainly at what people think and believe about the world in order to explain their actions. This perspective underlies what can be called *cultural economics.* The moral person's motivations are shaped by culturally specific belief systems and values. Their behavior and choices are guided by a desire to do what is right, and these moral values flow ultimately from a *cosmology*—a culturally patterned view of the universe and the human place within it. Moral human beings are "believers" whose actions are always guided by ideas of right and wrong, ideas they learn along with the rest of their culture as they grow up. This does not mean that people are religious fanatics, only that they have a moral sense grounded in a view of the way the world works. Symbolic systems and cognitive categories define the realm of the possible and shape choice. People internalize cultural value systems, so that acting against them produces internal conflict and even illness (psychologist Sigmund Freud depicted this as a conflict between the social *superego* and the personal *id*).

One variety of moral theory in anthropology examines each culture's unique system of language and classification. According to this theory, people make order out of the world by classifying things and phenomena into groups. In the process, their culture defines particular things as unclean and dangerous and classifies others as holy and good. Mary Douglas, in her famous *Purity and Danger* (1966), has asserted that the most dangerous and unclean objects and animals are usually the ones that do not fit cultural categories, the ambiguous and difficult things that are "neither fish nor fowl." Morality, thought, and behavior are therefore defined for each culture through language, symbols, and categories.

Anthropologists have spent an enormous amount of time and effort detailing the religious cosmologies of different cultures, always with the spoken or unspoken assumption that people's moral universes have direct effects on their choices and behavior. Michelle Rosaldo, for example, has argued that we cannot understand the practice of head-hunting among the Ilongot of the Philippines without tracing their cosmology and its effect on their emotions (1980b). The notion of moral motivation is often used to justify and stress the importance of subjective approaches to research, for this is seen as the only way to enter a different moral universe. And for many, a modern society is one that has lost the morality and ethics that guided behavior in traditional cultures, replacing them with amoral selfishness.

Again, there are stronger and weaker moral theories of behavior. No moral system can prescribe every action and option. And moral principles will always come into conflict with each other, so there will always be some flexibility. Although in the strongest terms, cosmology *determines* behavior, less stringent theorists would argue only that the moral universe *influences* or *modifies* behavior (see Medick and Sabean 1984).

The Combined Models

These three positions provide alternative explanations for almost any human choice or act; they also present very different solutions to human problems. Look, for example, at the care and attention that parents give to rearing their children. If we use a self-interested theory, we might say that parents are motivated by the eventual returns they expect from their children when they grow up. A social theorist could respond that parents have children because they want to build families, which are essential social units necessary to society, and because humans cannot live as isolated individuals. Moral theory would suggest, instead, that people take care of children because of their sense of moral obligation that stems from their religion and because they hold ideas of proper behavior learned in turn from their parents.

Now, if families fail to take care of children, leaving them alone in filthy apartments while the parents seek crack cocaine on the streets, what is the cause and what is the solution? The answer depends on the theoretical assumptions held about the basis of the family. Should we change the reward structure of the welfare system? Force men to support their children? Teach morality in the public schools and in churches?

The choices are usually not as clear as three simple alternatives. Many social scientists, from Weber onward, have sought ways to combine them, sometimes in a historical sequence and sometimes pointing to particular social or economic circumstances that favor the emergence of self-interested, social, or moral human beings.[3]

Some unorthodox economic theorists take a different course by accepting the objective reality of altruism, of a non-self-interested motive. Two arguments of this kind are Howard Margolis's "fair share" model and Amitai Etzioni's "moral economics." Both theorists think that humans have *two* discrete motivations (or utility functions) instead of one. Margolis (1982) sees the two as self-interested and group-interested, whereas Etzioni (1988) counterposes material self-interest to moral satisfaction.[4]

Humanity, to Etzioni and Margolis, is in a perpetual balancing act, caught between two basic urges, like the cartoon character struggling to make a choice, with a little red devil on one shoulder and a little white angel on the other. For Margolis, the two are self and the group, but for Etzioni, they are self and moral conscience. Both think these urges have a biological or genetic basis, as the products of human evolution as a cooperative primate (though of course nobody has ever found a gene that makes people sociable or moral).

Three Positions in Anthropology

Economic anthropology has been the scene of often passionate debate among proponents of all three views of human nature. The next three chapters will detail these debates and place them in a historical perspective. But before we proceed, I want to explain my own position on the three models of human motivations, since it informs most of the analysis that follows.

To begin with, I am skeptically unwilling to take *any* model of innate human nature as a fact. My understanding of human evolution is that the overriding characteristic of our species is adaptability and flexibility. Most of our species' capabilities appear to be cultural "software" rather than biological "hardware." People are always arguing that some human trait, like territoriality or the nuclear family, is "natural" and genetic, having evolved millions of years ago on the African savannah. These claims never hold up to hard scrutiny. We seem to be quite capable of almost any kind of behavior toward each other.

If we cannot settle the issue of what human nature is by an act of faith or through human paleontology, this leaves us with the skeptical empiricism of science. In other words, we have to make our choices about human motives by studying the ideas and behavior of real human beings. Therefore, instead of pinning down some illusory "human nature," I think the highest goal for economic anthropology is to find out what makes people self-interested, moral, or social. We need to think critically about the circumstances that can turn *any* human being into an altruistic saint or a self-interested monster.

I do not think the three models of human motive that I have outlined here are really discrete categories of behavior or motives. Like most anthropologists, my definition of "culture" is broad enough to encompass all three kinds of motives. Culture is really the sum total of social, self-interested, and moral behavior. The problem, however, is explaining why people are guided sometimes by one set of motivations and other times by the others. And how, in practice, do people balance these different motivations?

In Chapter 6, I discuss some of the more promising ways that anthropologists have brought all three aspects of human behavior together. My own suggestion is that we can find ways to think about all three as merely the extreme positions on several linear scales. In real life, people rarely work at these extreme margins. Instead, most of us live in the messy gray areas between, trying to balance self-interest, group interest, and moral precepts drawn from our cultural beliefs. As I will show in the next three chapters, setting up three simple categories is an excellent way to understand the literature in economic anthropology. But it has been a terribly clumsy way to try to understand the complex, textured decisions of flesh-and-blood people in real cultural situations.

Notes

1. Students can find both substantive and formal definitions of "the economy" and "economic" in most introductory economics textbooks. A classic is Paul Samuelson's often revised *Economics* (1948), and one that I find particularly clear is Waud's *Microeconomics* (1983).

2. I first found this three-part theoretical scheme in a slightly different form in an unpublished grant proposal by Henry Rutz, where it was presented with great clarity and elegance; I use it here with his kind permission. The scheme is quite similar to Max Weber's distinction between interest-oriented, tradition-oriented, and value-oriented behavior (1968).

3. The themes of morality and selfishness in anthropological critiques of the economy are admirably detailed by Kahn (1990) in his critique of a lecture by Geertz (1984). Kahn shows that many of the recent arguments by anthropologists about subjectivity, ethics, and positivism were also made by romanticist economists in nineteenth-century Germany.

4. The very idea that there could be two utilities flies in the face of the conventional economic definition of utility, which is a sum of all the possible subjective satisfactions that a person has at a particular time. Dividing those satisfactions into discrete "bundles" or types seems both inelegant and extremely difficult in the practice of real research.

3 ✍

Self-Interest
and Neoclassical
Microeconomics

"From now on, I'm thinking only of me."
Major Danby replied indulgently with a superior smile: "But Yossarian, suppose everyone felt that way."
"Then," said Yossarian, "I'd certainly be a damn fool to feel any other way, wouldn't I?"

—Joseph Heller, *Catch-22*

If all the economists in the world were to be laid end to end, they would not reach a conclusion.

—George Bernard Shaw

The History of Self-Interest

The individual human being has a special place in Western philosophy, theology, and politics. Since the Enlightenment, Western ideas about society have been cast largely in terms of individual rights and freedoms, elevating autonomy to a virtue, in opposition to the bonds and chains of tyranny and irrational superstition.[1] It should be no surprise, then, that Western economic thought also starts with the individual and tries to understand the whole of work, trade, and money by analyzing the behavior of the single human being. I label this approach *selfish* only because it begins with the individual "self," not because it always assumes that human beings act selfishly. On the contrary, most modern economists portray human beings as essentially ra-

43

tional and intelligent, and they specifically want to avoid the kind of value judgments about morality and motives that are implied when we use a term like "selfish" to describe someone's behavior.

This chapter outlines the intellectual history of the effort to build economics starting from the rational individual. The goal is to give a fair and balanced view of the dominant perspective in modern Western economics, to explain some of its results and conclusions, and to question why it has achieved such wide acceptance and power in the world. I include in the chapter some discussion of the internal criticism of Western economics by people seeking to qualify, modify, or improve its approach. But the more fundamental challenge is posed by the possibility of building economics on some other foundation than individual rational behavior, and these alternatives are treated in later chapters.

Adam Smith

In the Middle Ages, economic philosophy was inextricably tied to the moral theology of Catholicism—the concept of moral values based on God's law as opposed to earthly value. *Just* prices and *just* wages based on moral precepts were contrasted with unjust profits and usury.[2] As the amount of trade and the importance of economic activity to state revenues increased dramatically in the fifteenth and sixteenth centuries, scholars began to seek principles and laws to guide public practice. Their most urgent problems revolved around national finances, trade, and the regulation of money. Rulers and administrators needed to know how to set tariffs, raise revenues, and deal with shortages of goods, food, and cash.

In this setting, what we now recognize as macroeconomics began as a discussion of mercantile issues, part of the rapid expansion of the West into Asia and the New World. Economic philosophers asked what was good for the nation, reflected on whether the national good was aligned with or opposed to the interests of individuals, and pondered how much the state should intervene in economic affairs.

Seeking mechanical *natural laws* of economics on a par with physical laws, Sir Dudley North (1641–1691) argued that left to itself, trade would follow mathematical laws—and government regulation would only interfere with a self-regulating system. Others, like Sir William Petty (1623–1687)—who invented national economic statistics—favored government intervention and regulation. These economists felt that the government, for example, must keep gold in the country, because gold is wealth, so the state must encourage exports and discourage imports, look for raw materials, and set up foreign trade outposts.[3]

The notion of natural economic laws arose not as a philosophical speculation about human nature but as part of a complex debate about government policy, during the 1600s and 1700s, a period of mercantile expansionism and growth in the institutions of the nation-state. Issues of trade and money were pulled away from theology as a practical matter, in the name of national interests. This allowed, for the first time, an abstract and philosophical discussion of *value* as separate from *morality*, a crucial step in the development of economics.

The real start of modern Western economics as a discipline is usually traced to Adam Smith (1723–1790). Beginning as a moral philosopher con-

Adam Smith

cerned with human motives, Smith later wrote *The Wealth of Nations* in 1776 as a series of lectures on public policy. The task he set for himself was that of a natural scientist, to discover the workings of a vast machine—the economy. His book deals with the division of labor as a vehicle of progress, the role of money, taxes, wages, profits, trade, and the health of the national economy. He built a structure of logic, founded ultimately on a theory of value, leading to strong arguments against the intervention of the state in economic affairs.

The fundamental problem faced by early economists was to find some measure of value that did not make recourse to religion. To build an empirical science, they had to find some way to define "good" in a secular way, without reference to scripture or divine judgment; this was the central goal of Adam Smith's earlier *The Theory of Moral Sentiments* (1759). Economic philosophers needed a yardstick that was not blessed by God, because they were seeking rational science rather than theology. Smith's argument about value is therefore crucially important and is worth tracing in more detail.

In *The Wealth of Nations*, he first asserts that value cannot be measured by money, because sometimes money is artificially scarce (a shortage of coins was a common problem in his times). Value is also not the same as utility or usefulness, as is shown by the comparison of water (useful, low value) and diamonds (useless, high value). Therefore, because all labor is of equal value to the worker, labor is the best measure of value. The real or natural value of a good is the amount of labor it takes to produce it. Smith used contrasts between primitives and moderns to get at this natural scale of values. Among North American Indians, he said, beavers were traded for deer in a rate corresponding to the amount of time it took to hunt them. In this imaginary primitive "rude" society, all labor has the same value, labor is the only factor of production, and all resources are equally available.

In contrast, in "civilized" society, values are determined by exchange, not by production. Value is thus determined by the amount of supply (though not by the demand) and by disutility, or the amount of work a person can save by trading for something instead of making it. Rents and profits become part of the value of things, because they represent the cost of land, tools, and property necessary for production. Smith therefore has two theories of value, one rooted in the individual (labor) and one in society (exchange). He never quite solves the problem of linking together the two sorts of value (Gudeman 1978, 352–353), but he makes a clear statement of priority by identifying the value of an individual's labor as "natural."

Using his theory of value, Smith tries to reason out answers to pressing social and political problems and issues of the day through logic and empirical observation. His goal is to understand how the economy can work to make prices reflect natural values so that workers are justly compensated for their labors. And he wants to show how, at the same time, this can lead to the generation of wealth, in the form of productive resources, property, factories, and the like, that will build a powerful nation. His answer is the mechanism of the market, which acts like an "invisible hand" to bring prices and values together and to provide at the same time the rents and profits that make the accumulation of wealth possible.

People participate in this open market because of their own self-interested desire to get the best return for their labor by selling at the highest price. But they also exchange because of an inborn human nature to "truck, barter, and exchange one thing for another" (1937, 13). They do not stop exchanging when they have simply fed and clothed themselves. People also seek to accumulate riches because of their vanity and desire to be admired (to share in the positive sympathetic feelings of others) and also because people "naturally" love order, harmony, and design. They seek wealth because it satisfies their "love of system, the . . . beauty of order, of art and contrivance" (1966, 265, Myers 1983, 112–117). Smith's human being is selfish because of essentially positive natural impulses to make order in the world. These desires need to be cultivated through education and civilization and are hindered and restrained by politics, corruption, guilds, corporations, and organized religion, to the detriment of society as a whole (McGraw 1992).

From this philosophical foundation, Smith builds a powerful argument that the individual's self-interest generates the society's best interests. The more competition, the more production, exchange, and accumulation. Each person's struggle to get the most value balances everyone else's. Competition keeps down prices, costs of production, profits, and interest rates, and it controls the abuses of monopolies. When governments and guilds and other organizations intervene to regulate and control prices, trade, and markets, they impede the working of the marketplace and retard the greater good. The key element of Smith's argument is that human individual self-interest, working through the market system, produces the greatest possible good for the nation as a whole. In this calculus, there is no essential or inherent natural conflict between the individual's and society's best interests, as long as free individuals are educated and enlightened to act in rational ways.

The effect of Smith's calculus is to move moral issues (What is fair? How should government promote common welfare?) into the realm of logic, rationality, education, and science. Beginning with a rational individual motivated by positive natural impulses, he undertakes a series of dramatic political attacks on monopolists, corrupt governments, tariffs promoted by strong business lobbyists, guilds, colonialists, and "the capricious ambitions of kings and ministers" (1937, 460).

In Smith's economics, the central problem is the relationship of the individual to society. His theory was suited to a time when there was a huge growth in trade, a long series of wars over trade routes and the sources of raw material, and an active debate about the role of the government in people's lives. The degree of official intervention in the European economy during his lifetime would shock most people today. In France, for example, a huge and corrupt bureaucracy set prices for almost all goods, charged multiple tolls and tariffs on even short journeys, and required a license or concession (and usually a bribe) for every industry, from those that made pins to people hunting truffles.[4] But Smith also lived before the worst consequences of industrial capitalism and colonialism were inflicted on millions of people in factories and fields, so he never saw mass suffering or poverty being justified in terms of the "free market."

Smith is an enduring figure because the same public issues and problems are still with us, and the debates that he opened are still going on. The clear linkage that Smith established between self-interested human nature and the conduct of public economic life is still the basis of the discipline of economics, even as Smith's successors have drawn the discipline further away from issues of morality, following his lead in their efforts to create a "calculus of fact." As we shall see below, despite the best efforts of economists, those same issues of morality and human motivations keep popping up everywhere.

The Foundations of Modern Economics

After Adam Smith, the next great ancestor figure of economics was David Ricardo, a successful British financier and member of Parliament (1772–1823). He continued to place the concept of value at the foundation of economics. Value was the "atom" in a Newtonian-style system of economic mechanics. The pillars that he built upon that foundation are a series of assumptions, the basis of an economic universe in which human actions can be predicted. These are the basic rules within which all economic behavior takes place: We assume that (1) most property is privately owned, (2) labor time is the ultimate source of value, (3) economic actors have freedom of choice, (4) the economic human is a rational maximizer of economic gain (the utilitarian principle), and (5) all things being equal equilibrium is the natural state of the economy. Equilibrium is a key concept in Ricardian economics, for it represents an ideal state of balance between supply and demand, values and prices, input and output. Equilibrium is the "natural" state of an economy that is allowed to operate without interference. The idea of equilibrium rests ultimately on the belief that there are natural laws of the economy that are just like the natural laws of physics.

Ricardo saw all these assumptions as "natural" states of being (not descriptions of the real world) and viewed his deductions as scientific statements of mechanical laws, but we can see his axioms as social philosophy. They describe a set of values about the way things should be. But by stating these principles as plausible lawlike generalities of human behavior, Ricardo tucked the moral philosophy away under the cover of fact. The question was no longer, "what is human nature?" Now it was, "making these assumptions about human nature, can we make some accurate predictions and guide policy?" And certainly, his work on the laws of wages and on comparative advantage in international trade proved extremely useful in understanding economic history and changes in prices over time.[5]

The economic historian Karl Priban (1983, 593) said that the fact that Ricardo invented a theory of economic equilibrium during the incredible dislocations of the Industrial Revolution proves that "the development of economic reasoning is to a high degree independent of the actual course of economic events." Perhaps. But it is also possible that Ricardo's theories were a very direct reaction to the world but that he sought a theory of order and equilibrium as a form of consolation and a source of hope in turbulent times. It may be that theories of reason and order are most needed in times of upheaval.

Thomas Robert Malthus (1766–1834) was a friend of Ricardo's, and he applied the economic calculus to a different problem, that of the balance of population and resources. In his *Essay on Population* (1798), he wrote that war, famine, and disease were the product of geometric population growth overshooting arithmetic growth in food resources. War, sickness, and starvation would therefore level off the population, producing a kind of equilibrium. Here again is a model based on human rationality, on a utilitarian assumption that people will keep having more children because it is to their own benefit, though it hurts society as a whole. Reasoning mathematically from these first premises reveals a "natural" equilibrium. The goal is to find natural order beneath the chaos of human history.

Older histories of economics often make the direction set by Ricardo toward a deductive scientific economics based on the utilitarian mechanism seem inevitable. They present only a logical progression of ideas toward perfection through the scientific method. But more recent histories of science point to the ways in which economics was very much a product of its times and of dominant Western culture.[6] Even within the European traditions, there were other kinds of economics.

One of the most vibrant alternative approaches was offered by the German economist, whom Priban called "intuitional economists." He accused the Germans of mixing all kinds of nationalism, evolutionism, spiritualism, and eventually racism into their discussion of the economy. The moral seems to be that if we stray from the strict science of Ricardo, we end up on a dark slide downward into magic and evil. In a more subtle and sympathetic reading of the German tradition, Joel Kahn (1990) has argued that these nineteenth-century historical economists were the intellectual ancestors of modern interpretive anthropology. Some of the German historicists, such as William Roscher, thought that all people had *two* basic instincts, one self-interested and the other moral and ethical. Others, for instance, Karl Bücher and Friedrich List, thought human beings had no innate nature, that they were products of their particular historical and national contexts. They emphasized understanding economic behavior within the social fabric of each particular setting and built historical and evolutionary typologies. In general, they were much more sympathetic to government intervention in economic affairs than the British, for they had little faith in the wisdom of industrialists and capitalists who were out to pursue their own interests.

While Smith and Ricardo were "boosters" for industry and trade, the German historicists were more conservative and liked to think back to an idealized economy based on agriculture, in an era of peace and stability (that was largely imaginary). Like Malinowski, their critique of utilitarianism was grounded in a dislike of capitalism, commercialism, and consumerism; instead, they loved the peasantry, the old traditional moral values, and the little community. They idealized *national spirit* and argued that economics was only a reflection of the folk tradition of the fatherland. It is not too great a leap to find some of the intellectual roots of Nazism in their mystification of an "essence" in national identity. The other major alternative to Adam Smith's utilitarianism also grew out of this German romantic tradition: Marxism. We will follow this trail in the next chapter. For now, we need to build up a clearer conception of classical microeconomics as it has descended to us from Ricardo.

Neoclassical Microeconomics

Modern economics is conventionally divided into two parts: *microeconomics* and *macroeconomics.* Macroeconomics looks at whole economic systems—conventionally the nation-state, but more recently the world economy. It is concerned with modeling those systems in ways that will account for historical relationships between variables (rates of taxation and rates of inflation, for example) in order to develop advice for those whose hands are actually on the levers that run the machine. Macroeconomists are in the business of telling politicians, for example, "if you raise military spending by 20 billion dollars, it will decrease unemployment by 2 percent." The main tool of macroeconomics has been the increasingly elaborate formal mathematical modeling called *econometrics.*

Macroeconomists divide the economy into sectors—usually households, businesses, and government—make generalizations about how each one acts when variables change, and then draw flows between them, trying at each step to simplify, so the model doesn't turn into one huge tangle of spaghetti. More recently, econometricians have built huge computer models of national economies that can keep track of all the spaghetti.

Microeconomists are concerned with the internal mechanics of the little boxes that the microeconomists create in their models (e.g., "the firm," "the household") and with the operations of the markets that link the boxes together. Their main paradigm, which is based on Ricardo's utilitarian precepts and uses formal mathematical tools, is often called *neoclassical economics.* Their basic approach is to look at decisions made under rigidly specified conditions, decisions about how to allocate labor in production and money in consumption, with the goal of predicting scarcity, prices, demand, and the cost and output of labor.

Economic Language

The idea of a *model* is essential for understanding modern academic economics. The idea is to simplify the operation of the real world, taking away the random, complicating, or unique variables, in order to build a mathematical representation that still behaves like the real world. Simplifying assumptions ("assume that all consumers know the prices of all the products in the market") helps in the initial model building, with the idea that complications can be reintroduced once the basic relationships become clear. This is something like the way engineers might build a computer model of how water flows over a riverbed. They start with simple formulas with a single velocity and a straight river, then gradually add more complicated formulas to try to account for bends and obstructions.

Economics as a discipline is defined partially by the language it uses to build these models. Here we will only cover some very basic terms, but it is important to recognize that relationships and predictions within microeconomics can be expressed in any of four sets of metaphors:

1. Verbal language: "A decrease in the price of a product will lead to an increase in the quantity purchased."
2. Arithmetic: a table with two columns showing how much gas will be consumed at each price.
3. Geometry: a graph showing a demand curve, linking the points specified in the arithmetic table (this is the favorite means of exposition in microeconomics).
4. Algebraic expression: a function written to describe the geometric curve.

These metaphors are progressively more abstract, in the sense that they become less intelligible to a layperson moving down the list. However, the more abstract the concept, the greater the precision. Whereas an arithmetic table is usually produced from empirical observations of the world, geometric and algebraic expressions allow *extrapolation,* that is, a specified curve or line on a graph includes an infinite number of points that have *not* been observed. The combination of different geometric expressions has proven an especially powerful tool in building dynamic predictive models of behavior. A key problem in microeconomics is the reification of models; it is easy to begin treating curves and lines on graphs as if they were real, instead of being abstract representations that are full of assumptions.

Utility, Indifference, and Supply and Demand

Economics is an immensely influential and powerful discipline; when journalists or politicians want to know what will happen to the country next year or when they want to know the impact of a new law or policy, they will almost always call on an economist. This prominence is not simply because of economists' rhetoric or political influence. Rather, economics has sometimes been capable of providing practical guidelines and advice for decision-making that appears well grounded and justified. If you want to know what will happen to cattle prices during a famine in Ethiopia, how rising school fees will change Thai fertility rates, or why corn prices fluctuate in Guatemalan markets, the formal tools of microeconomics are often a good starting point, and they are often the only objective modeling methods available. If nothing else, they can provide a set of baselines, grounded in explicit assumptions. Then, if and when our predictions fail, we can better ask which of our assumptions is wrong, or we can ask what variables have been left out. Before we set about criticizing microeconomics, we should investigate how economists understand human nature and decisions.[7]

In trying to work from a set of scientific laws about individual behavior in order to establish the laws of motion for entire world economies, economists have built several distinct bodies of theory. Microeconomics begins with the theory of demand, grounded in the utilitarian assumption that each human being is a rational maximizer who seeks the optimum amount of satisfaction. Most economists make the simplifying ethnocentric assumption that the consuming sector of society is composed of households, each of which has a pooled bundle of resources to spend in the marketplace. Microeconomics also provides a model of production, grounded in the theory of the firm. Each firm seeks to allocate its resources most efficiently to create products, with the goal of maximizing profits. Production and consumption come together in the theory of markets, which is concerned with the regulation of prices and values and the circulation of goods. Beginning with a market where producing firms meet consuming households, macroeconomics then adds other institutions and traces flows of money and the effects of economic policies on the state of the system.

The theory of demand is the area where anthropology and economics intersect most closely, though in later chapters we will also look at anthropological theories of exchange and production. The theory of demand concerns the choices you make between options in a situation where the things you want and the things you have are scarce. The problem is to maximize your subjective satisfaction or well-being, what economists call your *utility*. Utility is simply satisfaction gained through consumption; its opposite is "disutility," or the dissatisfaction of unpleasant work. Utility is not an objectively measurable quantity, but it can be measured relatively in the form of rankings: You are assumed to have stable preferences for one thing over another, and these ordered preferences can be converted mathematically into a "utility function" that assigns a higher number to the options that rank higher.[8]

Maximizing in this way requires two sets of balances, between alternate ends and alternate means. The theory assumes that there is perfect competition and substitutability: Your choice between goods is free, and your means can be used to achieve any of the alternate ends. Utility can be provided by any of the possible ends or goods, in different quantities and combinations. Traditionally, this is taught with the examples of money as the means and goods as the ends, using the model of a shopping trip. But the same model can be applied to anything you want and anything you have to give up to get it—say giving up free time to study to get better grades or giving deference and "kissing up" to a superior in order to get a raise.

As soon as we accept that there are things that we want that can be ranked against each other, we have to add that when we do get what we want, we don't keep wanting it as much. In other words, satiation is possible, and this is formalized under the term "diminishing marginal utility." As you get more of something you value, each additional increment (the additions are said to be "on the margin") provides you with less *marginal* utility.

As you consume a good and its utility decreases, you begin to think of consuming something else instead, something that you originally valued less highly than the first good. Economic theory says that for any combination of goods there will be *substitutability* in maximizing total utility. Let's say we have two goods, shorts and T-shirts. Suppose you have no strong preference for one over the other, and in fact you would be just as happy with one pair of shorts and five T-shirts as you would be with five pairs of shorts and one T-shirt. Figure 3.1 shows a *straight indifference curve* that describes this situation. We have defined one person's preference in terms of the substitutability of the two goods, that is, a set of combinations, each of which produces the same total utility.

In reality, few pairs of goods have perfect substitutability because goods usually differ in their basic characteristics. Shorts don't substitute for T-shirts in most social situations! This calls for a notion of the *diminishing rate of marginal substitution* (Figure 3.2). In the middle of the curve, one T-shirt can substitute for one pair of shorts, but when we get toward zero pairs of shorts, twenty T-shirts may not substitute for a single one. This curve is therefore concave. As you get enough shorts, your need for shorts decreases and you are willing to substitute more T-shirts for each additional pair of shorts you give up. The idea here follows simple common sense: You will be more willing to substitute something else for a good that you have more of. As you satisfy urgent needs, you will begin to want other things more.

Indifference curves are useful because they can help predict how people actually behave. In a marketplace, the *price* of goods is independent of an individual's preference, so the cost or budget line is always a straight line.

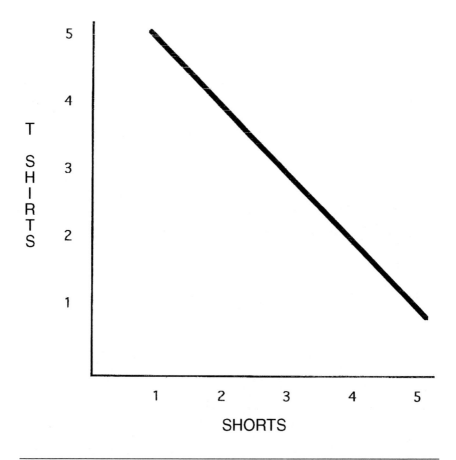

FIGURE 3.1   A straight indifference curve. The curve connects all possible combinations of two goods that give a consumer equal satisfaction. Any point above and to the right is preferred to any point on the curve.

There is a fixed combination of two goods that you can buy with a set amount of money (Figure 3.3). If T-shirts and shorts cost the same, the relationship will be plotted as a 45-degree diagonal line. The theory says that the *rational* consumer, not knowing the calculus, will still always choose the combination of the two goods that lies at A. The consumer *could* buy six pairs of shorts and no T-shirt or six T-shirts and no shorts, but given the indifference curve, the rational thing is to buy three of each.

Microeconomic analysis of demand can characterize individual consumers or groups of consumers on the basis of their different indifference curves, in order to predict how they will behave under changing parameters (e.g., the budget line). For example, what will happen if Fred's desire for shorts in-

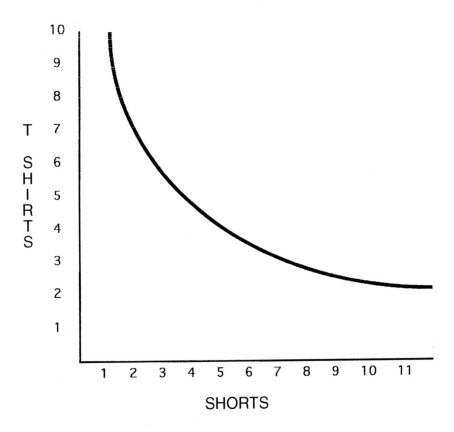

FIGURE 3.2　A concave indifference curve. The diminishing rate of marginal substitution reflects the fact that as consumers get more shirts, they are more willing to give up shirts for shorts. All the points on the curve provide the same level of satisfaction.

creases when shorts come into fashion and T-shirts go out? Before micro-economics, the commonsense answer was that he would stop buying T-shirts and spend *all* of his money on shorts, but that is not what happens, either in the model or in reality. He buys more shorts but still buys some shirts, and the change can be accurately predicted.

The Economics of Women, Men, and Work by Francine Blau and Marianne Ferber (1986) is full of examples of how demand analysis can be applied to current social and gender issues. For example, they analyze the tradeoff between home-produced goods and market goods, as part of their analysis of the role of tastes and preferences in determining the household division of

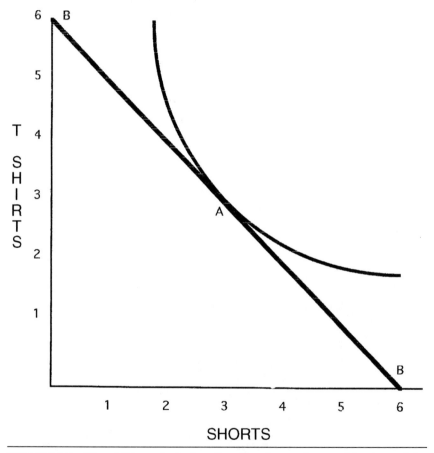

FIGURE 3.3   The addition of a budget line that shows what combinations of the two goods can be bought with the same amount of money. Point A is the highest level of satisfaction that can be obtained with the amount of money represented by the budget line BB, so it is the optimum choice (3 shirts and 3 shorts).

labor. Using a "production possibility curve" that defines all the total combinations of home-produced goods and housework that a couple could generate, they show how couples allocate their time between housework and wage work in order to reach an optimum combination of home-produced and market goods. In the process, Blau and Ferber demonstrate why unequal pay between men and women promotes task specialization in household labor, with men concentrating on wage work and women on housework. They show mathematically how households allocate their labor when wages rise and how government subsidies of child care affect wages and labor force participation.

It is important to remember that although the typical economic example deals with *dollars* and goods, what is really being maximized is *utility* and that means that the methodology can be applied to situations where very immaterial things are being traded off against each other—love and sex, security and excitement. Despite Harold Schneider's suggestion that microeconomic methods could be used in societies where there is no money (1974, 53–73), this has rarely been pursued by anthropologists, perhaps because it is so difficult to imagine measuring nonmaterial values and utility. But economists don't demand precise measures of utility for their model building, only rankings.

A major practical use for microeconomic consumer theory is in predicting demand at different prices. If you imagine a whole series of graphs like Figure 3.3 for two alternate goods at different prices for one of the goods, you get a demand curve—the basic tool for answering the most difficult questions in selling: What will happen to demand if I raise the price? Will my profit increase or decrease? This is the basis of market theories of the relationship between supply and demand, the foundation for macroeconomics.

Basic market *equilibrium analysis* is quite simple. Figure 3.4 presents an analysis of how the supply and demand for labor affects wages. The *demand* curve slopes down to the right because as wages decrease, the demand for workers increases (employers will be able to hire more workers and increase their efficiency). The *supply* curve slopes upward because as wages increase, more people will want to work (which has to do with their own indifference curves of labor versus leisure).

The two curves intersect at a theoretical point of equilibrium—where everyone who wants to work at a given wage can get a job—and *demand and supply are equal*. As Blau and Ferber demonstrate in their analysis of the shift from housework to wage work, a change in supply or demand will change the equilibrium—S2 in Figure 3.4 shows a situation where the supply of clerical workers is diminished (because other jobs for women open up), and this shifts the curve to the left, producing a higher equilibrium wage for the remaining clerical workers. The same analysis can also demonstrate why job discrimination against women in the workplace causes men's wages to rise (1986, 228–279). Their analysis does not presume to explain why there is

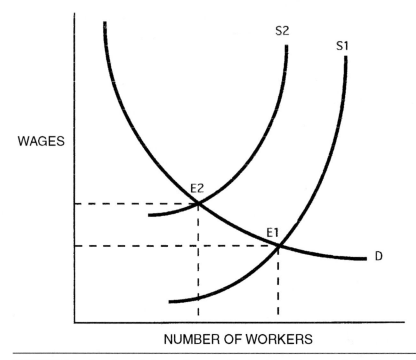

FIGURE 3.4   Supply and demand curves. D, the demand curve, shows that companies will hire more workers as wages fall. The supply curves S show that as wages go up, more workers will want to work and will enter the job market. The intersection of the curves is an equilibrium point where supply and demand are in balance. Where there are fewer total workers in the job market, as in S2, the equilibrium point is higher on the demand curve, and wages will be higher.

unequal pay for men and women in labor markets all over the world, but it does provide an explicit basis for understanding what kinds of economic policies and markets can be expected to reduce labor inequality. And these authors show how supply and demand are logically connected to each other throughout the economy.

Other elements of neoclassical economics have been used by anthropologists or have some potential for further use. I will briefly discuss some of them here and point out some of their assumptions and weaknesses.

Elasticity Analysis

The theory of elasticity proceeds from the observation that demand for some goods is quite flexible, responding readily to changes in price and supply. Demand for other goods is stable, regardless of the marketplace. Consider the demand for sorghum in a West African farm family. The family needs a specific ration of sorghum as a staple food and will work extremely hard, if necessary, to obtain it. Regardless of the price of sorghum in the market or the yield from their farms, the family will consume about the same amount of sorghum per person every year. If there is an exceptionally abundant harvest, however, the family will not consume a great deal more sorghum. Instead the surplus will be stored, sold, or traded for other goods. Demand for sorghum is therefore *inelastic* (if demand does not change at all when price rises or falls, economists say demand is "perfectly inelastic").

In contrast, in the same West African society, demand for ornamented metal serving bowls varies widely with price and production. In a good year when people have a lot of money, they will buy many. If trade is disrupted, supplies are cut off, and the price of bowls goes up, people will buy very few. Demand for bowls is therefore *elastic* (if demand goes down by the same percentage that prices go up, elasticity is said to be "unitary").

There is a third special possibility: What if when prices increase, demand increases instead of dropping or staying the same? The idea here is that for some kinds of goods, like Porsches, high price actually makes the good more attractive to consumers. This is called the *Veblen effect* after the economist Thorstein Veblen (1857–1929), who invented the term "conspicuous consumption."

Economists often assume that elasticities are qualities of goods themselves; demand for food is conventionally inelastic whereas demand for luxury clothing is more elastic. Anthropologists would generally find elasticity more grounded in cultural definitions of necessity and luxury, recognizing that needs have a strong cultural dimension (while remembering that the need for food also has a biological basis). By adding a cultural analysis to the study of demand elasticity, anthropologists make an important contribution to policy analysis.

For example, up until the "oil shocks" of the early 1970s, economists considered the demand for energy in developed countries to be highly inelastic. They planned for continuing major expansion of nuclear power and oil refineries and were taken by surprise by the effects of the OPEC oil embargo on Western economies. Energy demand proved to be much more elastic than it had been before, and when prices rose, demand plummeted, leading to the abandonment of many half-built power plants. Why did consumers suddenly become sensitive to energy prices, and why did energy demand become more elastic? An anthropological study found the changes rooted in environmentalism, political activism, and changing notions of domesticity associated with new gender roles and greater numbers of working women (Wilk and Wilhite 1984). Elasticity provides an important tool for linking the cultural behavior of individuals to flows of goods through the marketplace on a national and global scale.

Production Theory

People almost never work in isolation from each other; productive labor requires cooperation and the division of labor. Microeconomics provides a whole tool kit of concepts and tools for understanding how people combine their labors with goods and resources in order to produce efficiently.

My own work on agricultural production among the Kekchi Maya in Belize (1991) asked how farmers allocate their time among different productive systems and examined the way they use different sized labor groups to perform different tasks. Almost any anthropological study of hunting, gathering, or farming will use some variant of production theory to try to understand how and why people form particular groups and how they allocate resources and labor. Usually when we consider options—for instance, how much they would have to eat or how much money they would make using different systems—we find out that people are making rational choices, maximizing their yields from their labor, within the restraints imposed by their tools and environments (good examples can be found in Fricke 1986; Barlett 1982; Hill 1982; and Johnson 1971).

Two very basic and useful concepts in studies of production are *specialization* and *economies of scale.* Specialization refers to the ability to produce more efficiently by dividing labor among individuals or groups. Marshall Sahlins, for example, showed that farm families on the Pacific island of Moala were able to farm more effectively by sending work groups off to do different jobs in different parts of the island (1957). Because the taro patches were far from the coconut plantations and because some people could climb trees better than others, the whole group benefited by sending specialized teams off to do different jobs.

An economy of scale is the result of finding the optimum number of people to do a particular job. This part of production theory is concerned with the relationship between the size of an enterprise and its efficiency (usually measured in output per person). An economy of scale exists when each percentage of increase in input (labor or money or materials) produces a greater percentage of increase in output.

When the Kekchi Maya build a house, they call together a group of friends and kin to help. A single man alone simply could not build a house because it takes three people to hold beams in place while they are tied together with vines. When it is time to thatch the roof, the minimum number necessary is four—three to stand on the rafters and tie the bundles of palm leaves together and one down below to hand materials up. The efficiency of each person's labor increases with each additional person ("increasing marginal returns" in Figure 3.5); more hands means the work goes much faster. But this does not go on indefinitely. At some point, adding more workers increases the speed of the job, but not in proportion, so that a group of twenty-five people is only a little faster than twenty (diminishing marginal returns). At a certain point, adding more workers means people get in each other's way; a group of thirty-five has so many people standing around giving orders and suggestions that it actually gets less accomplished than a group of twenty-five (negative marginal returns).

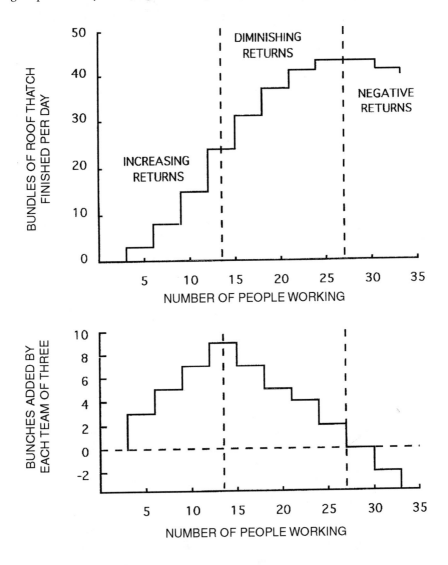

FIGURE 3.5 Economies of scale in thatching a roof. Each additional team of three increases output. The highest output per person is found in a group of 12.

Production theory has proven powerful in explaining differences between productive groups in different settings. James Loucky uses it to show why households are differently constituted in two Guatemalan villages (1979). In a farming village with limited land, households face diminishing marginal returns; they tend to marry late and have few children. In a rope-making community, additional labor increases the efficiency of the household by allowing a more elaborate division of labor. People there marry earlier and have more children.

Production theory is particularly important for anthropologists working with social groups that organize and divide up labor, including households, cooperatives, and some lineages and communities. Few people would argue that these groups are organized *exclusively* to achieve efficiency in production. But if we understand how they could best work together, we are then in a very strong position to identify the political, environmental, social, and cultural pressures and constraints that make people work harder or less efficiently than they otherwise could.

Institutional Economics

Most formal neoclassical economic theory assumes that producers, buyers, and sellers in firms, households, and markets have perfect knowledge of information. In other words, people know what their options are, and they know the outcome of their choices. More advanced models consider the cost of information and the possibility of imperfect knowledge. In particular, the field called *institutional economics* has built a sophisticated analysis of the origin and development of economic and political institutions. Beginning with neoclassical assumptions, institutional economists add the costs of information, the costs of making decisions, and the cost of institutional arrangements, including families, firms, and bureaucracies.[9] For example, a woman may find that it is economically rational to quit being a housekeeper and go to work outside the household—but the cost of renegotiating her relationships with her children and spouse may be so high that she puts off going out to work until the benefits are more clear-cut. This kind of resistance to institutional change is what economists call "stickiness." Many institutionalists have also pointed out that when information is hard to come by, there are many reasons for people to stick together and cooperate, even when they may otherwise do better on their own.

For institutional economists, the "transaction costs" of building relationships, changing organizations, and getting information are the key to understanding why people form groups and work together in the real world. This appears to make a space in mainstream economics for the subjects anthropologists so often study—kinship groups, clans, household organization, and political systems. Nevertheless, this often means that economists are going ahead and reinventing anthropology on their own, without the benefit of careful fieldwork (see, for example, Douglass North's 1993 Nobel Prize lecture).

Game Theory and Risky Choice

Although formal microeconomics often assumes that people know their options and can anticipate the results of their actions, many of the most important choices that people make are based on imperfect information. In real life, people make choices in different degrees of ignorance or uncertainty. Specialized formal methods have been developed, first in agricultural economics and then elsewhere, for choices made when people do not precisely know the consequences of their actions.

Theorists make an important distinction between *risk*, where an actor knows the rough probability of different outcomes (e.g., a farmer knows that 20 percent of seed sown will not sprout), and *uncertainty*, where the actor does not know the probabilities of possible results. Risk is predictable and quantifiable, whereas uncertainty is unpredictable. Microeconomists have developed a number of formal tools for analyzing choices under different degrees of risk, which often lead them to classify people or cultures as risk takers or risk averse, according to the ways they make their choices (see Ellis 1988, 80–101). Frank Cancian's study of innovation among Maya farmers is a convincing demonstration of the usefulness of risk theory in anthropology (1979; see also the recent collection in Cashdan 1990). He shows why the risk-taking and innovative farmers among the Maya were usually in the upper-middle levels of wealth—the richest had little need to take risks and the poorest could not afford to. Insurance of various kinds, long-term contracts, and various methods of "hedging" bets are other ways people deal with uncertainty.

Anthropologists have also done important research on *risk perception*, showing how culture affects people's ideas about what is risky or dangerous. It turns out that people are often much more afraid of very rare but dramatic disasters like nuclear meltdown than they are of the much more deadly and common but mundane dangers like car crashes and heart attacks (Douglas 1985).

In general, when farmers or shoppers make risky choices, their environment doesn't respond to their actions. If it is going to rain this summer, it rains whether you chose to plant corn or not. But when your decisions involve other *people*, who are also making choices that affect the outcome, you are playing a different and much more complex game. In the 1940s, mathematician John von Neumann and economist Oskar Morgenstern began to work out mathematical models for simple two-person situations where one person's choice affected the outcome of another's choice. This has since developed into a field called *game theory*, now considerably augmented by the use of personal computers to model games and simulate their outcomes.

Game theory asks how people can achieve an optimum outcome when others are trying to do the same thing and the consequences of their actions are linked together. A classic example would be when you are with a group that is dining out and plans to divide the check evenly. Should you order the cheapest thing on the menu or the most expensive? In a typical game, everyone benefits if everyone cooperates, but everyone except the selfish one suffers when someone acts selfishly. The question is, under what circumstances does it pay people to be cooperative, altruistic, or selfish? What happens when you allow people to play a whole series of games, learning from their experience?

Game theory had a brief flowering among anthropologists in the 1960s (see Buchler and Nutini 1969) and a more critical currency in the late 1970s (e.g., Quinn 1978; Gladwin 1979). It proved useful in understanding some kinds of hunting and fishing strategies and some kinds of tribal politics, mostly by providing a firm mathematical grounding for the intuitive understanding that sometimes "it pays to cooperate."[10] Recent computer simulations reach the same conclusion—that in the long run, cooperation and trust can emerge among competitive individuals pursuing their own interests (Lance and Huberman 1994). Some are tempted to extend game theory to explain the evolution of human societies. But like the rest of microeconomics, game theory begins with some basic assumptions about human nature and utility. As we shall now see, these assumptions have been seriously questioned.

Critiques of Formal Economics

Belizeans often say "The higher monkey climb, the more he expose his ass." Neoclassical economics has climbed about as high as is possible for a social science, and it has therefore attracted a crowd of critics. On the one hand, sometimes they seem like a legion of pygmies hurling sour grapes at a giant. On the other hand, they may be Davids who will one day bring Goliath crashing down. These critics have attacked many different aspects of economics, and we will next look at some of their most telling arguments. Economics itself is far from a unified field, for although there is certainly a dominant mainstream, there are also various "heterodox" schools of economics that disagree with most of the neoclassical assumptions (see Albelda, Gunn, and Waller 1987 for an excellent treatment of these deviant branches). I focus here on these internal critiques of the discipline by economists and economic psychologists. The anthropological criticisms of economics will be discussed again in Chapter 5.

Human Rationality

One line of criticism attacks the working details of microeconomic theory, looking particularly into assumptions about human beings as rational maximizers. Amos Tversky, a psychologist, has experimentally shown that the human brain is an imperfect decisionmaking tool, even when faced with relatively simple problems of choice. A basic example is the nonintuitive nature of the laws of probabilities. Even though we can easily demonstrate that the odds of a coin toss are fifty-fifty each time, humans insist on believing that a heads this time increases the chance of getting a tails next time (1981).

There is also now an extensive literature, based on the work of Herbert Simon, that examines the limitations of human reasoning power in complex decisionmaking environments. Simon invented the term *satisficing* to express the idea that people do not always seek the optimum solution—they usually do not work that hard. Instead, they set a minimum goal and adopt the first strategy they can find that meets that goal. People use "bounded rationality," that is, decisions that are limited by people's perceptions, imperfect knowledge, and subjective feelings, to make the best of an imperfect world. Simon argues that we should also recognize that making the best possible choices is often too costly; it would just take too much time and effort to find out all we need to know to make the "best" choices (1957; 1987).[11]

Many have questioned the reality of the economist's model of consumer behavior, which assumes that we all have a single unified utility in our heads, that preferences can be ranked, and that preferences are transitive (meaning that if you like apples more than chocolate, and chocolate more than cabbage, you therefore like apples more than cabbage). Economists also ask why we should we expect people's preferences to be stable for more than a few moments at a time (Tversky 1969). The whole notion that each person's utilities are internal and independent of everyone else's has been criticized as sexist and androcentric (built on a male point of view) because it ethnocentrically presumes that human beings can be emotionally unconnected to each other (England 1993).

Even if people do have stable and transitive preferences in their heads that they seek to maximize, how can we ever know what they are? Conventional economics says we can find out by looking at people's behavior, that when people act they reveal their preferences. But many critics point to the ultimate circularity of this argument. We know they have preferences because they made particular choices, and we know they made those choices because of their preferences. We have to *assume* people are rational in order to measure their preferences (Rosenberg 1992, 159; Downey 1987). The same circular argument appears in the notion of maximizing: We know people are maximizing because they survive, and we know they survive because they are maximizing.

The most fundamental criticism of rational choice theory is one that questions the whole notion of human behavior as decisionmaking. Jon Elster does not dispute that sometimes people do make rational, goal-driven decisions. But he also points to many actions taken without a clear goal, with no knowledge of the consequences, and because it is easier to conform than to choose. He says that for many choices, for example, choosing between careers, people simply have no objective basis for making decisions, cannot rank preferences, and make no decision at all or make the wrong choice. In other words, people can behave irrationally for very good reasons (1990).

The ultimate problem with all economic explanations of human behavior—and the concept that my students always have the hardest time accepting—is the idea of *rationality* itself. How do we tell if an action is rational or irrational? Sometimes it only looks irrational because we don't understand the setting, the meaning, or the history of a particular action. But maybe it really *is* irrational, and we are just making up a rational-sounding explanation based on our own ethnocentric principles. And what does it mean to argue that rationality is universal in all human decisions? Does this mean that rationality has been hardwired by evolution into all of our brains (as argued in the new field of evolutionary psychology), making cultural difference superfluous or trivial? These are very difficult, deep, and challenging questions that have no simple answers. On one level, the idea of universal rational principles seems quite absurd, given the wide variation in human behavior from culture to culture and across history. On another level, people from very different cultures are quite capable of understanding each other's actions and motives; they can communicate and evaluate each other's behavior. This would seem to argue for some universal properties of the human mind. As usual, the extremes of universal rationality or irrationality turn out to be untenable, and the truth lies somewhere in between, demanding to be defined along some other dimension than the one we are using (see Latour 1993 for some alternatives).

Economic Methods and Language

Another form of criticism looks more closely at the epistemology of economics, asking how economics gains knowledge of the world and how it expresses that knowledge. Economists themselves have been some of the strongest critics of the tools, arguments, and philosophical assumptions of their field. Their arguments range from friendly to hostile and are aimed at everything from the way economics journals select papers to the impossible complexity of national economic models. Economists have argued that modern economics is a poor guide to understand either the past, present, or future; hopelessly mired in Western philosophy instead of science, it is unable to predict a small thing like a price on the stock market or a large thing like the emergence of Taiwan as a world economic power (Fallows 1993; Heilbroner 1991; see also Rosenberg 1992).

Wassily Leontief, a senior economist, has written to *Science* magazine to express his disgust at the unreality of most academic articles in his field: "Nothing reveals the aversion of the great majority of present-day academic economists for systematic empirical inquiry more than the methodological devices that they employ to avoid or cut short the use of concrete factual information." He points out that more than one-half the papers in the *American Economic Review* are simply mathematical models without any empirical data: "Page after page of professional economic journals are filled with mathematical formulas leading the reader from sets of more or less plausible but arbitrary assumptions to precisely stated but irrelevant theoretical conclusions" (1982, 104). A review of extremely expensive large-scale computer models used by government economists for forecasting finds them wildly inaccurate; in practice, economists "fiddle and fit" until the model gives them the result they expect (Kolata 1986; Kuttner 1985).

When economists *do* use real data about the world in their studies, they tend to depend almost entirely on aggregate statistics produced by official government sources. Andrew Kamark, after working at the World Bank for twenty-six years, concluded that most of these official figures and measurements are too inaccurate for use in any kind of calculation. When they are added or multiplied, their individual errors compound, leading to numbers that cannot be used for comparison, much less prediction. He demonstrates that basic concepts like "unemployment" and "income" are arbitrary abstractions that do not fit reality and that cannot be compared across cultures or through time. Common measures like GNP and the balance of payments—the keystones of macroeconomics—are not accurate (or even vague) measures of human welfare or economic health and are often deceptively concrete (1983). As Susan Greenhalgh (1990) shows in her study of economic explanations for changes in fertility and mortality, when national statistics are aggregated and averaged (as economists usually do), they obscure all the important variability and become useless mute numbers.

Donald McCloskey stands out as a critic of economics who often sounds like an anthropologist. In two very readable books, *The Rhetoric of Economics* (1985) and *If You're So Smart: The Narrative of Economic Expertise* (1990), he attacks the language of economics, particularly for the way it insulates economists from criticism and hides their politics behind science.

To McCloskey, economics has become a cultural artifact of logical positivism, based on an outmoded idea that science is simply the discovery of facts and natural laws. McCloskey finds this model of science unconvincing and, following recent trends among philosophers, argues that instead science is *rhetoric* and *conversation,* merely persuasive argument based on selected and unsystematic observation. He says, "Science is Rhetoric, all the way down . . . Master scientists are master rhetoricians, word spinners in no dishonorable sense" (1990, 82). From here he argues that economic discourse is neither more nor less than stories built with all the common persuasive tropes used in rhetoric, including metaphor, analogy, symmetry, irony, and allegory. Economists, McCloskey says, tell magical stories, and by and large that is fine with him, as long as they do not pretend they are selling natural laws, immune from dispute. In practice, mathematical metaphors have become a language of power divorced from reality, a tool in the hands of those in power.

Economic philosophy, methods, and language, says McCloskey, are rooted in a "hard," extremely masculine model of science that excludes the whole world of experience, emotion, and personal insight (1993). Not by coincidence, it has also tended to exclude women from its ranks. Worse, economics lies about its essential nature, representing facts where there is only rhetoric. But like the other critics I have mentioned so far, McCloskey's solution is not to do away with the field. He wants economics to remain rational while getting away from the falseness, limitations, and hypocrisy of modernist methods. The problem he faces is that of many social scientists of this postmodernist era: How do we retain a sense of truth and contact with an empirical world of fact if we leave behind the notion of science as an objective search for natural law? McCloskey sees the division between science and the humanities as a historical artifact; he wants to build in the middle ground. The question remains, however, what kind of edifice should be built there? (Some answers may appear in the new journal *Feminist Economics,* which promises to take up many of these issues.)

Economic Immorality

One of the most persistent critiques of neoclassical economics is aimed at the utilitarian assumption that human beings are rational maximizers of their own utility. For some, this means that economists see human beings as innately immoral, hedonistic pleasure seekers, single-mindedly calculating their own advantage in every situation.[12] One alternative has been to keep the scientific form and tools of economics, while throwing out the utilitarian assumption (the opposite of McCloskey, who keeps some utilitarianism but throws out the science).

Instead, imagine that human beings maximize two or more different utilities that may be quite inconsistent with each other. What if human beings don't have a single rank order of preferences but instead have several different classifications. For example, a middle-class American could not compare the utility of a new Volvo with the value of a colleague's respect. Many schemes have been proposed that purport to divide "needs" from "wants" or to divine the basic impulses of human beings. The Enlightenment philosopher Thomas Hobbes, in *Leviathan,* argued for three basic urges: safety, gain, and reputation (1991, pt. 1, chap. 13). Another possible course is to follow Western dualist thinking about human nature and divide human impulses into a "higher self," that is, moral, altruistic, and driven by truthseeking, and a "lower self," which is selfish, subjective, egotistical, and driven by needs (Lutz and Lux 1988, 17).

This kind of dualism is elaborated by Amitai Etzioni in *The Moral Dimension: Toward a New Economics* (1988) into a new field called "socioeconomics" or "humanistic economics." This project has been very influential. Etzioni has formed an association, a newsletter, and a journal, and he appears frequently on news programs, arguing for a type of "kinder, gentler" capitalism, ideas that are fundamental to a political movement called the Communitarians.

Etzioni argues that humans are social beings as well as rational self-serving individuals, and he wants to find ways of combining these two aspects of the human experience. People make moral judgments on their urges, judgments rooted in their social experience, and these moral commitments are often stronger than their biological urges. For this reason, people often make their choices on the basis of social and moral judgment and only secondarily on logical grounds. He has three lines of argument to support this position:

1. *Humans are primarily illogical.* Creatures of habit and conditioning, they brush their teeth but do not fasten their seat belt; they smoke cigarettes even though they know it will kill them. People do not reliably connect cause and effect, and they do not do what is best for them, even when they do have good information.
2. *Institutions, not individuals, are the main unit of society.* Humans do not have free will the way neoclassical economics says. Instead, people act as agents of institutions, and they treat each other as members of categories instead of autonomous individuals. Institutionalized inequalities and power determine prices, not the free operation of the marketplace.
3. *Humans are often altruistic rather than selfish.* People do things like giving up food for Ramadan and Lent; they jump in rivers to save drowning strangers, they give gifts without expecting any return, they save for their descendants, and they don't leave when their spouses get Alzheimer's disease. They cooperate with each other at every turn, even when it would be in their best interest to go out on their own. All societies, he argues, follow moral codes, and everywhere only deviants are self-interested.

Many of these points are unquestionably true, and Etzioni combines and synthesizes many different economic critiques. But does he offer a viable alternative? The problem remains that Etzioni's idea of two basic urges is just as untestable as the utilitarian assumption of one basic urge. Neither Etzioni nor the neoclassicists can create a definition of "rationality" that avoids circularity and that most anthropologists would find acceptable when applied to other cultures. The "two urges" theory is very ethnocentric, and from a historical perspective, it can be seen as just another in a long line of moral critiques of modernity, individuality, and selfishness, extending back into Christian theology.

If, as Etzioni would have it, people are often illogical, then what *is* the basis of their decisionmaking? Surely it is not completely determined by their social setting, which would leave us all as automatons. I suggest that what is missing in this part of Etzioni's critique is exactly what anthropology has to offer—a concept of *culture*. The idea that culture patterns the way we think and the way we value different options allows anthropology to resolve the paradox of rationality and autonomy in a social setting. We will turn to this anthropological alternative in later chapters.

Summary

In this chapter I have only touched the fringes of a huge edifice of theory, observation, and method built on the basic assumptions of neoclassical microeconomics. If we are willing to assume that human beings are individual, rational maximizers of an abstract utility, we can move onward to some very complex and powerful inferences about the way the economy works. For some economists, the edifice has become an end in itself. Entranced by the elegance of their mathematics, they have often lost sight of the world it is supposed to describe and explain. Some argue that the study of economic management, firms, national accounts, and global institutions has moved so far that it can now stand independent of the microeconomic theory of rational maximizing. The managers of the Federal Reserve lose little sleep over the circular logic of revealed preference. Many economists argue that it doesn't really matter what is going on in people's minds anyway. They argue that they can go ahead and act as if people are logical maximizers, as long as it works.

The problem seems to be that for many kinds of situations, neoclassical economics doesn't work. Since many economists don't ever check their models against the real world, this doesn't bother them. But a vocal minority is worried, and the last decade has seen a real flowering of feminist, historical, philosophical, and critical scholarship in economics. In trying to understand what is wrong with the dominant academic neoclassical economics, many of the critics are drawn to that tiny human figure at the foundation of it all, that rational utilitarian called "economic man."

We began this chapter with Adam Smith, who defined two kinds of value. One was rooted in the individual's innate knowledge of the value of toil. The second emerged from social life, from the ownership of property and the division of labor. Although Smith deemed the first kind "natural," he accepted that beyond the earliest state of nature, all humans engaged in social life and derived their values from their relationships with others. We finished the chapter with Amitai Etzioni, still reworking the same problem of the contradiction between rational self-interest and the need for selflessness and community. But in the time between Smith and Etzioni, economics generally ignored the question of human nature. While economics rose to dominance in public life, other social sciences set about trying to find alternatives to utilitarianism.

Notes

1. The George Bernard Shaw epigram that begins this chapter is found in Winokur (1987, 14). The rise of individualism in the West is discussed in almost every history book, though Coontz's *The Way We Never Were* (1992) gives the theme a unique and timely context in the Western ideology of the family.

2. The medieval scheme was founded on a moralistic division of the economy into productive (agriculture and manufacture) and unproductive (lending and trade), established by the Greeks, as is well described by Booth (1993). Many other civilizations have targeted particular forms of wealth and work, usually trading and usury, as unclean or immoral.

3. Much of this discussion comes from Priban's *A History of Economic Reasoning* (1983) and Myers's *The Soul of Modern Economic Man* (1983). Another important work is Louis Dumont's *From Mandeville to Marx* (1977).

4. An excellent source on the economic context of Smith's times is Fernand Braudel's *The Wheels of Commerce* (1982). Thomas McGraw has written a short article (1992) that gives an extremely clear discussion of Adam Smith as a moral philosopher and details the way his ideas have been distorted and exploited by later generations to justify laissez-faire economic policies.

5. Ricardo's *iron law of wages* states that without outside intervention, wages will always tend toward the workers' subsistence level. *Comparative advantage* means that countries are better off producing the things they can make more cheaply than others and trading them to other countries than they would be if they tried to make everything they needed for themselves.

6. A fundamental and devastating critique of how economics developed in the Western tradition can be found in chapter 6 of Foucault's *The Order of Things* (1970). An even broader philosophical questioning of the history of economics is found in the work of the French surrealist Georges Bataille (see Richman 1982).

7. My goal here is not to write a condensed textbook in introductory economics; many good texts do a much better job than I could hope to. The examples here are meant to show how economic reasoning flows systematically from a simple model of human beings as utility-maximizing animals.

8. Utility and rational choice theory and its problems are simply and elegantly explained by Elster (1989). Amartya Sen (1990) provides a useful critique of the notion of utility, as does England (1993) from an explicitly feminist point of view. The classic critique of utility and indifference theory, still important and readable, is that of Georgescu-Roegen (1954). A more recent critique in a similar vein is given by Margolis (1982). The classic formulation accepts that utility is an internal and subjective value; utility can be measured only when it is revealed through behavioral choice (Houthakker 1950). For an intelligent defense of the notion of utility, see Stigler and Becker (1977). Heath (1976) provides a dense, but thorough and critical set of examples of rational-choice theories applied to anthropological topics. I also highly recommend Ellis (1988) for examples of different economic methods and theories applied to peasant farming. Machina (1990) gives a lucid but technical discussion of the theory of choice under uncertainty.

9. North (1990) has produced a readable application of institutional economics to history. Jean Ensminger is a strong proponent of institutional economics in anthropology (1992), and there are other good examples in Acheson (1994). Jennings (1993) discusses the ways that institutional economics can be sympathetically adapted to feminist scholarship.

10. The three classic applications of game theory in anthropology are by Barth (1959), Moore (1957), and Davenport (1960). An elegant critical review of these applications is provided by Goldschmidt (1969), who shows that the anthropologists misunderstood a lot of game theory. A classic and often-cited application of game theory to environmental problems is Hardin's discussion of the "tragedy of the commons" (1968). More recent game theory approaches in anthropology are converging with ecological studies of foraging and breeding strategies among other species (see Cashdan 1990).

11. This ties in to anthropological studies of decisionmaking that find that people use simplifying rules of thumb to deal with complex and risky choices. The Kekchi I worked with had a complex scheduling task involving planting corn and rice in relation to the start of the wet season. Their rule of thumb was that you should have half your corn planted before you start to plant rice. It may not have been optimal, but it was simple and reliable.

12. This is not quite what most microeconomists mean by utility maximizing, though at times the argument seems to split hairs. Microeconomists say that individual utilities often include the well-being of others. Thus, if I sacrifice my health to feed my family, it is because I rationally consider their well-being to have higher utility than my own. Utility is not the same thing as simple hedonistic or bodily pleasure. Since the argument revolves around what is going on in peoples' minds at a partially unconscious level, it falls more into the realm of cognitive psychology than economics. And who says that these are exclusive possibilities or that there aren't other options?

4 ↵

Social and
Political Economy

The Social Contract is nothing more or less than a vast conspiracy of
human beings to lie to and humbug themselves and one another for
the general Good. Lies are the mortar that bind the savage individual
man into the social masonry.

—H. G. Wells, *Love and Mr. Lewisham*

Social Humans

Most North Americans like to think of themselves as individuals first. We
are each unique, not reducible to a number or a category. The novelist Douglas Coupland has identified, with only partial sarcasm, an American "cult of
aloneness," consisting of "the need for autonomy at all costs, usually at the
expense of long-term relationships" (1991, 69). This ideology of extreme individualism coexists with its exact opposite, the idea that we all fall into
groups and "types," that most people are predictable because of their age,
gender, background, family, and ethnicity. We often explain a person's behavior as "typical eldest sibling" or "middle class," and we like to label
groups like yuppies, slackers, born-agains, and the silent majority. Modern
North Americans like to think they are unique individuals, but they also accept that other people can be lumped into categories, races, and occupations
(not least of which is the label "American" itself). The tension between individual and group identity is a central theme in our society; as we shall see, it
is also a basic problem in economic and anthropological theory.

Most humans grow up in family groups of some sort and therefore get
basic training in working together, sharing, and identifying as a member of a
collective with a group identity. This capacity to *belong* seems very basic to
many, a "natural" characteristic of the species. Because of this, most social

73

scientists treat human social groups, not individuals, as their essential analytical unit. Within disciplines of sociology, social psychology, social policy,
and social anthropology, we can find a huge variety of ideas and theories
about why people form groups, how groups create and enforce rules to regulate individuals, how groups adapt, evolve, and decay. Many of these theories have economic implications and relate in different ways to issues of economic behavior and economic institutions.

We have already encountered one of these perspectives in the last chapter.
The social exchange theory used by game theorists tries to show that individual maximizing leads people to form social groups as a rational solution
to real-world economic problems. In other words, people form groups out
of a kind of rational contract, because they correctly perceive that they will
all be better off together than they would be apart. This liberal notion of the
group as a voluntary product of a consensus, a social contract that benefits
all participants, comes down to us from the Enlightenment thought of people like John Stuart Mill and the founding fathers of the United States Constitution. Their idea was that people belong to groups because people are
logical, and they realize (with the help of education) that they are better off
belonging. They form social contracts out of enlightened, long-term self-interest. This implies that we all have the power to change the group if we
don't like it, to leave it, or to overthrow its leaders.

This chapter is concerned with another, radically different perspective on
social behavior that does not begin with rational maximizers and does not
end with efficient groups that serve the needs of consenting members. Instead of assuming that people are the atoms of social life and that human rationality shapes society, it begins with a fundamentally different view of
human nature. Instead, human nature is to be social, to think in groups, to
act in groups, and to live always in groups. To social theorists of this kind,
trying to deduce human history and social variety from the rational actions
of individuals is ridiculous. It would be like trying to understand an ant
colony by dissecting a single worker ant.

Why do we need a social theory? People aren't ants. But social theorists
can point to some common aspects of human life that don't seem to fit the
idea of individual rational choice and mutual benefit. For example, it is obvious that some groups *do not* serve the needs of members. Some groups of
people, slaves, for example, suffer terrible exploitation, whereas others, like
kings and nobles, benefit out of all proportion to what they contribute. To
argue that the slaves are freely entering into a social contract with their masters, to the benefit of all, is clearly absurd. Instead, some people have more
power and have the means to make the weak consent through threats and
coercion.

From this observation that social groups do not serve the needs of all their
members, we can move back to question the assumption that people are

freely seeking individual satisfaction from a range of possibilities. Instead, we may be born into groups, forced into them, or classified as members against our will or consent. And groups can have power over their members, forcing them to conform despite their own individual's needs, desires, or strategies. Groups contest for power with other groups, seek to limit each other's options and choices, and impose their group interests. By focusing on power rather than choice, we have a very different perspective on social life, which in turn reflects distinctly on human nature. Instead of rational maximizers, we have political animals seeking power and followers by using persuasion, the power of ideas and images, physical force, and fear.

Power and Politics

Of course, the idea of human beings as political and social animals has a pedigree and a history. At the end of the European Enlightenment in the late eighteenth century, optimism in the ability of individuals to make rational choices for the betterment of society began to run aground on the harsh rocks of the Industrial Revolution. The nineteenth century brought tremendous social dislocation and change, accompanied by unprecedented economic growth and huge disparities in the distribution of new wealth and power. New social theories developed to account for these changes.

Robert Nisbet divides the nineteenth-century post-Enlightenment social theorists into three groups.[1] First were *liberals,* ranging from Jeremy Bentham to Herbert Spencer, who continued to stress the central importance of individual freedom. Like modern Libertarians, they saw both the modern state and traditional social institutions as repressive and dangerous, as obstacles to progress and prosperity. Their modern intellectual descendants are neoclassical economists like those discussed in the previous chapter.

Second were the *radicals,* who also thought the state, the church, and established wealth were oppressive obstacles to social justice. But radicals like Karl Marx did not find the answer to social problems in greater individual freedom; instead, they sought to attack the social and economic *system.* They did not see the oppressive state as the creation of rational individuals, which could therefore be changed by rational action. Rather they saw the state and the industrial economy as a vast machine of tyranny created by a privileged few for their own purposes.

Last were *conservatives,* who thought social problems were caused when people lost their respect and belief in old traditions, authorities, and affiliations. Theorists like Edmund Burke and Frederic Le Play thought that individualism and utilitarianism were the basic *cause* of nineteenth-century economic and social problems, because they had led to a breakdown of old institutions like the family, church, and aristocracy and had caused the decay of traditional moral values. The conservatives believed that people needed more and stronger social institutions, not more freedom. They thought that human beings were never happy unless they were playing their part by serving a complex social machine.

These three perspective are still very much with us as recognizable political philosophies. The important point is that each is based on a concept of human nature, on a set of assumptions about what people need and want and how they behave. But until the middle of the ninteenth century, there was no systematic attempt to collect empirical real-world information to support or attack these assumptions. Social science as we now know it really began in the first efforts to systematically collect information to prove or attack one or the other of these political and philosophical positions. Over time, the overt political content and mission of social science has become less blatant. Some social scientists portray themselves as objective, detached observers who are simply pursuing truth. But many others argue that the political issues remain a powerful underlying motivation and that all science remains at least partially shaped by political agendas.[2]

My goal in bringing this up is not to undercut social science but just to be realistic about its limitations and to argue that we need to read social science, especially that concerned so directly with public policy, intelligently and perceptively. If Marx had a political agenda, that does not mean his analysis or theory is wrong. Conversely, we may agree with Adam Smith's politics, but this does not necessarily make his economic theory correct. In either case, it helps us understand and judge an author's theory if we know something about that person's life and politics.

For this reason, and because the topic of human social nature is so volatile, the first part of this chapter revolves around two famous theorists, Emile Durkheim and Karl Marx. They present two clear contrasts. First, Durkheim was politically in the mainstream of society, an esteemed public figure and scholar who had tremendous influence in conservative circles. He was "establishment" all the way, though he did take unpopular political stands during his lifetime. Marx was the quintessential radical, whose life was spent in poverty as a journalist and writer outside of any institution. His influence was great, but only in revolutionary, utopian, and subversive circles until long after his death.

Durkheim and Marx also present two very different perspectives on human nature. Although both are social theorists, in the sense that they believe that human beings live and act in groups, they disagree fundamentally on what kind of social animal *Homo sapiens* really is. Both reject the radical individualism and utilitarianism of Adam Smith and the mainstream of economic theory, but there the agreement mostly ends. As we will see, for Durkheim, social life is a magical thing, a source of harmony and strength. I will discuss his work under the general label of *social economy*. Marx, in contrast, found an eternal struggle in society, an arena where powerful contradictions drove conflict founded in a history of inequality. His theory is the foundation of *political economy.*

For reasons of clarity and continuity, I will discuss Durkheim first, even though Durkheim was born forty years after Marx. In fact, some of Marx's most influential works were published before Durkheim was born in 1858. However, even though I will discuss Durkheim first, I do not want to imply that his ideas or theories are in any way prior to or more fundamental than those of Marx. After discussing the two emblematic social theorists, the second half of the chapter will trace their intellectual descendants in more recent economic anthropology.

Durkheim and the Social Organism

Emile Durkheim (1858–1917), a French author and professor, is a principal founding figure for social science. He combines some of the threads of nineteenth-century thought in new ways, but in the balance he belongs firmly in the conservative tradition. He provides an especially clear alternative to the utilitarian perspective of microeconomics.

Durkheim's most fundamental point about human nature is that human beings are social; they live in groups and their consciousness is shaped by their interactions with others. Therefore, we cannot understand human social behavior by looking at individual psychology; the collective cannot be explained by looking at the individual. Unlike the utilitarians, Durkheim did not believe that self-interest draws people together. Instead, he thought that

Emile Durkheim

people's individual interests pit them against each other; people cooperate only when they have submerged their self-interest in that of the wider group. Society gets individuals to suspend their self-interest through a system of "beliefs and sentiments" that make social life feel quite natural, a system Durkheim labeled their *collective unconscious*. These collective beliefs have the tangible power to deflect and channel natural individualism: "When a group is drawn together for some common purpose, when its members feel a sense of unity, they set aside their own personal interests in favor of the collective pursuit. In this way they are drawn outside themselves" (1958, 105).

Durkheim thought that society impresses its will on the individual through both the carrot and the stick. The carrot is the system of belief in the sacred that gives order to the world and lets each individual share contact with a power greater than the self. The power of society produces a deep emotional response from the individual and a transcendent feeling of "effervescence." Ritual is a conscious expression of human togetherness, of authority and power rooted in the collective. The stick is a set of sanctions and punishments. When we try to go against social beliefs, we find out how very powerful they are—we can be shamed, shunned, or even burned at the stake. We encounter a moral outrage grounded in collective belief. In other words, when we break social rules we are being punished not so much for a particular crime but for deviating from the group, from the established social order.

Durkheim did not think humans are mechanical mindless conformists. He portrayed social life as a constant interplay between the individual, private, and everyday world and the sacred and timeless traditions of society. His famous study of suicide was meant to demonstrate the dangers of these extremes. He thought that *egoistic* suicide results from "excessive individuation"; when alienated from family, religion, and community, people feel lost and unable to cope. *Altruistic* suicide is a product of "insufficient individuation"; completely submerged in their social worlds, people lose sight of their own interests and give up their lives as sacrifices, in warfare, for example, or for honor (Durkheim 1963, 212–217).

This idea that human beings will die if they are not properly socialized and given some wider identity in a group is very appealing and makes intuitive sense. Of course, Durkheim's opinions on many other things have made sense to generations of readers and scholars. Beyond the idea of the socialized human, Durkheim establishes three themes that have become important for later anthropology, especially economic anthropology. These are *anti-utilitarianism, anti-individualism,* and *typological evolutionism.*

Anti-utilitarianism

The foundation of neoclassical economics is the idea that individuals make practical choices among options, based on their perception of the intrinsic worth of those options. To the utilitarian, a person's knowledge and attitudes may ultimately be derived from other people, but their choices are ultimately personal and *internal*. Their judgments are based on intrinsic characteristics of the things they choose, so value has some real basis in the natural world. As we have seen, Adam Smith thought this value was grounded in the labor that goes into production, although other values were created in the physical process of market exchange.

Durkheim attempts to sweep all of this away. He argues that the value of things is entirely a social construction, having no basis in utility, labor, or need. A flag, he says, is an almost worthless piece of cloth, but a man will die for it. Value does not come from reason, but rather from social conventions. We want things not because we figure their utility but because of the absolute power of collective representations to convince us that things are good: "Society substitutes for the world revealed to us by our senses a different world that is the projection of the ideals created by society itself" (1953, 95). Thus, *values are social products.*

The microeconomist's world begins with unlimited wants. A reasoned, ordered society emerges from each individual pursuing those desires through production and exchange in the marketplace. Durkheim saw unlimited wants as the very root of evil, the source of an anarchistic battle among interests that destroys society instead of building it. To Durkheim, unlimited desires are *antisocial*, not a true form of freedom (1961, 45; 1969, 21). Instead, real freedom only emerges in the context of strict rules and regulation. Society sets limits on needs and desires and therefore makes satisfaction possible. Becoming a social human being means learning to control passions, in the interest of social cooperation. But people do not just follow these social rules because they reason that "this is best for everyone." They follow them because the rules are part of a system of *sacred* collective representations. The value of the flag, for example, is rooted in a whole series of social values and beliefs about goodness, unity, and sacred force. Therefore, burning the flag is likely to bring down the wrath of society, for it attacks the sacred roots of order.

The utilitarians thought that the government should keep its hands off the economy, which would work to everyone's best interests if only it was left alone. Because Durkheim thought individual desires destructive and believed that society must function to control material desires, he had no compunction about social and political regulation of the economy. After all, the economy is a *product* of social life. Where utilitarians saw healthy competition in the marketplace, Durkheim saw "chronic warfare and perpetual discontent." Where utilitarians saw progress bringing increased standards of living, Durkheim perceived an increase in discontent and "impatience."

> It is forgotten that economic functions are not their own justification; they are only the means to an end; they constitute one of the organs of social life, and that social life is above all a harmonious community of endeavors, a communion of minds and wills working toward the same end ... If industry can only be

productive by disturbing that peace and unleashing warfare, then it is not worth the cost. (1958, 16)

For these reasons, Durkheim advocated direct government intervention in economic affairs. He believed that the economy throughout history was subordinate to and controlled by political, religious, and social institutions. Problems occurred in industrial Europe because society had lost control of the economy; the solution was a reassertion of traditional institutions and an expansion of government powers, more regulation, and stronger churches, schools, and associations.

Durkheim's notion that the economy is embedded in and subordinate to the rest of society surfaces over and over again in economic anthropology. As we have seen, it was a pillar of later substantivism founded on Polanyi's economic history. But in Durkheim's work we can see the political agenda behind substantivism more clearly. It is aimed at taming the economy, in direct contradiction to the "free market" philosophy of the English utilitarians who thought markets were a liberating source of justice and equality. Durkheim argues that *real* values come from social life; wealth and freedom are shallow modern replacements for the transcendent and magical emotions of unity with others.

Anti-individualism

In Durkheim's sociology, the individual really does not exist. One of his "rules of the sociological method" is that you cannot explain the behavior or beliefs of society by reference to the individual. A group is not the sum of its individual human parts—it is instead something greater, following rules and laws of its own. Everything about society has to be explained by reference to social needs, social functions, and social history, not by examining the ideas or motives of individuals. Society is a thing in and of itself; it is always the cause and never the consequence.

> When the individual has been eliminated, society alone remains. We must, then, seek the explanation of social life in the nature of society itself. It is quite evident that, since it infinitely surpasses the individual in time as well as in space, it is in a position to impose upon him ways of acting and thinking which it has consecrated with its prestige. This pressure, which is the distinctive property of social facts, is the pressure that the totality exerts on the individual. (Durkheim 1938, 102)

The collective consciousness is not the same as the individual's. And by extension, even human reason and self-awareness are only the products of society. The very ideas that we think with—ideas of time and space and causality—are simply reflections of the kind of communities and social groups that we live in (see Nisbet 1966, 95–97). Does Durkheim's collective consciousness turn human beings into conditioned, brainwashed dupes who carry out the dictates of a nebulous "group mind" (Harris 1968, 473)? The answer is that Durkheim never completely does away with the reasoning individual. His normal and healthy human acts in an economically self-interested way much of the time. But then there are rituals and gatherings, social events in which the same person gives up individuality and acts with emotion. The Australian Aborigines, he says, lead a "double existence" and have a "double nature" (1947, 219). But since in every place individual rationality is the same, the individual can never be called upon to explain the particular shape of any society or the variation between societies.

If people are not always acting out of rational self-interest but instead express the collective consciousness, where does that collective consciousness come from, and what shapes it into so many different forms? Here we encounter Durkheim's functionalism. His simple answer is that society functions to maintain and perpetuate society. You have to explain individual customs and practices by looking at what they do to maintain the solidarity, cohesion, and order of the group. Again, this remains a common theme in economic anthropology. Many substantivists still seek to explain economic customs through reference to their function in maintaining social life (see, for example, Robben 1989). This is a very different explanation from that given by utilitarians, who see customs as the result of individual rationality and consciousness.

Typological Evolutionism

Like the utilitarians, Durkheim used non-Western societies as a tool for understanding European society. He accepted the prevailing wisdom of his time by thinking about contemporary people around the world as representatives of earlier forms of European societies, which were therefore important keys for understanding the starting point and stages in the development of the "modern" from the "primitive."[3] Durkheim used this method, in combination with a detailed study of what was known of Australian Aborigines (representing what he thought was the most primitive form of society), first, to isolate the most essential and basic features in all social life and, second, to build an evolutionary model of directional change from the simple and "primitive" to the complex and "modern."[4] His entire approach was founded on this evolutionary distinction, so fundamental to Western social science, to enable him to find some simple way to divide a collective Western "us" in the present from everyone else on the planet, past and present. (I believe this need for distance lies behind a lot of evolutionary thinking in social science.)

In Durkheim's version of social evolution, the opposite poles are societies dominated by *mechanical solidarity* at one extreme and by *organic solidarity* at the other. In the "lower" societies, mechanical solidarity prevails, change is slow, property is collectively owned, everyone conforms, and individual life is not worth very much because everyone shares the same exact set of collective representations and has the same consciousness. Society is divided into numerous, small, identical units like clans. People's needs and desires are set and regulated entirely by custom.

> The group has an intellectual and moral conformity of which we find but rare examples in the more advanced societies. Everything is common to all. Movements are stereotyped; everyone performs the same ones in the same circumstances, and this conformity of conduct only translates the conformity of thought. Every mind being drawn into the same eddy, the individual type nearly confounds itself with that of the race. And while all is uniform, all is simple as well. (Durkheim 1926, quoted in Voget 1975, 493)

For this reason, economic activity in primitive societies can only be seen as an expression of social solidarity, as a form of collective representation that brings people together in mechanical solidarity. But as population grows more dense, the intense face-to-face interaction of mechanical solidarity can no longer be maintained, and society threatens to break apart. People begin to specialize in different kinds of work and activity, forming social subgroups like guilds and corporations. This *division of labor* leads to a society where subgroups relate to each other functionally, like the organs in a body. The whole economy becomes integrated because people are more dependent on one another, and people are now grouped together by the kind of work they do. They develop rules and laws to regulate their cooperation; they need laws because the collective consciousness is weaker, religion is less dominant, and people develop a limited sense of their own individuality (Durkheim 1933).

There is no room for a full dissection of this story here, though its factual failures and ethnocentric weaknesses are a tempting target. The most important point is that Durkheim *submerges economic change within social evolution.* The utilitarians also saw cultural evolution as a product of the increasing division of labor through specialization and intensification. But they thought that people specialized in order to be more efficient and productive. Durkheim turns the story around; he thinks that people specialize in order to reduce competition and conflict and to maintain social solidarity in the face of increased population (Harris 1968, 476). Since human motives don't enter Durkheim's world, it is impossible for issues of efficiency, profit, or demand to enter his evolutionary scheme. This is why his approach should be considered *social economy.*

Durkheim established the basic foundation of a social economic perspective by arguing that human consciousness was a product of society, not of individual reason. By this device he absorbed the economy into society as a whole. Economic behavior became an expression of social structures; the economy changed because society became more complex. For this reason he is usually considered the intellectual ancestor of classical British social anthropology, discussed later in this chapter. What is lacking in both Durkheim's theory, and that of many of his later followers, is a notion of politics—that instead of everything simply functioning smoothly to maintain equilibrium, there are different interests within society and groups struggle, often violently, to advance those interests. The foremost theorist of struggle is Karl Marx, to whom we turn next.

Karl Marx: Putting Politics into the Economy

Karl Marx (1818–1883) produced thousands of pages during a writing career that spanned forty years, covering philosophy, history, economics, politics, and a broad range of current events. His political and academic followers and critics both during and after his lifetime have produced an avalanche of words and paper, in hundreds of languages. In anthropology alone, a Marxist bibliography would easily fill this chapter. In a few pages I can scarcely do justice to more than a fragment of this literature, so I will focus on Marx as a philosopher of human social motivation to show how Marx's social human is crucially different from Durkheim's. For Marx, consciousness was not simply defined by cosmology or ritual experience of group membership but rather by what he saw as a more fundamental human activity: *work.*[5]

Marx injected politics directly back into the study of economics. The neoclassical school of individualism is explicitly not concerned with power; individuals are autonomous decisionmakers. Their choices reflect their preferences and interests directly and are limited only by the kinds of information available to them. They work together only when it suits their purposes, and they create society as an extension of individual choice. If people breathe polluted air, drink impure water, and eat unhealthy foods, they have chosen

Karl Marx

to allocate their effort to those ends. If they want clean air and healthy food enough, they will pay for it. The sovereignty of the individual, in this view, is absolute. If the government passes clean air and water laws, it limits people's choices and shifts the cost of goods to people who do not want them.[6]

Marx, like Durkheim, argued to the contrary that people's economic rationality is deeply embedded in society, that they belong to groups, and that their choices reflect social and historical structures over which they have no power. Where Marx parted ways with Durkheim was in his assertion that society is not a unity, a single interest group. Instead, within society there are *classes* of people defined by the kinds of property they own and the kinds of work they engage in. These classes are in contention and conflict with each other. They struggle for dominance and control, with a consciousness defined by their position, putting politics into all social life. To Marx, politics was not individual leaders or parties, platforms, and programs but was instead the inevitable clash between classes defined by their economic interests. Classes, not societies, he thought, define the consciousness of their members and the divisions within society. Marx therefore began his analysis with inequality and domination, with the unequal distribution of power and property in society—exactly the issue that neoclassical individualism does not address.

Although Marx said that class shapes consciousness, he never asserted that class or social forces mechanically *determine* human consciousness. He always argued that human beings make the world they live in and that they can therefore change it. To understand this relationship between society and the individual, we need to learn something of Marx's notion of human nature and delve into his analysis of history.

Marx, Human Nature, and History

Marx said that we human beings are different from other species because we think symbolically, we form images of things before we make them. Furthermore, in the process of acting on our mental images, we work with each other and thereby find new needs and develop new goals. We discover, and in a sense *create*, ourselves through labor. And unlike other species, we work even when we have no immediate needs, because "free conscious activity" is part of our "species-being" (Marx 1975, 328–329; Donham 1990, 56–57).

Productive work therefore lies at the heart of Marx's analysis of social life. Through work we express ourselves, exercise our freedom, and remake ourselves and our consciousness. Labor is also, in Marx's economic system, the ultimate and only form of value. But people do not always keep the products of their own labors; they cooperate with each other and exchange their products back and forth. If products are exchanged at the ratios of the amount of work put into them, they are reflecting their true value. Marx thought this might be the case in early, extremely primitive societies. But in all later groups, people receive either greater or lesser value for what they have produced and contributed.

The difference between the true value of what people produce and what they need to survive is what Marx called *surplus value.* This surplus is key to understanding the economy, for it is what people produce beyond what they need to survive and reproduce—it is the fund of "extra" that can be invested or used for improvement or change. And the nature and dynamics of society can ultimately be defined by tracing the flow of surplus value and the means through which it is extracted from some and taken by others (Marx 1983, 394–433; Mandel 1990).

Drawing on European history, and on the ethnographic research of Lewis Henry Morgan in the United States, Marx traced the development of the extraction of surplus value through a series of stages of types of society. Using Marx's notes after his death, Friedrich Engels wrote *The Origins of the Family, Private Property, and the State,* in which he said that the first forms of extraction took place in the household, as the surplus value produced by women and children was taken by husbands and fathers (see Folbre 1993 for a critique of these ideas). In later societies, surplus value was extracted through slavery and forced labor, through tribute and taxation. Finally, in capitalism, surplus is taken from the worker in the form of the difference between the value of what a worker produces and the value of the wages that worker receives. Marx and Engels argued that all these systems of inequality are based ultimately on *private property,* on social systems that protect property and assign special rights to property to particular kinds of people (men, household heads, nobles, or factory owners, for example). Private property is the basic means by which surplus value is taken from some and accumulated by others.

At the time that Marx studied at the Universities of Bonn and Berlin (1835–1841), history was understood mostly in *idealist* terms. People's ideas changed over time, their consciousness was transformed by learning, revelation, and experience, and gradually, society changed as a result. For philosophers like Georg Hegel, writing history meant tracing the development of ideas and beliefs through time.

Marx said that Hegel had things exactly backward. Ideas did not shape history. Instead, history had to be understood primarily in material terms, by looking at systems of production, at real people involved in struggle over the products of labor. Ideas, said Marx, were largely a product of class, economic structures, and social position. Ideas justified or rationalized the economic structure at any one time—they did not *cause* that structure.

The mode of production in material life determines the general characteristics of the social, political and spiritual processes of life. It is not the consciousness of men that determines their existence, but, on the contrary, their social existence determines their consciousness. (Marx 1904, 11–12, quoted in Harris 1968, 229)

   To show how the material basis of society moved history, Marx divided
social systems into three parts. First, there is an *economic base*. This includes
the tools and technologies, the skills and labor that people use to produce, as
well as the social groups that people form for the purpose of work (the *forces
of production*) and the specific relations of inequality between people that
move surplus around and leave some people with less than others (*relations
of production*). On top of this base there is a *superstructure* with two parts.
The first is the legal and political system, which orders and regulates society,
usually in the direct interests of the social groups that are economically
dominant (the *juridico-political superstructure*). The second part is the system of ideas, including religion, philosophy, and cosmology, that rationalizes
and explains the economic system and convinces both the haves and the
have-nots that the way the society works is "natural" (the *ideological superstructure*). The whole bundle of base and superstructure together is usually
called a *mode of production*, though that term is sometimes restricted to the
base alone (see Donham 1990 for a clear discussion; see also Jessop 1990). A

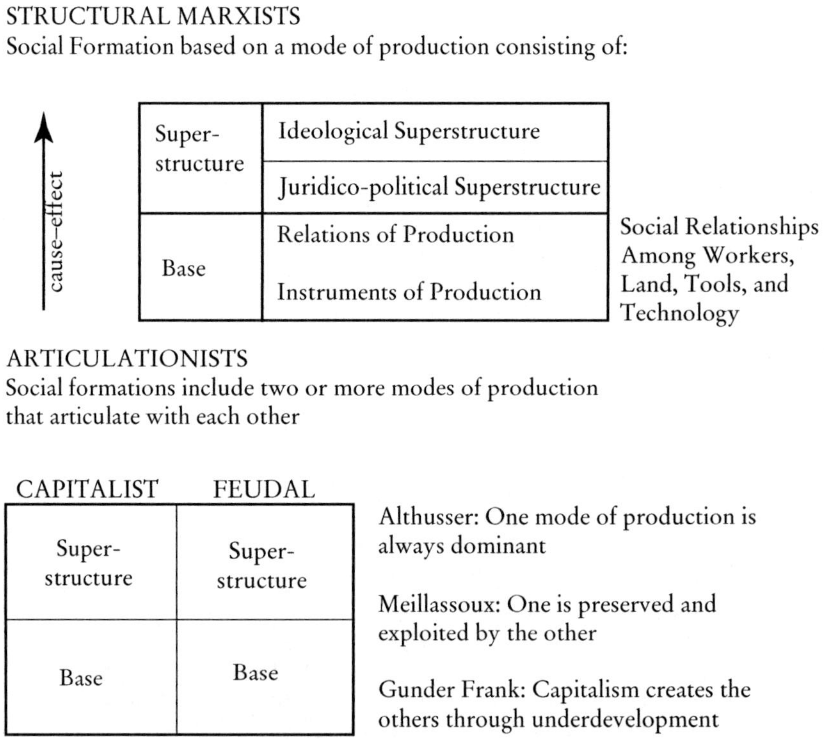

STRUCTURAL MARXISTS
Social Formation based on a mode of production consisting of:

ARTICULATIONISTS
Social formations include two or more modes of production
that articulate with each other

FIGURE 4.1 Marxist models of society. The French structural Marxists see the base
as the determinant of the superstructure. Articulationists argue that capitalist modes
of production are always connected with other modes.

rough diagram of the concepts is given in Figure 4.1. The dynamics of a society and its historical development are determined by the mode of production. Marx defined several types of modes of production, including the feudal and capitalist; later scholars have tried to define other types, using the much broader range of comparative social and economic data on world history that became available after Marx's death.

There is no question that Marx saw the base as the dominant element in each mode of production. This has led some to accuse him of being a *mechanical materialist* who thought that the material economic world directly determines all of human society. This accusation is weak, however, because he always argued that the base includes human relationships. He also emphasized that there is constant interaction between all parts of society, that one part does not simply determine all the others. The parts do not fit together seamlessly—there are always contradictions and conflicts that threaten order, and this lends a constant dynamism to history. In particular, the ideology that masks, rationalizes, and justifies such an unequal system can never work perfectly.

The role of ideology and ideas has become one of the most interesting areas of controversy and theoretical debate among modern anthropological Marxists. Early followers of Marx were mainly concerned with discovering, nurturing, and encouraging class consciousness, making workers aware of how they had been exploited and divided by capitalists. It was presumed that such awareness would cause workers to recognize their common interests and work together to overthrow the system. Early Marxists thought that class consciousness was rational and independent, far from the position of Durkheim, who thought group identity operated at an unconscious deeper level. But in time it became clear to Marxists that other things besides class position, like nationalism and gender, affected the way people saw themselves and understood their place in society.

The Marxist rethinking of consciousness and ideology began with the Italian theorist Antonio Gramsci (1891–1937), who asked how it was that workers and even slaves came to accept ideas (like Fascism and racism) that are used to oppress and harm them. Gramsci's term "hegemony" refers to this power of beliefs and ideas to mask or blind us to our own best interests. It is based in the Marxist notion of *false consciousness,* a state in which people do not clearly see the relations of domination and exploitation in which they are bound. Gramsci was the first Marxist to focus on the important role of *popular culture*—popular music, arts, religion, and mass media—in affecting consciousness and identity. Popular culture and mass media make the prevailing unequal social order seem natural and inevitable. They put words and ideas into people's minds and mouths in ways that make it very difficult for exploited people to challenge the system.

The idea that popular culture is the key to class dynamics in modern capitalism is a major thread in more recent Marxist theory. It was the key focus of the influential Frankfurt School of Critical Sociology and Philosophy (see Habermas 1979) and is the central issue in the work of the very influential British Marxist theorist, Raymond Williams (1980; 1985). After the 1980's anthropologists broadened the concept of hegemony from Gramsci's original narrow meaning. Gramsci originally spoke of class consciousness, but anthropologists now discuss the concept of *cultural* hegemony. They ask how ideology, ritual, religion, art, and other symbolic systems work to make people believe their world is natural and accept situations where some have power over others. This more general discussion of hegemony and power can be traced to Pierre Bourdieu's very influential book *Outline of a Theory of Practice* (1977; for a more recent example, see Comaroff and Comaroff 1986). Although based ultimately on a Marxist approach, such research tends to give the world of ideas, beliefs, and symbols much more power than Marx himself did. Marx always brought the conversation directly back to systems of work and production.

Marx on Capitalism and the Future

Marx was not as concerned with anthropology and sociology as he was with understanding capitalism—the economic system that was exploding across the world during his lifetime. In his analysis, the foundation of capitalism was private ownership of the means of production, which turned the common property of all into the private property of the few. This in turn transformed human labor into a commodity, meaning that it was bought and sold in a marketplace just like potatoes or any other good.

In a capitalist system, said Marx, society is divided into a small class that owns the means of production (capitalists) and a broad mass of people who own nothing productive and can only sell their labor to survive (proletarians). The capitalist keeps the surplus value produced with the workers' labor and uses it to further accumulate and build capital. From this basic analysis, Marx worked out a series of "laws of motion" of the capitalist mode of production that have proven remarkably accurate. He predicted that companies would get larger and larger and seek to establish monopolies, that capitalists would invest more and more in machines and technology, driving constant technological innovation, and that there would be continuing cycles of boom and bust, expansion and contraction in the economy.

He also made a number of predictions that have not been fully realized. First, he envisioned a tendency for the economy to become more and more under state or central coordinated control (this clearly happened in only a part of the world). Second, he predicted ever greater social polarization, in the form of greater divisions between rich and poor. He did not anticipate the success of labor unions and the continuing growth of the middle class. Finally, he expected that workers would show growing class consciousness, leading to more class conflict as the inequalities of capitalism increased.

Eventually revolutions would return the ownership of the means of production to the people.

Durkheim, Meet Marx

At this point, we should go back and look at the differences between Marx and Durkheim. Both of them argue for the social nature of humanity and see the economy as a product of social forces, not as driven by individual decisions or actions. They think that human consciousness is determined by social relations and have little faith in common sense and practical reason. Both offer a *holistic* perspective, in that they do not separate the economy from the rest of society; economic activities are part of social relationships. And both Durkheim and Marx use an evolutionary, historical framework, through which they divide all societies into a limited number of types and stages.

But where Durkheim stresses the functional unity of all societies, Marx is directly concerned with the conflict that arises from inequality, which inevitably leads to change. Where Durkheim exalts social integration and functional stability, Marx elevates class conflict based on the relations of production to the status of prime mover. And because Marx divides societies into groups that may act together for their own collective interest, he aims our attention at issues of power, control of resources, and politics. Because he pays close attention to economic differences, he provides a much more detailed terminology for different kinds of societies than does Durkheim.

There is a broad range of economic anthropologists who draw their inspiration from Marx. Marxist scholars still argue over the interpretation of Marx and fight over what often seem minor issues to outsiders, in anthropology as in many other social sciences (there are a number of lively journals with titles like *Rethinking Marxism* and *Dialectical Anthropology*). But the general thrust of all "Marxian" anthropology is quite clear:

1. A focus on issues of power and exploitation
2. A concern with conflict and change
3. A starting point in the material system of production and the ownership of property
4. An analysis of action as political power struggles between social groups defined by their control of property

Although economic behavior, in the form of production, shapes political and social structure and although classes often act in their own self-interest, there is not much place for individual rational decisionmaking in Marx's scheme. Therefore, the key similarity between Durkheim and Marx, despite all these differences, is in their view of human nature. Neither of them have time for the microeconomic self-interested human being so beloved to the Enlightenment utilitarians and rational choice theorists discussed in the last chapter. And for both of them, expressive symbolic culture—art, ritual, religion—that is, all the ideals and ideas that Marx places in the "superstructure," are not fundamental motivations for human behavior. For Durkheim, ritual is a sort of magical glue or lubricant, whereas for Marx, it can be the ties that either bind people together or blind them to their own best interest. But the human being described by both Durkheim and Marx is basically a social animal rather than a symbol-using one.

Varieties of Social and Political Economy

Three main streams of anthropological economics descend directly from Durkheim and Marx. First, there is the British social anthropology of E. E. Evans-Pritchard, A. R. Radcliffe-Brown, and Meyer Fortes, drawing inspiration from Durkheim. The second includes neo-Marxism of separate French and North American varieties. Third, we have historical macroeconomics grounded in Marxism, which has now acquired various labels, including *dependency theory* and *world systems theory*. The rest of this chapter will touch on each of these and point toward some of their applications and implications. For each topic I suggest some readings that explain the complexities that cannot be explored here.

Social Anthropology

During much of this century, British anthropology was dominated by an approach that has come to be called *structural functionalism*. In its broadest outlines it accepts most of Durkheim's assumptions about human nature: that people are basically social, that individual consciousness is shaped and formed by social context, that those social contexts form "types" of societies, and that society is bound together by functional relationships between parts and institutions. In his first ethnography, *The Andaman Islanders*, Radcliffe-Brown states this position quite clearly:

> (1) A society depends for its existence on the presence in the minds of its members of a certain system of sentiments by which the conduct of the individual is regulated in conformity with the needs of society. (2) Every feature of the social system itself and every event or object that in any way affects the well-being or the cohesion of the society becomes an object of this system of sentiments. (3) In human society the sentiments in question are not innate but are developed in the individual by the action of the society upon him. (4) The ceremonial customs of a society are a means by which the sentiments in question are given collective expression on appropriate occasions. (1948, 233–234)

Any attempt to explain social life by reference to the activities or thoughts of rational individuals was condemned as inherently *psychological* rather than anthropological. Economics was seen in this way as part of society, to be sure, but only because the economy was a public expression of social life. The Andaman Islanders traded with each other in order to build social ties. The hard daily work of obtaining food was a means to teach children their social obligations and responsibilities. To Radcliffe-Brown, people may *think* they are planting crops or building houses, but they are really building social relationships.

Radcliffe-Brown's primary unit of analysis was the *social structure*, consisting of different groups of people, organized according to social statuses (usually based on kinship in nonindustrial societies), carrying out their social roles according to rules, rights, and obligations. They *had to*, in order to keep the system functioning properly. Because no system could work perfectly, there was always a judicial system that resolved disputes and put things back onto a smooth functioning track. People remained committed to these structures and rules, even when it was not in their own immediate physical best interest, because of the power of "myth, dogmas, ritual beliefs and . . . mystical values" to make people think of the common interest (Fortes and Evans-Pritchard 1962, 18). Societies were grouped into types on the basis of the kinds of social rules they followed and the kinship relations between the people who formed groups. The economy was just another social institution, in which people followed the rules and worked, exchanged, and consumed according to the customs appropriate to their social position:

> The economic machinery of a society appears in quite a new light if it is studied in relation to the social structure. The exchange of goods and services is dependent upon, is the result of, and at the same time is the means of maintaining a certain structure, a network of relations between persons and collections of persons. (Radcliffe-Brown 1965, 197)

If we follow this logic to its conclusion, we find that the economy is not particularly interesting, since the *real* puzzle is social structure. This comes across very clearly in a classic work like Evans-Pritchard's *The Nuer,* about a group of pastoralists in the Sudan. The first two chapters of the book describe the Nuer system of production and exchange in some detail, explaining the importance of cattle in the Nuer way of life and outlining the ecological context of their social organization. But the exposition is a static collection of facts, meant mainly to show "the limitations imposed on Nuer economy by their environment and of the way they manage to overcome the natural poverty of their country" (1969, 87).

Although Evans-Pritchard tells us that social structure is closely related to economic life, there is no question about which causes which. The Nuer depend heavily on millet and other crops and on fishing, but their attention is riveted on cattle, because of the social function of cattle in kinship and politics. Early in the work, we find that "it is unnecessary to write more on what are generally called economics . . . One cannot treat Nuer economic relationships by themselves, for they always form part of direct social relationships of a general kind" (1969, 90). As in the rest of structural-functionalism, the economy is never a source of contradiction or dynamism; it produces only equilibrium, limitation, and the fuel to keep the social structure going. And economic behavior, in the sense of goal-seeking decisionmaking, hardly enters the ethnography at all. Instead, "the behavior of persons to one another is determined by a series of attachments, to family, joint family, lineage, clan, age-set, etc., and by kinship relationships, ritual ties and so forth" (1969, 264). Any observation that turned things around and tried to show how social organization made economic or ecological sense was labeled "determinism" and rejected by structural functionalists (Fortes 1969).

Neo-Marxists

As noted, there are two modern streams of Marxist anthropology. The first is the French, dominated by figures like Maurice Godelier and Claude Meillassoux and grounded in strict and detailed reading of Marx and careful discussion of his ideas. The second strain is an American variety, which built on the work of Eric Wolf and Sidney Mintz and is grounded in Julian Steward's cultural ecology rather than in direct interpretation of Marx's texts. The French and American Marxists alike have asked if and how Marx's ideas can be applied to nonindustrial societies and have looked for connections between politics, social organization, and the economic base.

Marx saw the historical development of capitalism as an essentially linear process, and he did not pay a great deal of attention to the inner workings of precapitalist systems outside of Europe. The idea of class consciousness was applied mainly to capitalist societies. But what determined consciousness in societies *without classes?*

Meillassoux and other French Marxists say that Marx's concepts of exploitation, ideology, and power can indeed be used to understand societies that had no states or elaborate political hierarchies.[7] They argue that kinship is *part* of the political economy, that even in "traditional" egalitarian communities and households there are groups that exploit others, and that much of the "traditional" ideology and symbolism beloved of anthropologists actually serves to justify and hide this exploitation. Meillassoux (1981) defines a "domestic mode of production," in which elder men exploit younger men and women by controlling their labor; they do this through what most previous anthropologists had called a system of *kinship*. Elder men control bridewealth, lineages, and the marriages of their daughters. Whereas in the capitalist mode of production, wealth is based in the control of *property*, in the domestic mode, wealth is based on the control of *people*. Instead of owning factories or land, lineage elders control the labor of their wives, children, and relatives by controlling their access to property and spouses. The elders decide who gets married to whom, what lineage children belong to, and who gets to farm which piece of land. Control of economic surplus is achieved through custom and family connections, not though wages or tribute.

For British structural functionalists, kinship was a wonderful expression of social structure, a system that gave a distinct identity to each culture as well as a basis for grouping them together into classical categories like "patrilineal" and "matrilocal." For the French Marxists, however, kinship was a system of power, grounded in the concrete control of labor and the products of labor.

This may seem like a major break from previous anthropological thought. But the French Marxists tended toward the same kind of abstraction and devotion to "structure" and types found in British anthropology. They never bring the individual into the picture and share the assumption that human beings are submerged in the social whole. The economy is no more than a static, stable base, on which the more dynamic and interesting social superstructure is built. In the end, their major goal is traditionally anthropological—to show that the economy is a social product, *part* of the social order but not logically preceding it.

This becomes most clear in the specific ethnographic case studies done by French Marxists, of which Godelier's *The Making of Great Men* (1986) is perhaps the best example in English (also Godelier 1977). The book is about the Baruya, a horticultural group of about fifteen hundred people in highland New Guinea. They also produce blocks of salt from the ashes of a kind of grass, which they use for trade. The major thesis of the book is that there is *no* relationship between economic power and political power in this classless society. Some Baruya men become wealthy through their salt trading, gardening, and hunting, but they cannot convert their wealth into power and become chiefs. Instead, political power comes through success in war, through control of magic and ritual, and most of all through manipulation of *kinship*. Kinship is the true basis of all power differences in Baruya society. Rooted in a religion that gives most of the power of fertility to men, power is exercised as the domination of men over women through lineage rules and marriage exchange. The whole society is held together and given meaning by ritual and ideas of the sacred that bind people together into a social unity that overcomes their differences.

Godelier therefore owes as much to Durkheim as to Marx. The only thing that makes his view Marxist at all is the attention he pays to power and exploitation, the presence (though not the power) of an economic base, and the idea of cultural evolution that seeks "types" of society based on the ways that politics and social organization control people and surplus wealth. Whereas Durkheim dissolves consciousness and the economy into society and Marx submerges the individual in class, Godelier eliminates the individual person and substitutes categories of gender, age, and kinship nested in a web of religious ideas about supernatural power. People may act out of "self-interest," but their interests, and even their idea of "self," are a product of their social position and their gender. All together, says Godelier, the social organization of the Baruya defines a "type" of society, where the economy is entirely dominated by kinship. But why this type of society in this particular place? He has no answer. And how and why would this type change into another? Again he is silent; the Baruya political economy appears as a frozen, integrated whole. As William Roseberry says of structural Marxists, all the conflict takes the form of contradictions between *structures,* not people. Any reference to an active human subject is considered a "dark sin" (1989, 160–161).

Modes of Production.   The only time the economy becomes a dynamic element in the French Marxist scheme is when different economic systems come into contact with each other and "articulate" (meaning connect with each other in a way that affects both). Marx had an essentially linear idea of social change and thought societies went through a series of stages on their way from primitive communalism to capitalism and then on to socialism and communism. French Marxists, especially Pierre-Philippe Rey and Louis Althusser, took up Marx's notion of the "mode of production" and tried to use it to build a more detailed and accurate world economic history.[8]

Their basic plan was to define a series of precapitalist modes of production. They argued that in the modern world capitalism has not simply *replaced* these previous forms. Instead, capitalism in the colonial era captured and transformed other economies, then turned them to its own purposes, while retaining some of their original features. To use their jargon, capitalism *articulated* with precapitalist modes of production in various ways, though capitalism always maintained its domination.

Meillassoux, for example, demonstrates that the arrival of capitalism in West Africa did not cause the complete transformation of all previous social and economic systems. Rather, the development of colonial capitalism in each area was dependent on the exploitation of precapitalist economies; capitalism therefore tries to encapsulate and preserve precapitalist modes of production, exploiting them through control of trade and exchange. The end result is still one in which capitalism is dominant, and the other forms of production are determined by the way they articulate with capitalism (Binford and Cook 1991). Nevertheless, Meillassoux made an important point: Societies that are not themselves capitalist—even those that do not use money at all—may still be part of the modern world capitalist economic system.

Dependency and World Systems Theory. The French Marxist work on modes of production converged with another analysis of the global economy—*dependency theory*—developed largely by economists and historians associated with the Economic Commission on Latin America. In the 1940s and 1950s, the dominant philosophy of economic development was *modernization theory*. In this view, there was a single road from primitive to modern, a pathway of economic change that each country had to follow. In a flush of postwar optimism, economists thought that every country could follow in the footsteps of the United States, moving through agrarian capitalism to modern prosperous industrial consumerism (see Myrdal 1957; Rostow 1960). For a while, it was thought that modernizing countries might end up in a phase of "dualism," with a dynamic, modernizing prosperous sector, side by side with the archaic, impoverished traditional sector. The world was reassured that this was just a temporary, transitional condition that would pass in time.

Dependency theorists made the unpleasant observation that the predicted transition was lasting an uncomfortably long time, that in fact in many parts of the world things were getting worse, not better. By the 1960s, it was becoming clear that the modernization miracle was a mirage for most of the world's people. Paul Baran (1957) responded by setting modernization theory on its head. He argued that the "modern" countries, rather than paving the way for the poor countries to follow, were actually *blocking* development and growth in the Third World. Growth in Europe and North America was actually, he said, achieved by systematically draining surplus and raw materials from the poor countries. Instead of creating modernization, "development" created *dependency* and *poverty*. Poorer areas lost their ability to feed and educate their people and required loans and aid to finance economic "growth," which actually made the problems of poverty worse instead of better.

Andre Gunder Frank (1967; 1969) applied dependency theory to Latin American culture and history. He argued that the whole notion of dualism, of the gradual evolution of the primitive into the modern, was an illusion. Instead, the Latin American societies that appeared most "traditional," those that were isolated, impoverished, and dominated by old customs, were *made that way* by capitalism and colonialism (the "development of underdevelopment"). They had once been, like China and India, great civilizations and economic powers. Mercantile capitalism had systematically drained them and turned them into stagnant backwaters (see also Rodney 1972; Amin 1976; Cardoso and Faletto 1979). What they had in common culturally was *not* the product of some previous *precapitalist* state. What anthropologists had been calling "traditional" societies were mostly a direct *product* of capitalism and had become a distinct *peripheral* (meaning marginal, or at the edges) variety of capitalism.

While the economists argued against prevailing ideas about development, academic studies of European history were also transformed. Most traditional histories treated the history of European development from the Crusades through the Industrial Revolution as an internal matter, as if Europe were an isolated area. History in the traditional sense did not start in the rest of the world until Europeans conquered and colonized. The new version of history concentrated on the economic connections that had tied Europe to Africa and Asia long before the colonial era. Immanuel Wallerstein rewrote world history as a series of cycles of expansion and collapse of economic systems, which he called "world systems theory." He said that all the modern world's wars, battles, and conquests, as well as the world's cultures and political systems, were tied together by the logic of trade and production. Global geography could at any one time be divided into "cores" that accumulated wealth and "peripheries" from which it was drained (see Chase-Dunn and Hall 1991 for a clear discussion).

Neo-Marxism, world systems theory, and dependency theory forced anthropologists to look more closely into the economic and political history of the people they studied. These theories are largely responsible for a shift from thinking about culture change as "acculturation" (the simple adoption of modern Western culture by previously isolated primitive people) to much more complex and interesting studies of the political, economic, and cultural impact of Western expansion on the rest of the world. This has been the special province of a renewed neo-Marxist political economy among North American anthropologists, which I will discuss next.

The American School.   Whereas French Marxism is clearly descended from Durkheim, the American Marxists have their intellectual roots in a native anthropological tradition concerned with the physical environment, with a strong empirical base in fieldwork. Julian Steward's version of *cultural ecology* that emerged after World War II placed the productive economy firmly within the "culture core," at the very base of society (1955; see also Netting 1977 and Orlove 1980). The rest of society is functionally shaped by the necessity of survival and by the tools and technology that together constitute the "subsistence system." Cultural ecology was ecological because it focused on processes of cultural change and on the interconnections between the human and the natural environment; it was also neo-evolutionary in reviving earlier anthropological ideas about regularities in long-term cultural change, and it was functionalist in its assumption that culture took a particular shape because it improved efficiency and survival. But most cultural ecologists avoided rational choice theory; the logic of adaptation was not an individual form of maximization but operated at the level of the social system as a whole. Entire societies adapted to natural environments to improve the efficiency and stability of the system. Here was something similar to the Marxist notion of a mode of production, but without conflict, inequality, or the contradictions that Marxists think always drive social change.

The next generation of American anthropologists working within Julian Steward's framework, particularly Eric Wolf and Sidney Mintz, put these elements of conflict and politics back into cultural ecology. Instead of studying the evolution and adaptation of isolated or ancient societies, they were interested in long-term dynamics and conflicts that occurred when societies became enmeshed in expanding Western capitalism. Mintz in particular did ethnographic and historical research in Caribbean island cultures built on slavery and sugar production that had *never* been isolated and self-sufficient.

This generation studied peasants, slavery, rebellions, and warfare, and the transformation of independent farmers into landless workers.[9] Other neo-Marxists used anthropological tools to expose nontraditional subjects, as with June Nash's study of Bolivian mine workers (1979), Scott Cook's on Mexican brickmakers (1984), and Aihwa Ong's on Malaysian factory women (1987). Some form of neo-Marxism lies behind almost all the recent economic anthropology in the United States.

The constant element at work in this tradition is the encounter between a global system of production based on wages, factories, or plantations and local economies grounded in locally controlled farming, crafts, and small-scale industry. The American school is distinguished from the dependency theorists and French neo-Marxists by the way it depicts this encounter. The American school allows for a variety of outcomes, for resistance and accommodation as well as domination. Local cultures are not merely hapless victims; they fight back instead of being crushed, pushed aside, marginalized, or encapsulated and exploited. Sometimes they even win.

Two excellent recent examples of this tug-of-war historical approach are Donald Attwood's *Raising Cane* (1992) and Michel-Rolph Trouillot's *Peasants and Capital* (1988). Attwood shows how peasants took control of large-scale sugar production in western India. Far from being passive and exploited, these farmers are socially mobile and politically engaged. They successfully defended their interests in their conflict with the government and large factory owners. Instead of a few huge sugar factories teeming with thousands of landless workers, Attwood found a landscape of prosperous independent farmers who managed factories cooperatively. Trouillot studied the long history of banana farming on the Caribbean island of Dominica; peasants end up as much more than a "mode of production." Rather, they have a history; they resist and strategize in various ways to retain some autonomy and control over their lives. They struggle to retain their local identity and economy while remaining part of a larger world market.

Eric Wolf's *Europe and the People Without History* (1982) takes American historical neo-Marxism to a global scale. Like many anthropologists, he found dependency and world systems theory too schematic and mechanical;

capitalism appears as a uniform juggernaut, and everything else becomes merely "precapitalist." By contrast, Wolf shows that over a five-hundred-year period, capitalism itself took different forms, and Western economic expansion dealt very differently with hundreds of different cultures around the world, cultures that had their own distinct modes of production.[10] But the force driving this expansion was essentially economic, and the structures it encountered were defined by their systems of production. This is definitely economic history with the politics included, not cultural determinism or functionalism. Wolf recaptures the lost histories of collision between cultures, histories previously covered over by the textbook story of steady and uniform Western expansion. In the process, he moves economic anthropology to a global scale. He redefines the subject of the discipline as the ongoing encounter between different kinds of economic systems, the political struggle over the outcome that defines winners and losers, and the cultural consequences as reflected in people's diverse experiences.

In the 1990s the American neo-Marxist school has started to grapple with contemporary problems of trade, the expansion of tourism and factory production to new parts of the world, and the growing network of communication technology that makes global advertising, marketing, and consumerism possible. Multinational corporations freely move capital across national boundaries; workers respond with their own mobility and migration by building "transnational" communities that connect Third World villages with First World cities. Culture no longer appears rooted in a single place, and new kinds of cosmopolitan and hybrid cultures are emerging.[11] There is some convergence between this American school of global political economy and a British Marxist-inspired subdiscipline of "popular culture" studies, which has worked for decades on television, pop music, street festivals, and other kinds of mass media.[12] All of this work is Marxist in that it always keeps an eye on the bottom line, asking these questions: Who controls culture? Who owns the means by which culture is produced, sold, and communicated? Who owns the factories and the phone lines, and how does money wield political influence over cultural policy? A Marxist scholar faced with growing ethnic warfare might ask this: Who benefits from the strife? How is ethnicity manipulated and shaped by media, politicians, and powerful financial interests?

Summary: The Problems of Structure and Agency

On Wolf's global scale, history appears as conflicting forces, as modes of production colliding with each other across the landscape, and there often seems little room for human action. Groups have interests in seeking wealth and power, and in a general sense, people seem to know what is good for them; but we are never clear on who is making the decisions or what reasoning is going on in their minds. On that scale, human actors seem like tiny cogs on giant gears in some huge satanic factory. How can we put the people back into this picture? Many modern neo-Marxists are concerned with this problem, which has been labeled "structure versus agency" (drawing on the theoretical work of the sociologist Anthony Giddens). How can we account for the reality, force, and power of social structures and at the same time grant some "agency," some autonomous decisionmaking power, to individuals? Structure makes everything seem mechanical, determined in advance ("overdetermined"). Yet individual behavior often appears unpredictable, even unfathomable.

Most neo-Marxist studies these days try to grapple with this problem in one way or another.[13] Neo-Marxists are deeply concerned with ideology, hegemony, and consciousness. Writers often show that local people have a variety of responses to outside pressures, that the outcomes of struggles are not determined in advance, and that people therefore can change their world through group action and organized resistance (see Scott 1990). At the same time, these authors want to show how power, rooted in control of governments, land, money, and factories, is exercised to exploit and dominate. They tell us that people often cannot recognize what is in their own best interest because of a long history of oppression and because they have been divided to the point where they are unable to work together. But their religious or cultural beliefs, especially those grounded in family and ethnicity, are also a source of resistance to oppression, solidarity, and community (for example, see Comaroff 1985).

As statements about the way the world works, these are all undoubtedly true. Sometimes people do act together as a group, recognizing their own interests. But sometimes they don't. Sometimes people recognize that they are being exploited, but at other times they are loyal to people who ruthlessly exploit them. The problem is that a social theory of human action, whether grounded in Marx's political economy or in Durkheim's social economy, gives us no grounds to predict why people are sometimes *not* social or why selfishness sometimes overcomes altruism. Because these theories begin with an assumption that consciousness and action are social products, they cannot deal very well with situations where society itself is in question, where individual interests tear the social fabric apart.

Political economy clearly provides a powerful alternative to utilitarianism, a solution that dovetails with the traditional interests of anthropologists. It is concerned with long-term change, helps divide economic systems into historical types so that we can compare them, and makes us pay attention to exploitation, inequality, and conflict. But because it leaves no theoretical place for individuals, it cannot help us understand pragmatic decisions in the way a utilitarian theory can. Nor does political economy deal directly with the cultural values and knowledge or with the unique local configurations of language and belief that underlie all behavior. We turn to that missing piece in the next chapter.

Notes

1. Nisbet (1966) remains an essential guide to social theory. For further reading on Durkheim I suggest Lukes (1973) and Hatch (1973), though Marvin Harris's treatment of Durkheim in *The Rise of Anthropological Theory* (1968) is much more critical and makes more interesting reading.

2. Bourdieu (1988) provides a sustained critique of the politics of academic research and the role of social science in modern society. On a more general level, Michel Foucault has written extensively on the ways that science organizes knowledge in the service of power. Once again, feminist scholars have been at the forefront in revealing the political agendas of modern science; in particular, see Martin (1987) and Schiebinger (1993).

3. I use the terms "primitive" and "modern" in quotes to indicate that I do not agree with the assumptions so often concealed in using these terms. I do not use them myself in my own ethnographic work and consider them generally discredited, laden with bad associations and imprecise meaning.

4. Many early anthropologists used other cultures to represent earlier stages in European history, a practice thoroughly discredited by later generations (see Harris 1968). Later social scientists have built theories around a notion that there is some kind of "great divide" between modern or Western cultures and the rest of the world. We seem to need some kind of "other" in order to think about ourselves and our past, but as Edward Said argues in *Orientalism,* in the process we usually do violence or injustice to the "other" (1978). James Carrier makes the interesting point that when we stereotype the exotic "other," we also manipulate our image of "the West," eliminating diversity and conflict through what he calls "Occidentalism" (1992).

5. For a basic, amusing introduction to Marx that concentrates on his political philosophy more than on his economics, I recommend Rius's *Marx for Beginners* (1976). *The Portable Karl Marx* (1983), edited by Eugene Kamenka, is a usable collection of Marx's original writings. A superb discussion of the development of Marx's economic theory extending up to the present can be found in the volume of the New Palgrave Series entitled *Marxian Economics* (Eatwell, Milgate and Newman 1990). Elster has written two recent books that introduce Marx's social theory in a readable and concise fashion (1985, 1986). Bloch (1975) and Littlefield and Gates (1991) are good collections of Marxist anthropology. The introduction to Eric Wolf's *Europe and the People Without History* (1982) has one of the best discussions of what Marx provides to anthropology, as well as a concise discussion of Marxian theory; Donham (1990) has an excellent commentary on how neo-Marxism is applied to noncapitalist societies.

6. Landsburg's *The Armchair Economist* (1993) makes this argument, carrying out the utilitarian method to the point where it seems to be a parody of itself.

7. Meillassoux (1972) gives an excellent summary of the French Marxist approach. Godelier (1977) is a good collection; Terray (1972) is perhaps the most rigorous and readable application of French Marxism in English, though Meillassoux's *Maidens, Meal, and Money* (1981) is the most frequently cited. The earlier French work is well reviewed by Kahn (1981). Molyneux (1977) takes the French Marxists to task for their sexism and makes important points about the notion of "exploitation" along the way.

8. The recent literature on modes of production is voluminous, complex, and difficult. Roseberry (1989, chap. 6; see also his 1988 article) gives a clear but brief critical

commentary, Foster-Carter (1978) has a more detailed discussion, as does Carol Smith (1984). The best original sources in English are probably Althusser and Balibar (1970) and Rey (1975). Perhaps the best, sustained application of the concept of modes of production to actual cases is by De Janvry (1981). There are some excellent neo-Marxist papers on the Andes in a volume edited by Lehman (1982).

9. Mintz's early work on the Caribbean plantation is collected in *Caribbean Transformations* (1974). His *Sweetness and Power* (1985) connects sugar production in the Caribbean with the increasing sugar consumption of European elites and the growth of an industrial working class that required cheap energy foods. The main thrust of Wolf's and Mintz's work is already clear in their early work with Steward in Puerto Rico (1956). Wolf's work on peasants remains a landmark (1966, 1969). Roseberry provides a thorough and thoughtful review of recent political economy research in the *Annual Review of Anthropology* (1988).

10. Wolf (1982) provides a succinct definition of the different modes of production that form the political economic basis for all cultures. Because it is so clearly stated and succinct, it is worth summarizing here. Capitalist: Wealth can buy labor power; (1) capitalists control means of production, (2) laborers denied access to means of production, and (3) surplus accumulates to owners, so this is a growth system. Tributary: Wealth is not used to control means of production; (1) extraction is through political, not economic means, (2) struggle between local and central powers for control of surplus, and (3) civilization is the justifying ideology, and there is a cosmology of hierarchy. Kin-ordered: Wealth consists of labor and social relations; (1) labor is locked into social relations of consanguinity and affinity, (2) people circulate between groups, and control of people is key, (3) accumulation comes via control of people and through war, limiting the possibility of expansion. By basing his typology on production, Wolf directly contradicts Polanyi and Sahlins, whose typologies were based on different kinds of *exchange* (market, redistributive, etc.) instead of being based on control over the means of production.

11. Gereffi and Korzeniewicz (1994) provide an excellent survey of recent trends in global political economy. Basch, Schiller, and Blanc (1994) discuss transnationalism and the cultural connections between dispersed migrant communities. Ulf Hannerz is one of the most interesting and readable theorists of the emerging global culture (1990, 1992), though there is also a spate of more academic discussion of how culture is being affected by new communication technologies, consumerism, satellite television, and the like (e.g., Robert Foster 1991; Friedman 1992, 1994, 1995; Tomlinson 1991; Featherstone 1990; Wilk 1995).

12. This British school was largely inspired by Raymond Williams. There is a good representative book by Morley and Robins (1995).

13. Mark Moberg's study of Belizean citrus farmers, *Citrus, Strategy, and Class* (1992), is a good example of the problems neo-Marxists have in bringing together structure and agency. He suggests that the farmers are crafting their own futures, but by the end of his story they are the helpless victims of national and world economic structures. Other sources on the structure versus agency debate include original works by Bourdieu (1977, 1990) and Giddens (1984) and a collection of papers by Held and Thompson (1989).

5

The Moral Human:
Cultural Economics

What is morality in any given time or place? It is what the majority then and there happen to like, and immorality is what they dislike.

—Alfred North Whitehead, *Dialogues*

He is a barbarian, and thinks that the customs of his tribe and island are the laws of nature.

—George Bernard Shaw, *Caesar and Cleopatra*

Virtue is its own punishment.

—attributed to Aneurin Bevan

Morals, Ideology, Symbols

The newspapers and magazines in the United States in the early 1990s are full of discussions about "family values" and the collapse of public morality. I live in a small midwestern town where increasing family violence, teenage pregnancies, drunk driving, and handguns in the high schools are leading church and community leaders to describe a "moral crisis." They say that these terrible things are happening because parents are not teaching proper moral values at home and because the schools have given up teaching morality in favor of "secular humanism" and moral relativism.

Although many of the professors who teach at my university do not agree with Fundamentalist clergy about the causes of the rising tide of crime and violence in town, many of them do share the same basic assumptions about human nature. This is a moral model of human behavior, which assumes that people are guided throughout their lives by a set of principles that they learn as children. These principles divide actions into good and bad and provide a moral compass of values that should be followed in life. An ordered society results when people all learn a stable, coherent value system, because people's actions are determined by their moral values. Therefore, if people learned values like "fairness" and "self-control," society would improve.

Fundamentalist ministers and liberal college anthropologists part company on the issue of the origin of values and moral systems. On the one hand, some people believe that moral systems are eternal commandments of gods or prophets and are thus natural laws. Most social scientists, on the other hand, believe that moral codes are cultural products of particular times and places.[1] One of anthropology's fundamental contributions to knowledge is that in every society, people believe that their own values are part of the natural order. When anthropologists set out to explain why people in other societies do things that seem, from a Western point of view, bizarre or irrational, they show that within other cultural systems of morality they make a great deal of sense. Human sacrifice, to us a grossly immoral form of public murder, was considered by the ancient Aztec civilization to be an immutable part of the natural cycle, a valuable and highly moral public display of faith necessary to feed gods and perpetuate the world.

Many economists have no trouble accepting the general proposition that culture shapes human values, since economists do not pretend to explain where values come from. But they believe that once people acquire moral values, they all use them in the same basic, predictable ways. Although values may be culturally relative, they say, logic and rationality are not; no matter what culture people belong to, they use the same logical tools to translate their values into ordered preferences and then seek to maximize them in a predictably rational way.

Anthropologists often disagree with economists on this point. Some use the Sapir-Whorf hypothesis, an anthropological proposition that the different grammar and lexicon of each language affects the ways native speakers of each language think about objects, time, and causality (Whorf 1956). Some anthropologists go back to the work of the French sociologist Lucien Levy-Bruhl (1857–1939), who argued that there was a "primitive mind" and that premodern people did not think in the same way we do. (This is not to say he thought primitives were completely irrational, only that their rationality took a different form. He said primitive thought was primarily mystical and communal, incapable of finding linear chains of cause and effect [1966].) Anthropologists can also draw on studies of literacy, which say that members of cultures that depend on oral tradition instead of written records have different logical processes (Goody 1986; Walter Ong 1982).[2]

There is not universal support for any of these propositions among the current generation of anthropologists, which is generally uneasy about any suggestion that people in other cultures are not as logical or rational as Euro-

Americans. Any argument of difference can become a statement of superiority. Instead, anthropologists are more likely to use the notions of *ideology* and *symbolism*. Ideology became a crucial concept in the Frankfurt School of Critical Sociology and Philosophy (which was mentioned in chapter 4, including Max Horkheimer, Jürgen Habermas, and Herbert Marcuse) and more recently in the work of the French social theorist Michel Foucault (e.g., 1980). An ideology is much more specific than a general set of values; it includes real logical statements about the world like "Everyone has the right to own a gun," or "Blondes have more fun." What makes these statements ideology is that many people accept them as facts, but they are only partial and relative truths. Ideology always has some basis in observable reality, but it is much more than a statement of simple fact about the world. And in this age of advertising, it should be no surprise that ideology can be promoted or influenced by powerful interests. The Frankfurt school Marxists proposed that ideology always supports ("legitimizes") groups in power, while concealing their direct interests. Foucault argues that the modern state maintains order and discipline among citizens through ideologies that classify and regulate (including notions of hygiene, crime, deviance, and sexuality).

Symbols are another way to understand how culture affects the thought and behavior of individuals and groups. To a neoclassical economist or a Marxist, the ultimate reason that objects and things are desirable is their utility, their concrete physical use in achieving practical goals in the world. The bias here is that objects are in some sense ends in and of themselves, because they have *intrinsic* value. In contrast, symbolic anthropologists, think objects are desirable because of their *meaning*, because they stand for something else, for ideas and concepts, and because they trigger powerful emotions. From this perspective, you go to jail for burning an American flag because your violence against the flag is an attack on what the flag *symbolizes*. "Guess" jeans are valuable because of what they mean, not because of their utility (see Lurie 1981 for more on clothing symbolism).

Most anthropologists agree that symbols are basic tools of thought and action in every society and that the dependence on symbolic communication is indeed one of the basic traits that sets the human apart from other animals. Many anthropologists define *culture* as a system of symbols and define anthropology as the study of symbolic culture (though of course many other anthropologists disagree).

But there is a lot of disagreement about the degree to which symbols affect thought and rationality. Victor Turner argues that symbols provide unique cosmological order in every society, that humans make order out of a chaotic universe with symbolic structures (symbols organized by contrasts and similarities), and that these symbolic structures shape both everyday behavior and ritual. People themselves may not even be aware of these symbolic structures; the symbols may influence behavior even though they remain *unconscious* (1964). Many other anthropologists are reluctant to delve into the unconscious minds of their informants and think it dangerous to start explaining other people's behavior by reference to analytical models that really exist in the anthropologist's mind.[3]

Clearly, we can take the importance of symbolism too far and end up depicting other peoples as inhabiting a dreamworld of mystical symbols, as primitive existential philosophers, sitting starving in the dust while debating the balance of the cosmos. Given the difficulty of dealing with meanings and values that cannot be easily measured or even discussed, many economic anthropologists would just like the whole issue of symbols, ideology, and values to go away. But others have sought a middle ground, an economic anthropology that uses the anthropological concepts of symbolic culture and also looks at the practical, rational behavior of making a living. Following the model of previous chapters, next we delve back into Western intellectual history for the roots of this movement and then look critically at the ways in which recent anthropologists have used symbolic approaches to economic behavior.

The Roots of Moral Economics

The New Testament is full of admonitions about the corrupting power of wealth, the purity of poverty, and the evils of avarice and greed. In reading through the sacred texts of the world's religions, Russell Belk found that the same sentiments occurred over and over, from Buddhism to Orthodox Judaism (1983). And in many great civilizations, from Aztec Tenochtitlan to the Tokugawa shogunate in Japan, merchants and moneylenders were social outcasts; making money through trade and industry was considered unclean and dangerous.

These values should not be totally alien to modern Americans. The established society circles of New York and Philadelphia still look down their collective blue-blooded noses at the vulgar newly rich, with Astors excluding Trumps from the highest social ranks. In a large portion of the world, investment and merchant banks follow Islamic principles and do not collect interest (though they have other ways of making money on loans). In the Midwest, there are Christian business seminars and associations whose members try to follow biblical morality in their daily business. Society has always struggled in various ways to control the economy. Moral issues are never far from economic life, and the two are often hard to separate.

To medieval European philosophers and theologians, there was no question that the economy was subordinate to Christian morality. At the same time, the worldly church often pursued its own material wealth and power in what can only be considered an extremely rational way. The wealth and economic activities of the church were justified as furthering God's plan.

It is hard to imagine that most medieval Europeans did not perceive that there was sometimes a conflict between moral philosophy (Blessed are the meek) and everyday common sense (You cannot eat blessings). But this conflict did not break into print until the Enlightenment, when ancient Greek ideas about reason and rationality were revived and placed in opposition to the moral theology propounded by the church. For David Hume (1712–1808), religion was not based on reason; it came from emotions, passions, and appetites, especially fear (1964). All people had the capacity for reason, but few exercised it; human nature emerged from an interplay of emotions and appetites, on the one hand, and practical physical and social experience, on the other.

Reason became the great intellectual theme of the Enlightenment.[4] We have seen what Adam Smith and the utilitarians did with the concept. Yet scarcely was absolute rationality separated from religious thought than philosophers tried to limit it once again. Immanuel Kant (1724–1808) wrote *Critique of Pure Reason* to argue that all people are born with mental equipment and concepts ("transcendental consciousness") that limit and shape reason and rationality. Kant used unconscious patterns in human society (the seasonal rise and fall in marriages and births, for example) to argue that things that appeared to be the products of decisions and reason were actually determined by something else.

Many people jumped into the business of explaining what that "something else" was. German romantic philosophers started down a trail of ethnic and biological determinism that led to both important modern social sciences and to the abusive philosophies of racial superiority that legitimized Fascism and Nazism. Johann Herder (1744–1803) thought that by adapting to local circumstances and environments, each culture developed its own unique character and "genius." These *Volk* cultures were naturally harmonious, enshrining unique patterns of thought, speech, and action in their history and traditions. The patterns were unconscious and powerfully determinative. They explained why the Spanish were lazy, the Gypsies dishonest, and the English successful in business. The romantic nationalists believed that economic success and aptitudes for different kinds of work came from the unique genius and mind-set of each people. Each nation was like a person, with a personality formed through history (though most of these "personalities" were really just stereotypes).

Although later scholars have accused Herder of racism (e.g., Stocking 1968), he did not try to reduce national characteristics to biological race. The distinct economic behavior of different peoples was clearly a product of history and culture, not of physical or mental capabilities (De Waal Malefijt 1974, 99). But other German scientists like Gustav Klemm *were* quite willing to explain cultural differences as the product of biological race: Germans were *born* "active," whereas most of the rest of the world's peoples were "passive" (see Harris 1968, 101–102).

The main argument of the German romantics is instantly recognizable to modern anthropologists: Human nature is embedded in a particular time and place. Furthermore, this human nature could not be measured objectively or explained by universal laws—the only way to understand it was subjectively, through experience and the detailed study of individual cases. The romantics also believed that they were in the midst of a great historical watershed in the development of culture; they were seeing the death of *real authentic Volk* cultures and their replacement by grasping, calculating, and materialistic modern capitalist values. Their political goal was to save some of the authentic peasant culture of the German past and to carry its best values forward.

In Western academic economics, the Germans romantics never overcame the dominance of the utilitarianism of Smith and Ricardo. But in the other social sciences, their ideas had much more influence. In anthropology and sociology, Max Weber was the key figure who translated romanticism into a systematic foundation for ideas about the relationship between culture and economic behavior.

Max Weber: Rationality and History

Weber (1864–1920) grew up in Berlin, the son of a prominent politician, during a time when the German economy grew explosively and the country became a world power.[5] Weber's scholarship ranged across many disciplines, from philosophy to political science, though today Weber is remembered mainly as a sociologist. He did not subscribe to any simple moral or utilitarian view of human nature, nor did he believe that there was a universal natural impulse behind all action. He identified a number of different human motives that were determined by context; sometimes people were value oriented, sometimes interest oriented, and other times bound by tradition (see Weber 1968). He also argued that humans were often collective and social because they shared material goals or were forced together by common oppression or because they shared ideals, world views, or feelings.

Weber believed that the ideas and values produced by historical circumstances make people act in a particular way. Each culture therefore has to be understood as a unique whole, and if we could place ourselves in the minds of its members, we would see things from their point of view. We could then see how their actions, which might seem strange or irrational to an outsider, made sense from the inside. Weber studied a number of world civilizations with the goal of understanding how each saw the world, explaining the economic and social behavior of Hindus, Jews, and Chinese by using "values" and "spirit" as key concepts. The specific spirit of a culture shaped its economic fortunes; for example, the spirit of the caste system kept India from developing a modern capitalist economy (Käsler 1988, 115). Weber's idea that each group had its own values that gave its civilization a unique character is close to the modern anthropological concept of culture.

Weber's studies of other cultures were also used to critique the modern world. What makes modern industrial capitalism unique in history, he said, is the extent to which "rationalization" has invaded and captured all human relationships: "The fate of our times is characterized by rationalization and intellectualization, and above all, by the disenchantment of the world" (1946, 155). Weber thought the modern bureaucratic state is founded on utilitarian principles and impersonal legal ties between people, all based on rational calculation and secular materialism. Its progress crushes "the traditional, the patriarchal, the communal, the 'enchanted,' along with the irrational, the personally exploitative, the superstitious" (Nisbet 1966, 294). Weber recognized some of the drawbacks of traditional society, but he was not optimistic about what capitalism and the state were erecting in its place. He mourned the loss of the venerable and ancient world based on religious morality, personal relationships, and kinship, but he also sadly recognized that there was no going back.

Weber tells a marvelous and persuasive story: Once there was a world of tradition and harmony, though it was often cruel and unequal. Then in Europe, modern *rationality* arose, a way of thinking that fed like cancer on tradition, spreading and destroying everything that came before it. This model of a global transition from traditional to modern has become so pervasive in Western science and popular culture that it is often accepted as a simple fact and an article of faith. But as mentioned in Chapter 4, it has been attacked by historians and social scientists because it does not fit "the facts" as we know them. And neither does Weber's idea that modern Western society is impersonal, for personal and kinship ties continue to be important in our lives. The theme of the death of superstition and the rise of rational religion cannot survive a trip to the supermarket tabloid racks.

McCloskey thinks that the idea that modern bureaucracy is rational and efficient can only be maintained by someone who has never worked for one or who has served in the armed forces. McCloskey says that the whole Weberian lament about the increasingly material, secular, and rational nature of

Max Weber

society emerges from the deep hostility that intellectuals have toward the middle class. This is why they write so much that portrays the bourgeoisie as crass, small minded, grasping, materialistic, and the "embodiment of rationality," and it explains why they long for the good old days when people respected the elite (1994, 189).

Whatever the fate of Weber's historical analysis, his underlying model of human behavior demands closer scrutiny, specifically his proposal that rationality is a product of a particular time and setting. This may sound in some ways similar to what I have said about Marx in the last chapter, but there is a crucial difference. Marx thought individuals were indeed created in a particular historical context, but they held the potential for a *class* consciousness founded in the material realities of their lives as producers and workers. Weber, working in the German romantic tradition, thought a whole society shared a set of values and ideas that transcended class or economic status. Weber believed that all Hindus—whether workers or owners, priests or peasants—share a basic set of beliefs about the world and its moral values that bind them together and make them act in very similar ways, in the home, in the temple, and in the marketplace. In Weber's logic, economic behavior is therefore deeply embedded in culture and beliefs, whereas Marx saw things very much in the reverse. In every society, Weber thought, economic acts are a product of personal, ethical, and social considerations; only with capitalism does an abstracted and separated notion of rationality emerge. These ideas are most fully developed in his most famous book, *The Protestant Ethic and the Spirit of Capitalism.*

In this work, Weber first establishes the difference between modern capitalists and people of the Catholic Middle Ages. The "spirit" of capitalism is one of open competition and "survival of the fittest." People make agreements with each other for individual advantage in the pursuit of wealth. Benjamin Franklin is the pragmatic philosopher of capitalist avarice, with such aphorisms as "Time is Money," and the like.

In contrast, there are traditional peasants. They are so set in their ways and so limited by their conservative notions of what is right that they cannot respond to the profit motive. Weber's example is worth quoting in full.

> A man, for instance, who at the rate of 1 mark per acre mowed 2.5 acres per day and earned 2.5 marks, when the [wage] rate was raised to 1.25 marks per acre mowed, not 3 acres, as he might easily have done, thus earning 3.75 marks, but only 2 acres, so that he could still earn 2.5 marks to which he was accustomed. The opportunity of earning more was less attractive than that of working less. He did not ask: how much can I earn in a day if I do as much work as possible? but: how much must I work in order to earn the wage 2.5 marks, which I earned before and which takes care of my traditional needs? This is an example of what is here meant by traditionalism. A man does not "by nature" wish to earn more and more money, but simply to live as he is accustomed to live and to earn as

much as is necessary for that purpose. Wherever modern capitalism has begun its work of increasing the productivity of human labor by increasing its intensity, it has encountered the immensely stubborn resistance of this leading trait of precapitalistic labor. (1958, 59–60)

The capitalist employer faced with this behavior learns that to get more work he must *lower* wages instead of raising them. Coercion may be necessary; Weber goes on to state that "an almost universal complaint of employers of girls, for instance German girls, is that they are almost entirely unable and unwilling to give up methods of work inherited or once learned in favour of more efficient ones, to adapt themselves to new methods, to learn and to concentrate their intelligence, or even to use it at all" (1958, 62).

Why does the peasant or working girl behave this way? Weber's answer is that of every employer who has ever had to deal with a labor force or market that does not respond "properly" to higher prices or wages: *It's their culture.* They *cannot see* the clear sense of making more money, investing it in more land or buying better clothes. They are *irrational*. It is not that they are stupid; they just want to live the "leisurely and comfortable life" they have always led, in their traditional families and institutions. This is not a matter of nature, but of the particular moral code ("ethos") of medieval Christianity. The philosophy of the church specified that money and its pursuit was unclean and that everyone had a divine calling in life, a station, that should not be changed.

What happened? Weber is quite willing to admit that historical changes in commerce, the growth of cities, and population increase were fertile ground for the development of capitalism in northern Europe in the seventeenth century. He does not deny that there was a lot of *traditional* capitalist trade and wage labor. But the key cultural change was the Protestant Reformation of Calvin and Luther, which changed people's fundamental ideas about God, fate, and work. The whole structure and nature of economic life changed because of a transformation in "those psychological sanctions which, originating in religious belief and the practice of religion, gave a direction to practical conduct and held the individual to it" (1958, 97).

Weber goes into a great deal of theological detail to find the roots of rational calculation, material satisfaction, and the work ethic in the teachings of early Calvinists. The crucial lessons in Protestant theology, he says, were that people can improve their station in life as a sign of God's grace and that hard work is an act of piety in and of itself (the work ethic). The Protestants found a way to allow the pursuit of wealth to coexist with an ascetic morality by finding a distinction between bad wealth (wasteful display and luxury leading to sloth) and good (just rewards for hard work and proof of genuine faith). This is not to say that on a personal level Protestants were more rational than Catholics, but only that Protestant beliefs made capitalism *as a system* more efficient, rational, and expansive.

Therefore, for Weber, it was ultimately a set of *ideas,* a moral philosophy, that let the cat of capitalism out of the bag of tradition. From the Reformation it was an easy step to the exaltation of rationality in the Enlightenment and to the progressive extension of "victorious capitalism" into every nook and cranny of personal daily life. Weber cautions that the capitalist revolution was not *purely* or simply a product of new religious ideas, that there was always a difference between philosophy and fact (1958, 284). But taken as a whole, Weber argues firmly that economic behavior is entirely subject to moral codes and cultural values.

Generations of scholars have attacked Weber's *The Protestant Ethic.* Most of his historical facts have been disputed. His characterization of the hide-bound tradition-minded peasantry, incapable of responding to market incentives, has been repeatedly shown to be false. James Scott's *Weapons of the Weak* (1985) exposes peasant conservatism as a condescending myth; peasants often resist change because they quite rationally recognize a real attempt to exploit them or take away their autonomy. Weber's account distorts and exaggerates both the unreason of traditionalism and the rationality of modernity.

But many who reject Weber's history still embrace his ideas about motivations and rationality. Like most anthropologists, he was striving for an explanation of the relationship between belief and behavior that would take into account individual people's subjective understanding and experience. And like many modern anthropologists, his answer was that religious interests and cosmology influence and shape concrete actions and social relationships and even mundane economic behavior (Parsons 1963, xxi). For Weber, rationality is not a principle in and of itself; it is a social product. Although we all have some degree of freedom of action (and this degree varies according to how traditional our culture is), our goals and values are given us by culture, which also sets the rules of what is acceptable behavior.

Weber's formulation of moral economics is the basis of early economic anthropology and remains a powerful theme in the work of prominent twentieth-century anthropologists like Marshall Sahlins and Clifford Geertz. Next, we will trace the theme of moral economics through other major figures in early anthropology and then examine the more recent variations on the theme, finishing with some examples of how Weberian economics appears in modern anthropology.

Bronislaw Malinowski: The Magic of the Kula

Malinowski (1884–1942) was never a central figure in the British social anthropology movement discussed in Chapter 4 because he did not submerge the individual in society.[6] Throughout his career, he was deeply interested in individual motives, in finding the reasons people did things that were more direct than the structural functionalists' explanation—"to maintain the social structure." For this reason, he built his theory of behavior on human *needs,* not the needs of society but those of the individual. He provided lists of needs (e.g., "bodily comfort") and the cultural responses that fulfilled them ("shelter") (1944, 91). He created a hierarchy of needs, some of which were primary and immediate and had few solutions when denied (breathing), whereas others were secondary and could be satisfied in a number of ways (raising children). He argued that no trait, action, or custom survived if it did not satisfy a need; there were no useless or ornamental customs (1944, 28–29). Because he was more interested in individual motives than other social anthropologists, he was more willing to debate with economists' rival theories of motive.

His relationship with economics was extremely ambivalent. On the one hand, he fought throughout his career to show that the exotic customs and practices—the "apparently senseless antics" of people in other cultures— were actually reasonable. The famous Kula exchange system of the Trobriand Islands, in which armshells and necklaces were solemnly moved over thousands of kilometers, seemed like just another crazy native practice or primitive biological instinct to ethnocentric missionaries and colonial administrators. To others, these native people were of an inferior race. Malinowski showed that, from the Trobriand point of view, Kula made great sense and, furthermore, that it served basic economic and social functions in

Bronislaw Malinowski

their society. He told colonial officials to keep their hands off primitive customs they did not understand; customs were not isolated traits but part of a complex social fabric that satisfied basic biological needs.

On the other hand, Malinowski argued that the economists' idea about rationality being motivated by selfish and utilitarian material needs was ethnocentric and did not work even when applied to modern Western capitalism (which is, he said, full of magic and symbolism [1931, 636]). Instead, he believed that primitive motives are deeply social and symbolic, and people are motivated to economic action by desires for prestige, by beliefs in magic, by tradition, and by a desire to follow custom. As he said of the Trobrianders, "It must not be forgotten that there is hardly ever much room for doubt or deliberation, as natives communally, as well as individually, never act except on traditional and conventional lines" (1961, 62).

This contradiction is basic in the moral economy model of human behavior. In one sense, humans are rational and driven by reasonable and universal human needs. In another sense, the actual form of most needs is culturally variable, and solutions to those needs are dictated by custom. When the Trobrianders slave for months in their fields to produce huge numbers of yams, which are put on competitive display in elaborate yam houses and used in magic garden rituals, they are rationally pursuing a way to satisfy needs, though within a fabric and context dictated by custom. Malinowski's famous explanation of magic falls into the same mold; magic is the result of individuals' rational attempts to make sense out of things they cannot explain, in ways that satisfy their basic biological need for security.

Malinowski's solution to understanding human action and human nature has a strong appeal. Anthropologists are always engaged in the dual task of trying to explain how all human cultures have common ground and how each one is also distinct and different. This theory tells us that all human cultures have something in common—rationality based on universal needs. But at the same time, each culture is unique. Through ideas of custom, culture, and tradition, anthropology engages us in the mystery of difference. Then it pulls us back to the mundane and tells us that no matter how exotic the setting, people are really all pretty much the same. Learn the language and spend a year or two there, and you can understand how reasonable they really are.

Despite this appeal, Malinowski's approach is problematic because it leaves everything in the anthropologist's uniquely qualified hands. Only the anthropologist is capable of explaining when and why people are behaving in universally understandable ways and when they are acting according to unique custom and tradition, since we have no external guidelines for judging when people are one and when they are the other. This problem appears in an even more dramatic form in the economic anthropology of the American tradition.

Franz Boas: Economy as Culture

Boas (1858–1942) studied physics, mathematics, and geography in Germany before becoming an ethnographer during research on the Baffinland Eskimo. He took individual cultures as his unit of analysis but argued with cultural evolutionists about the causes of similarities and differences between cultures. Boas thought cultural similarities, rather than fitting a grand evolutionary scheme or being the products of common environments, should be explained by tracing specific historical developments and connections between groups (*historical particularism*). His connection with German romantic economic philosophy (which he learned in college) is clear; every culture is a unique historical product that can only be understood from the subjective perspective of those who share its "spirit" (Hatch 1973). Like the romantics, he found among non-Western native peoples the positive virtues that he thought were so lacking in modern industrial society.

Boas believed that all humans have the same kind of rationality: "There is no fundamental difference in the ways of thinking of primitive and civilized man" (1963, 17). But he also thought that each culture was a tightly integrated system, which determined the behavior of individuals with an "iron grip" (1940, 259). Culture shaped behavior through the emotions and through habit. Actions that are repeated over and over become habits and therefore become unconscious. Once we have absorbed cultural ways of doing things as habits, any other way of doing things seems unreasonable, even dangerous (1962). When people do give reasons for their actions, they are usually just after-the-fact rationalizations rather than the real cause of their behavior. Thought, action, and decisions were always a product of culture, according to Boas, never the other way around (see Hatch 1973, 56–57).

Here is the basic contradiction of moral economics in the hands of modern anthropology. Boas's respect for the essential humanity of non-Western people demanded that he reject Levy-Bruhl's dictum that the "primitive mind" was somehow different and incapable of logical and rational thought. Therefore, everyone must be capable of rationality built on common "basic psychological processes." Even so, most people did not really use that rationality on a daily basis; instead, they followed customs and traditions dictated to them by their culture. In practice, then, people *do not* all think alike, and there is no universal rationality, only some vaguely defined common thought "processes" that could mostly be revealed by studying the common structures of language.

Later in his career, Boas became more interested in the effect of culture on individual personality and came to believe that individuals could also change the culture in which they lived (e.g., 1940, 285). The "creative factors" that gave each culture its unique historical development were in the individual

Franz Boas

mind, as shown in his work on American Indian art (1940, 578–589). Most art, like the rest of culture, is the product of simple unreflecting habit. People make an object in a particular shape because that is how they have always done it. But now and then an artist adds features or makes modifications through the creative "play of imagination." Thus, *artistic creativity* is the only form of free will that Boas allows people, certainly not anything like calculating self-interest.

Anthropology in Boas's time was a young science fighting racism, ethnocentrism, and various kinds of evolutionary foolishness, all of which depicted non-Western people as inferior, irrational, or survivors of earlier evolutionary stages. His response, like Malinowski's, was that you have to understand people's behavior *in context* and from their point of view. The context of all behavior in all societies is tradition, not rationality or the functioning of the social organism. Economic behavior is simply that part of tradition and habit concerned with production, exchange, and consumption.

Two Paths from Boas

Boas's students and followers in American anthropology generally took two paths to later cultural economics. The first was an elaboration of the notion that culture is *irrational* and can only be understood from an insider's subjective point of view. The second was the idea that a culture is an integrative system, with an internal coherence that can be empirically studied through painstaking detailed fieldwork.

Ruth Benedict (1887–1948) was Boas's student at Columbia University and took the first path. Her particularism led her to say that no two cultures are ever really alike, that each culture has its own particular obsessions and preoccupations. This *ethos* or *configuration* was like a personality; each culture was dominated by unique emotions and attitudes (1932). Particular practices and behavior can only be interpreted and understood in the context of this configuration, not through general theories or comparisons with other cultures.

Rather than being rational decisionmaking human beings, Benedict's people are caught in the grip of powerful emotions. The Melanesian Dobu Islanders appear treacherous, deceitful, paranoid, and jealous, or "passionate," in their pursuit of Kula wealth and sex. But their attitudes become reasonable and understandable in the context of the overall cultural pattern (1934, chaps. 5, 7). In *Patterns of Culture* Benedict argues that we cannot explain cultural difference through biology, geography, functionalism, or psychology; instead, culture, shaped by a unique history of borrowing and integration, explains everything.

Her study of the Kwakiutl of the Northwest Coast shows how much she thought economic behavior was determined by culture. Rivalry is "the chief motive that the institutions of the Kwakiutl rely upon" (1934, 227); "the whole economic system of the Northwest coast was bent to the service of this obsession" (1934, 178). Her explanation of the Kwakiutl *potlatch* feasts, where wealth is given away with the object of shaming another and gaining prestige, is based on the idea that rivalry is an overriding imperative value for all Kwakiutl.

> Rivalry is a struggle that is not centered upon real objects of the activity but upon outdoing a competitor. The attention is no longer directed toward providing adequately for a family or towards owning goods that can be utilized or enjoyed, but toward outdistancing one's neighbours and owning more than anyone else. Everything is lost sight of in the one great aim of victory ... In Kwakiutl institutions, such rivalry reaches its final absurdity in equating investment with the wholesale destruction of goods. They contest for superiority chiefly in accumulation of goods, but often also, and without a consciousness of the contrast, in breaking in pieces their highest units of value, their coppers, and in making bonfires of their houseplanks, their blankets and canoes. The social waste is obvious. It is just as obvious in the obsessive rivalry of *Middletown* [middle-class Muncie, Indiana] where houses are built and clothing bought and entertainments attended that each family may prove that it has not been left out of the game. (1934, 228)

Culture sets the goals, provides the rules, and gives people the emotional rewards that keep them playing. "The vast proportion of all individuals who are born into any society always ... assume as we have seen, the behavior dictated by that society" (1934, 235). The few who do not conform are deviants or outcasts. The whole idea that individuals have different interests from society at large, says Benedict, is just one of the ethnocentric cultural beliefs of modern Western society.

Benedict's idea that people are essentially conformists was probably shaped more by the rigid and narrow cultural restrictions of 1930s intellectual circles in New York than by the Dobuans, Zuni, or Kwakiutl. From the perspective of 1990s anthropology, in which people are seen as creative and often rebellious improvisers and manipulators, this seems a very dated and static picture. For all the talk of "seeing things from the native point of view," there seem to be very few real natives in this anthropology, just generic characters following customs, reciting myths, and staging rituals. Benedict shows us one logical extreme of cultural economics: that *there is no economics,* only a cultural configuration.

The second direction of Boas's work was an approach to economics that I call, quoting *Dragnet,* "Just the facts, Ma'am." During his entire career, Boas instilled in anthropologists the need for meticulous documentation of every aspect of cultural life. Explanation and comparison were premature without "the facts," that is, customs, social organization, language, and beliefs. (Actual daily pragmatic behavior did not usually appear on this list.) Given that so many cultures seemed to be disappearing, this was also an ethical incentive to document things before they were gone.

Economic activities, or at least customs and traditional practices of production, exchange, and consumption, were included on the Boasian list of facts. Boas and Benedict said that in each culture, particular activities were a primary focus for custom, emotion, and power, so there were good reasons to document economic behavior as part of any well-rounded ethnography and to go into special detail on economic institutions when they were central to emotional and ritual life.[7] One goal of the Boasian program was to compile a complete catalog of the huge variety of exotic and intricate economic practices, customs, and institutions that are or have been practiced by all cultures.[8]

Manning Nash's *Machine Age Maya* is a fairly standard example of the just-the-facts approach, published in 1958. This is a study of a Quiche-Maya–speaking village in the Western Highlands of Guatemala, where a textile factory had been established in 1876. At the time of Nash's fieldwork, more than one-third of the village was employed in the mill, where the workers had a labor union. In a dry, descriptive tone, he notes the traditions of the farmers in the village, the differences in lifestyle between field and factory workers, and the social life of the community. Farmers are more "traditional" and mill workers are more "modern"; for workers, the family and kinship is less important and voluntary associations more common. But by and large, everyone in the community shares the same set of folk-Catholic beliefs and worldview. Although the villagers have been exposed to "rational" modern ideas through their work in the factory, they have not allowed this rationality to creep out of the mill into the rest of their lives (1958, 96). Just as Boas would have expected, the traditional culture and cosmology absorbs foreign practices and keeps the people in its power. Factory work only affects the Maya by changing their personalities and by introducing new objects and concepts, not by transforming their circumstances or social organization.

A theme that arises in Nash's ethnography, as well as in a number of other factually oriented economic ethnographies from the 1930s to the 1960s, is the notion of a *prestige economy*. People in the village did not usually invest their money in businesses but instead spent it on the lavish requirements of serving public political, religious, and ceremonial offices. In the Mayan *cofradia* system, for example, men acquire respect as they pass through different offices and eventually become seniors who make important political decisions. The idea is that people are rational, but they do not seek wealth or leisure like "we" do. Rather they seek status, rank, and power in their community (women are typically marginalized by this account; their position is seen as only a consequence of their husband's actions). Here is the classic formulation of cultural economics: that people have autonomy—but only to satisfy goals that are culturally programmed (some autonomy!).

The *just-the-facts* thread of economic anthropology rarely makes its assumptions clear, because they are taken for granted. As Sol Tax says in *Penny Capitalism,* his ethnography of the highland Maya, "There is no economic theory in this book. I am simply describing the way a people live, picking out those elements to describe that I understand fit under the rubric of *economy*"(1953, ix). The lesson these ethnographies teach is a liberal story of cultural diversity, that each culture is different and that economic behavior is therefore different in every setting. Some of the factual ethnographies discovered people who were not very different at all. Leopold Pospisil's encyclopedic compendium of facts about the economy of the Kapauku of western New Guinea concludes that the average Kapauku is just as economically minded and individualistic as any Chicago shopkeeper (1963).[9] Although the Kapauka have Stone Age technology, they own private property, use cowrie shells as money, make loans, buy and sell everything, and generally work hard to acquire wealth and prestige. Like a good Boasian, Pospisil concludes that evolutionary models don't work, because here is a case of "primitive" people who do have money, wages, and markets.

Most of "the facts" collected by neo-Boasians sit quietly, dead, on library shelves these days. When I went to find Charles Wagley's *Economics of a Guatemalan Village* (1941) in the library while writing this chapter, I found that some of the pages had never been cut, and it had not been checked out since 1952. In anthropology, the facts emphatically *do not* speak for themselves. When cultural economics became simply the documentation of all the wonderful ways that cultures shape production, consumption, and exchange, it became a dreadful bore, a trivial pursuit. Worse, it was unhinged from the controversies about politics, ecology, and ideology that were changing anthropology into something Boas would barely recognize. Only when anthropologists began to question and challenge the Boasian concept of culture as a collection of customs or a state of mind did economic anthropology come to life again.

The Question of Rationality and Culture

A key term in all the discussion so far is "rationality." Microeconomics carefully defines rationality as a form of instrumental logic based on goal seeking and efficient allocation of resources. Social economics defines rationality at the level of the group, as effective class struggle or group survival. Moral economists do think there are universal mental abilities, but they differ on precisely what they might be. For some, they include goal-seeking rational capacities to connect cause and effect, to solve complex allocation problems, or to bargain. For others, the universal human capacity is to symbolize, categorize, and communicate with language.[10] The values and goals that motivate people to use these innate rational capacities are entirely relative, the province of each unique culture. Modern symbolic anthropologists are especially clear on this point; for this reason I will use the label *cultural economics* to refer to the recent school, which uses some variant of symbolic anthropology and a moral model of human nature.

The American symbolic anthropologist Melford Spiro illustrates the logic of cultural economics with unusual clarity in his short paper "Buddhism and Economic Action in Burma" (1966). In northern Burma, he observes, many poor Buddhist farmers and townspeople spend their meager incomes on things that seem, to many Western eyes, superfluous and useless: religious rituals, feasts for monks, and building elaborate pagodas. This expenditure is not stupid or irrational, he says. Nor does it result from people following the Buddhist doctrines of charity (*dana*) and submission to fate (karma). Most of the people he interviewed, who were uneducated farmers, didn't *know* the basic tenets of Buddhist philosophy.

Instead, he says, the Burmese are rational *within a particular cultural and economic context*. First, they really wouldn't be able to make a difference in their standard of living if they saved their money instead of spending it on ritual (this assertion is unsupported by figures or details). Second, life in Burma is risky and uncertain, so even if you become wealthy, you may not be able to keep your wealth, thus, it's probably better to spend it (this contradicts the first point). Third, even if most Burmese do not know Buddhist theology, at an *unconscious* cognitive and symbolic level, they have absorbed Buddhist ideas about rebirth, karma, and building merit through charity. These beliefs are part of everyone's moral worldview and cosmology; by following them, people rationally conclude that spending money on monks, rituals, and pagodas is a reasonable way to acquire prestige and respect, ensure an advantageous rebirth, and have a good party at the same time. They do not have to consciously *know* Buddhist philosophy in order for it to affect their worldview and behavior.

Spiro concludes, "In the Burmese behavioral environment, religious spending is by far the more rational decision to make" (1966, 1168). Thus, the Burmese are not especially "spiritually minded" or "otherworldly." They are rational maximizers, driven by culturally defined needs, who have very different values from the average American.

Here I want to quote Spiro's position on human nature, because it is such a clear statement of cultural economics and because it neatly links Boas and Weber with the later theorists we will discuss next.

I assume that the behavior of any well-socialized adult is instigated by some need . . . I further assume . . . that for almost any need this well-socialized adult has a fairly wide behavioral repertory, that is, a set of potential acts, all of which are instrumental for the satisfaction of the need. Hence, any observed act represents a *choice* from among a set of alternative, often conflicting, potential acts. I further assume that this choice of the one from the many is based on the actor's *perception,* or *evaluation,* of the relative instrumental efficacy of the members of the set for satisfying the need. I assume, finally, that this perception is importantly determined by his *cognitive* system and, specifically, by that part of his cognitive system that constitutes his conceptions of nature, of society, and of culture. For it is from these conceptions, among others, that actors evaluate their projected actions as being possible, desirable, meaningful, and so on, or their reverse [emphasis in original]. (1966, 1164)

Problems with Cultural Economics

To reduce Spiro's argument to its kernel, all human beings are reasonable, but their environment is shaped by culture and so are their perceptions, values, and desires. Here is the same double-edged argument that Malinowski made—on the one hand, "they" are just as rational as anyone else, but on the other hand, their rationality can only be judged within their own cultural context. On the face of it this is a very attractive argument, which has driven an enormous amount of productive ethnographic fieldwork aimed at finding out other peoples' worldviews, motives, and values. It retains some of the form and power of Western economics by retaining the idea of rationality. Yes, everyone *is* indeed maximizing. But it adds cultural relativism, as well as ethnographic knowledge of how cultures work from the *inside,* by arguing that people's ideas about *what* is to be maximized and the possible *actions* that can be taken to achieve those goals are determined by *culture.* Culture writes the menu and tells us what tastes good, but it leaves us free to choose what is best at each meal from the list. And nature is what makes us hungry to begin with.

But there are some logical problems with this scheme that need to be examined, because they surface over and over again in later economic anthropology. To begin with, cultural economics tends to take the issue of rationality for granted, translating it into a very general sense of "reasonable": It is simply action that can be explained. But rational for whom and in what way? Spiro tells us that it is rational to spend money on entertaining ceremonies because investing it or accumulating it is too risky and ineffective. But how do we know this is true, if he did not gauge the return from other possible activities? And since he rejects a comparable universal measure of value in terms of money or labor, how *could* we compare the return of other possible ways for the Burmese to spend their money? Without a yardstick, "rationality" becomes meaningless. We merely discover what people do and then invent plausible reasons for it. Anything that doesn't actually kill the actor could be rational by this definition. And there might even be perfectly good reasonable explanations for self-destruction, too.

The social and ecological functionalists at least argue that what is rational is what is good for the society as a whole. An example is Marvin Harris's well-known analysis of the sacred cow in India. Like the Kula system, allowing cows to run around the streets while people are starving appears to many outsiders as "irrational" behavior (1966). Harris shows that society as a whole is better off, and has more money and food by keeping the cows as draft animals and using their dung for fuel and fertilizer, instead of eating them.

The problem with *both* social functionalism and Spiro's cultural economics is that neither puts rationality into the conscious minds and goal-seeking behavior of individuals. Malinowski said that the way Trobrianders thought about and explained their Kula trade had nothing to do with its rationality or social functions (Leach 1957). Similarly, Spiro's informants never told him that they spent their money on monks and pagodas because it gave them a better return on their money than land or a gas station. Rationality is seen from above, as an analytical judgment by a trained scientist from a distance. *Culture* is what is really "rational" here, not individuals, who are just creatures of culture. It is hard to see what remains of the economists' notion of rational maximizing when it is used in this way, since it is no longer a form of decisionmaking that is going on in an individual's mind. If it is not in people's minds, where could rationality possibly be?

The American sociologist Talcott Parsons put his finger right on another key problem with this loose systems definition of rationality (1957, 57–67). He said it never manages to link *motives* with *behavior* in any concrete way. It rests ultimately on psychology and on socialization as the process that implants culture in each person's mind as the person grows up. But Malinowski, Boas, and Spiro never tell us how culture becomes implanted in individual psychology or how the conscious and unconscious minds work together.

For all Malinowski's talk about biological needs, in the end, both the needs and the rules for satisfying them are a product of culture, so instead of being rational in any objective sense, people are cultural robots. This analysis begs the question "Then where does the culture come from in the first place, and how can it change?" Given Malinowski's theoretical framework, culture is not changed or altered through the actions or decisions of individuals. It is a concrete structure of traditions and customs, a unique historical product that is changed only through the impact of external forces or through the adoption of innovations from other cultures.[11]

Cultural Economics, Round Two

Geertz and Sahlins

Despite its logical problems, cultural economics has definitely been the thread that connects economic anthropology most clearly with the mainstream of modern sociocultural anthropology. As symbolic anthropology has grown in reflexive, interpretive, and postmodern directions, many scholars have developed new strains and variations of cultural economics. How have later symbolic anthropologists developed and extended the Weberian tradition, and how have they tried to transcend its limitations?

Clifford Geertz is perhaps the most famous American anthropologist of the 1970s and 1980s, known for his view of culture as something alive and fluid that requires subjective understanding and "thick description."[12] Much of his early ethnographic work was concerned directly with ecology, with systems of production and exchange in markets. But his point was always to show that economic behavior is a unique cultural product; he always relativizes economic practice.

In order to move away from the static Boasian idea that culture, through psychology, determines behavior, Geertz adopts a more complex model derived from Talcott Parsons (and through him from Weber). He recognizes that neither the Boasian model nor social functionalism can effectively account for social change. His solution is to separate culture from the social system (1957, 233). Culture includes language, systems of meaning, values, and symbols. The social is actual "interactive behavior" and the structure of groups and associations that guide it. Culture is a set of ideas, whereas society is an observable ordering of people and behavior. Using the example of a Javanese funeral, he shows that culture and society often conflict with each other; people's beliefs and customs tell them to do one thing, but actual social relationships and loyalties push them to do something else. In this situation, change occurs. Behavior therefore results from a collision of forces, in this particular case from an urban social structure and a peasant religious system. Despite Geertz's careful discussion of the individual people who played out the conflict, they appear as almost helpless onlookers, struggling to deal with the contradictions of their lives. Their decisions are about how to cope with their culture and social organization—not with problems of economic gain or self-interest.

Peddlers and Princes is Geertz's most developed cultural economic ethnography. He contrasts a bustling Muslim commercial market town in Java with a sleepy Hindu temple town of nobles and peasants in nearby Bali. The Muslim Javanese town is dominated by individualist entrepreneurs, and the culture encourages rational maximizing. The Hindu Balinese are enmeshed in traditional social relations, and the culture stresses group cooperation and harmony. The Javanese are *Homo economicus,* whereas the Balinese are *Homo politicus* (1963, 131–132). Economic growth causes different problems in the two settings. In the Javanese town, there is not enough cultural constraint on the economy, and there is not enough trust among people. The result is too much open competition and struggle. The Balinese town has the opposite problem: too many cultural restraints and too many limitations and obligations, which bog down enterprises and force them to become inefficient.[13]

At the time Geertz was writing, in a rush of postwar optimism, many social scientists thought the "developing" world was just at the point of "takeoff," on the verge of becoming modern wealthy consumer cultures. The reason some groups lagged while others forged ahead was explained mostly by looking at their culture and society. The more "traditional" cultures, in Weber's sense, were hindered by their lack of capitalist spirit. Economic success could be explained by culture. Geertz argues with some of Weber's details but never questions Weber's assumptions about human nature. He concludes by arguing that both Java and Bali are developing, but each in its own way because each has a unique history, religion, social system, and culture. He finds similarities in the process of modernization, however, that link the two cases together.

The problem that Geertz studied should be familiar to any urban North American. Take a look around and you quickly see that some cultural or ethnic groups are more economically successful than others. All the Italian greengrocers in New York's Greenwich Village, where I went to college, are now displaced by Koreans. Go almost anywhere in the developing world and you find Indian shopkeepers and Chinese restaurants. In Belize, where I have done most of my fieldwork, German-speaking Mennonite farmers have pretty much driven locals out of commercial farming during the last twenty-five years.

The easy answer is to argue that there is "something in their culture" that makes a group especially good farmers, smart shopkeepers, savers, or hard workers or lazy, spendthrift, and, as Belizeans say, "good fa nut'n." Clearly, Hindu shopkeepers have different religious values from Italian grocers. But one could also point to differences in social organization—to Chinese family structure, for example. Or to differences in historical experience, by comparing Mexican farm workers with Russian political exiles. Or you could look at the wealth people have to work with, at their education and skills, or at their political organization. Mennonites in Belize are successful because they work hard, but they also started with a lot more money and land than the average Mayan farmer.

Geertz's bottom line is that Balinese and Javanese cultures are different, and he argues his case persuasively. But he never looks closely at alternative causes, and he never explains exactly how it is that culture makes some people entrepreneurial and leaves others subject to tradition. And if we follow Geertz's analysis to its logical conclusion, we come back to the thesis that each culture has a unique historical identity that determines its development and change. This can either lead us back to a frustrating particularism (culture is the cause, and every culture develops from a unique past) or to a very dangerous kind of *blaming the victim*. If culture is the ultimate cause, when some group or country *fails* in some way, then culture is also the culprit.

Taken to an extreme, we end up blaming the *culture of poverty* for people's destitution. Or we can follow Lawrence Harrison, whose *Underdevelopment Is a State of Mind* blames Catholicism and laziness for the economic failure of Latin American economic development (1985).[14] Harrison's historical and social analysis is full of holes and errors, but his book was widely read and praised in U.S. government policy circles because it gives us a comforting fatalism and an excuse for inaction; if the problem is social inequality, land distribution, the wrong technology, bad management, or inefficient markets, then poverty can be overcome. But if the problem is the *culture,* what can we do? We can't expect people to respond logically to the right incentives. "They" are stuck in tradition, whereas "we" are modern and rational. From this perspective, the only solution to poverty is to send missionaries and teachers to change the culture.

The problem with cultural economics is that once you make rationality relative and culturally embedded, you only have two choices in evaluating or analyzing people in other cultures. The easiest course is to portray some groups as more rational than others, with all the chauvinism such a judgment implies. The second is to relativize *all* rationality and conclude that *no* culture is more rational than another and that scientific, objective knowledge about other cultures is therefore impossible. This last path leads toward the subjectivist, introspective kind of anthropology that is often labeled "postmodern," an anthropology that radically questions the anthropologist's authority to even define rationality.

Marshall Sahlins is perhaps the theorist most responsible for pushing economic anthropology in this direction. Sahlins's *Culture and Practical Reason* is a manifesto of cultural economics, an extended argument for the priority of meaning over pragmatics. For Sahlins, cultural categories of meaning come first; these in turn order people into social groups, which are then projected onto material objects and things: "Any cultural ordering produced by the material forces presupposes a cultural ordering of these forces" (1976, 39). It may *appear* that people's behavior is a response to land shortage or the desire for money, but land shortage and money are themselves cultural creations. The idea that self-interested people pursue economic interests is simply a smoke screen, the "origin myth of capitalist society." Economics is just the dominant idiom of capitalism (1976, 53, 205–207).

Sahlins says that values are arbitrary, not universally grounded in labor or property. Value is symbolic, a system of signs with its own logic and order that can be studied using tools like those derived from linguistics by the structuralist anthropologist Claude Lévi-Strauss. Sahlins tells us that modern bourgeois capitalism merely collapses the *cultural* order into a material order—so the way economists think about the world is purely symbolic even though they believe they are dealing with tangible things. Sahlins, like Malinowski and Weber, thinks that the symbolic aspect of cultural order is the most basic and that this is why it is revealed most clearly through the study of primitive economic systems (1976, 213–214). But even the economic order of modern society, Sahlins claims, can best be understood as a symbolic structure of meanings. We eat beef instead of horses and dogs, not because beef is cheaper to produce or more suited to the ecology of the United States Great Plains, but because of the way American culture symbolically orders and organizes the animal world, making dogs and horses taxonomically closer to inedible humans than to edible cows. Thus, he finds the whole political economy of cattle production and the historical ecology of rangelands on the American frontier totally irrelevant for understanding why Americans eat so much beef.

If we carry Sahlins's argument to its logical conclusion, there really is no such thing as economic anthropology. Instead, there are general principles of cultural order and symbolic process that can be extended to any kind of human activity, from reckoning clan membership in a tiny New Guinea village to trading wheat futures in the Chicago Mercantile Exchange. Economics is just an arbitrary part of the whole, which we choose for our own convenience to reflect our own concerns. (Obviously I don't agree with this position or I would not have written this book!)

In cultural economics, the key to understanding how people behave in relation to work, trade, and consumption is to see things from their own subjective and culturally determined point of view. What are their ideas about the good life, about the proper way to cooperate, about the morality of consumption and the value of money? Understanding economic behavior depends on mapping the symbolic and social order that underlies it, gives people the values they pursue, and constrains the strategies they follow. This indigenous subjective interpretation could be described as a *folk model* of the economy. Most of recent cultural economics sets out to describe these folk models, using the tools and concepts of interpretive and sometimes symbolic anthropology.

Is Max Weber Alive and Well in the 1990s?

Stephen Gudeman and Alberto Rivera set out to understand the economic folk models of peasants in *Conversations in Colombia* (1990), using an experimental subjective style.[15] Their book is presented as a sequence of conversations between the two anthropologists and among the anthropologists and the Colombian peasants they meet as they drive across the countryside. Instead of presenting facts and figures or observations of behavior, they provide fragments of discourse and conversation, with each other, with the peasants they meet, and with long-dead economic theorists they find in books.

They say that the Colombian peasants' ideas about the economy are really very similar to those of European economic writers before Adam Smith. The

Colombian farmers believe that the only true increase in wealth comes through farming and stock raising. Their goal is to preserve their house and farm (their "base"), to feed their families and livestock, and to put back any increase into the base. The economy is symbolically organized around the central metaphor of a *house,* and their strategy is to "keep the base within the doors." This mental model, say Gudeman and Rivera, accounts for behavior that often seems, from the outside, irrational and conservative. The peasants do not value their labor in monetary terms when they work "inside the house" (on their own farm), so they work long hours for much less return than they would get working for wages. The farmers concentrate on ways to save and be thrifty instead of figuring how to invest and profit outside the house for future returns. Culture appears as a set of *metaphors,* which provide the framework within which people think about their options and choices.

The point that peasants also have economic models and that these models make a difference in their daily lives is argued with clarity and force. Unlike Weber's peasants, who are just stuck in customary ways of doing things, these Colombian peasants are quite rational and even sophisticated. But their rationality runs along deep cultural grooves that often leave them working a tiny plot of potatoes harder and harder while their families starve. And this cultural model ends up monolithic and uniform, as if every peasant thought the same thing. Why should they all share the same model? Just as with Boas, there is also the problem of accounting for change. If behavior is so deeply shaped by *unconscious* mental models learned from parents, then how can people ever consciously change their behavior? Like Weber's peasants, Gudeman and Rivera's Colombian farmers will never respond to market incentives, land tenure reform, or other opportunities, because they are stuck with a restrictive and static worldview.

In the end, we are given no evidence that this cultural analysis explains Colombian behavior better than neoclassical or political economics. In other words, cultural economics done this way *appears* to explain things quite well, but only if we accept the subjective judgments of the authors and only if we do not try to compare this mode of explanation with other possible explanations. How do we know these peasants are not expressing class consciousness or that they are not making perfectly rational microeconomic decisions? Certainly the dynamic history of the Colombian countryside, full of rebellions and rapid economic change, cannot be explained by static models of peasant mentality.

Sheldon Annis's *God and Production in a Guatemalan Town* (1987) tells a remarkably similar story. In the highland village of San Antonio Aguas Calientes, Annis worked with poor Maya weavers, many of whom also kept small farms (milpas) and livestock. Through the efforts of American missionaries, a significant portion of the village had abandoned its traditional Catholicism and had embraced evangelical Protestant sects.

Robben's book is like *Conversations in Colombia* in its careful attention to what people themselves have to say about their economy, and he often quotes his informants directly from his field notes. He brings important social theorists into his discussion and makes sensible use of trendy anthropological concepts like "structuration" and "discursive conflict." Like the practice theorists he cites, Robben seeks a way out of the "culture determines behavior" problem, by putting culture closer to the ground and allowing the possibility that people can transform their own culture. As he puts it, "Traditional practices have to be reproduced through actions, and here there is always the possibility that established customs are reinterpreted and challenged, or that old ways cannot respond to new contexts. This historical dimension makes the transformation of routine practice possible" (1989, 10).

Robben's updated cultural economics trims away Weber's ideas about evolution from traditional to modern. He also cuts out the assumption that every culture has its own single, unique worldview and allows for diversity within a culture. But what is left sounds an awful lot like Boas: The economy is a product of cultural imagination, and there is no universal rationality. Robben's own words are therefore a succinct restatement of the most recent and also the most essential elements of cultural economics, in the language of current anthropology:

> This book wants to challenge the persistent myth that the economy is a bounded domain of society and culture that therefore can be truthfully represented in models, structures, laws, and principles. I will argue that the conflicting interpretations among our informants about the place of the economy in society and culture can neither be ethnographically ignored, nor theoretically reasoned away by assuming that ultimately everybody in a particular culture makes economic decisions in the same manner because of an underlying folk model, a universal drive towards maximization, or an all-embracing form of social integration or opposition. (1989, 2)

Summary: How Much Does Culture Determine?

A moral view of human nature says that people are essentially bound by cultural rules, which define the categories of action. People are *moral* in this sense, because they seek to conform to abstract principles of behavior that are deeply encoded in language and thought. (This is not to say that they always follow those cultural rules but only that they evaluate all behavior according to them.) Moral humans neither follow their own self-interest nor the interests of their group or class, except insofar as the rules of their culture allow it. Because culture creates the categories and the values, all human behavior is, in this view, a cultural product. There is no place in moral economics for underlying universal human impulses or universal rationality. Instead, the only basic human capacity is to understand and act in a world created through symbolic and metaphorical communication; all other human thoughts and actions follow from this.

For a moral theory of human behavior, rules and categories of thought take priority over the physical measurable aspects of the world. This is perhaps why the concept of *the gift* has been so central in defining the cultural economic perspective in anthropology. The concept of the gift is powerful because it demonstrates that all values are produced through human relations and cultural conventions. Value is therefore not an inherent or intrinsic property of things themselves.

For these reasons, cultural anthropologists are drawn like flies to the complex gift and barter economies of New Guinea and nearby islands. In *Inalienable Possessions* (1992), Annette Weiner tells us that in the Trobriand Islands, many objects are culturally imbued with a spiritual essence of the gift giver; when they are physically transferred from one person to another, they retain meaningful links with the giver. Gifts are culturally an entirely different kind of substance from the alienable, independent commodities that we know in the capitalist marketplace. We cannot understand their production or circulation with universal ideas of utility or scarcity (Gregory 1982). In an extreme form, this argument says that since the New Guinean person as a separate self is created through the gift giving of marriage and fertility, even the idea of "self-interest" is a purely cultural construction, which varies from place to place.[16] Anthropological categories of personhood and social group, the very language of microeconomics or political economy, has no meaning or relevance in Melanesia.

The theorists of the "otherness of the gift" economy sound a lot like Malinowski. They ask us to imagine another world, where cultural difference is so great that the basic concepts of economics cannot be applied. The Melanesian gift is the *icon of otherness* because it breaks all the rules Western people are used to. The gift has no inherent utility that can be separated from the relationships among the people who own it. It cannot be sold for money. It is often more valuable to a person after they have given it away than while they hold it. But yet, we are told, people think about and use gifts in quite rational ways, and that rationality is discoverable by anthropologists, who can then explain to us the unique rules that make that society work.

Malinowski's version of cultural economics always kept one foot on the ground in physical reality, by referring to basic human physical needs. His Trobriand Islanders gave gifts and practiced magic, but they still had to eat, reproduce, and find shelter. The more recent run of cultural economists have often forgotten that part and have acted like the *only* thing people do is communicate, symbolize, use metaphor, and "construct personhood."

Carried to this extreme, the culturalist position makes no sense. Surely there are some universal pragmatic principles that make it possible for even the most culturally different people to find ways to understand one another (see Jackson 1989). In their desire to tear economics apart and portray it as a naive tool of Western imperialism and ethnocentrism, many anthropologists seem to forget that economics began as the search for exactly those universal human qualities. Few anthropologists would deny that culture makes a difference in the way people think and behave—culture is after all still the discipline's central concept. But surely culture cannot determine *everything*? And if it doesn't, there is still something else of human nature that needs to be defined. The real issue that cultural economics often avoids, then, is *how much* does culture determine? Does it always determine the same amount? Are some human beings more influenced by cultural rules than others? Are some kinds of behavior more under cultural influence than others? As I will suggest in the next chapter, these questions have rarely been clearly phrased by any of the theorists discussed in the book so far. Are these questions that can be answered by theorists at all?

Notes

1. The anthropological idea that all moral systems are cultural products does not mean that anthropologists do not believe there is such a thing as general moral principles. Humanists are often accused of a lack of morality because they say that all moral systems are ultimately human creations. On a personal level, however, most anthropologists are quite willing to state a number of general moral principles and values, like equity, nonviolence, and self-determination. Hatch (1983) summarizes the history of anthropological relativism.

2. I find Stanley Tambiah's *Magic, Science, Religion, and the Scope of Rationality* an excellent survey of these themes in anthropology, with particularly clear discussions of Levy-Bruhl, Malinowski, and the problems of relativism.

3. Kaplan and Manners (1972, 116–119) have a brief and clear discussion of the problems of attributing behavior to unconscious symbols, values, and norms.

4. The Enlightenment philosophers are treated especially well by De Waal Malefijt in *Images of Man* (1974), though her main interest is in theories of cultural evolution. I continue to depend on Kahn (1990) for the German romantics and Harris (1968) for a critical edge.

5. The classic intellectual biography of Weber is by Bendix (1960), though Käsler (1988) is more dense but complete. Nisbet (1966) provides some useful insight on his philosophy of human action.

6. *Man and Culture*, edited by Raymond Firth (1957), provides a highly critical summary of Malinowski's social theory by his most famous contemporaries. His first publication, in Swedish in 1912, was a discussion of the economic aspects of an Australian ceremony, and he was a pioneer in the study of land tenure, property, work, exchange, and consumption in non-Western societies. His clearest early statement about primitive economics is in a 1921 article published in the *Economic Journal.*

Probably his most complete theoretical work is *A Scientific Theory of Culture*. Voget (1975) places Malinowski in historical context.

7. Almost any of the standard ethnographic works in the descriptive tradition can be taken as an example of just-the-facts economic anthropology. Just look for the chapter titled "economic life" or "the economic system." Fieldwork guides and cross-cultural comparative data systems like George Murdock's *Outline of Cultural Materials* (1961) have lists of economic information the ethnographer should obtain.

8. An early example of the factual approach can be found in Goodfellow's work on the Bantu (1939). Melville Herskovitz and Raymond Firth are the two major figures in the economic anthropology of the 1930s and 1940s, and both of them produced a great deal of descriptive empirical ethnography of economic life. But neither really fits the "just the facts" category I have established here. Both took a very general sort of formal neoclassical model of rationality and set about showing how culture and social organization established the context in which people tried to maximize their satisfactions (see LeClair and Schneider 1968). Thus, unlike the Boasians, they did have some explicit theoretical goals. But like the Boasians, they worked at cataloging some of the enormous variety of "economic" institutions to be found among exotic cultures.

9. Sol Tax, Nash's teacher at the University of Chicago, in his just-the-facts study of a Guatemalan village economy, concluded, like Pospisil, that the Indians were quite as economically rational as the average North American. He addresses Weber's famous story about peasant logic, but argues that the Maya peasant *would* keep working long hours when wages were increased (1953, 204).

10. An excellent, though complex guide to recent thought about universal human symbolic, grammatical, and classificatory abilities is Lakoff's *Women, Fire, and Dangerous Things* (1987). An easier introduction to cognitive anthropology is Lakoff and Johnson's *Metaphors We Live By* (1980).

11. The most interesting and important anthropologist to take up the issue of cultural and economic change, from within the Boasian tradition, is Fredrik Barth (see particularly his 1967 paper).

12. The best guide to Geertz' theory is Geertz himself, in *The Interpretation of Cultures* (1973) (the word "economy" does not appear in the index). His sociocultural approach to the economy appears in his first book (1956). His intellectual development follows a common pattern; he began with highly empirical fieldwork on material and economic problems. Later, he became less and less interested in behavior and more of a "high" theorist of meaning, symbol, and culture. Marshall Sahlins has followed much the same path.

13. The contrast between Java and Bali reads, at times, like a parable about American capitalism and Soviet communism. This was not a conscious theme of Geertz's, but given the times when the book was written, it could hardly have been absent from his mind.

14. Harrison draws directly on Weber and suggests that until Latin Americans become Protestants, there will be no sustained economic growth in Latin America. The book is terribly condescending and consistently ignores the historical causes of poverty in Latin America.

15. Gudeman's earlier book *Economics as Culture* (1986) provides a detailed argument for cultural economics that is more historically grounded and constructive than

Sahlins's *Culture and Practical Reason.* My selection of these three books here is quite arbitrary; other excellent examples of this genre include Weismantel's extraordinarily textured and highly readable ethnography of diet in highland Ecuador (1988) and Shipton's admirably clear and concise discussion of the cultural limits on money in Kenya (1989).

16. The most extreme culturalist argument about the radically different essence of the gift and the self in New Guinea is Strathern's *The Gender of the Gift* (1988). Battaglia provides a complex but interesting case study of the meaning of gifts in creating a sense of time and in marking the stages of life in Melanesia (1992). A less extreme position is taken by Pnina Werbner in her work on gift giving among Pakistani migrants in England; she shows how gifts can coexist with commodities and how both can be strategically used in creating social ties and building hierarchy. But in the end she still argues that all values are culturally constructed (1989, 1990).

6 ✍

Conclusions: Complex Economic Human Beings

To see what is in front of one's nose needs a constant struggle.

—George Orwell, *In Front of Your Nose*

The Case of the Leaking Houses

In 1982, I began working with another anthropologist on an ethnographic project among an exotic tribe: middle-class suburbanites in Santa Cruz County, northern California. At that time, energy conservation was a major public concern. The United States was then, as now, highly dependent on foreign oil, and public utilities could no longer afford to build new nuclear power plants. Energy conservation was state policy in California, and the public utility companies were mandated by law to begin programs to encourage the public to cut down on energy consumption.

All was not smooth sailing in the process of getting people to use less energy in their homes. The largest use of energy in California homes was for heating and cooling, so programs were focused on getting people to make this more efficient. The common perception was that saving energy meant putting on sweaters in winter or opening windows in the summer. Utilities and state agencies tried to educate the public about other options with programs to encourage simple ways to insulate homes, use weatherstripping, and improve the efficiency of their water heaters and other appliances. Simply caulking and sealing a house in northern California could save, at that time, up to $1,200 a year for a minimal expense. But despite public education programs, television advertising, mass mailings, incentives, and even free weatherstripping services, the number of households that were improving their energy efficiency was disappointingly low. In some areas, flashy and expensive energy-saving devices like solar hot-water heaters were proving more popular than simpler, cheaper, and more effective things like hot-water heater blankets.

Unable to understand the public response, the state government made some money available through the University of California for basic research on how people make decisions about energy consumption in their homes. And that was why Hal Wilhite and I were running around the hills of Santa Cruz asking people questions about their thermostats, their political opinions about energy companies, and who liked the shower the hottest.

This seemed like a perfect topic for our anthropological and ethnographic skills and knowledge. After all, the basic problem was about domestic life, about house and home, and about the way families interact—all things in which anthropologists have great interest. We also thought that detailed interviews and close daily contact with people—the basics of ethnographic method—were the best way to throw some light on energy consumption.

On a theoretical level, the problem was also something right at the heart of economic anthropology: Here was an example of "uneconomic" behavior. The people we spoke with were not ignorant of the costs and benefits of home weatherization. They knew that for a small investment of a few hours of time and a few dollars' worth of materials, they could save hundreds of dollars on their electric or gas bills. Some of them had even bought the materials and had them stored in the basement or garage! But only fourteen of the sixty families we interviewed had weatherized. In contrast, eighteen had installed a wood stove, and fourteen, a solar water heater. According to simple microeconomic models, people were behaving in an irrational way. They were spending $3,000 on solar hot water, an investment that would not be paid back in savings for ten years, instead of spending $75 on weatherization, an expense that could be recouped in a few months.

Of course, as anthropologists, our first goal was to understand the way *culture* could explain this behavior. We quickly found several clear cultural explanations. First, most people we spoke with did not have an accurate idea of energy usage in their homes; they were not usually aware of how much they were spending on heating, cooling, water heating, or lighting. They tended to overestimate the cost of lighting and judge electricity costs by tracking the pump price of gasoline. Second, heating and cooling were often tied up with ideas about "homeyness" in ways that made it difficult for people to admit that there might be something wrong with their house. Finally, people thought weatherizing their house was a "dirty" job, and a simple ethnosemantic analysis explained why.[1]

Anthropologist Mary Douglas has shown that people tend to categorize their world, to impose cultural order on nature. But no system of categories is perfect. Those objects and actions that cross categories, that do not fit into the cultural scheme of categories, tend to be considered dirty and unclean, even dangerous (1966). In talking with Santa Cruzans, we found that people clearly divided the things they did to their house into discrete categories: adjustments (like changing the thermostat setting), maintenance (changing furnace filters), repair (patching roof leaks), and improvement (adding a wood stove). When we asked people to categorize weatherizing, they usually could not decide in what group it belonged. Was it a kind of maintenance, a repair, or an improvement? Therefore, one reason people were so uncomfortable about weatherizing was because it did not fit into any cultural category.

Could we just go back to Pacific Gas and Electric and tell the company that reluctance to weatherize was an entirely cultural issue and that there was nothing economic or social about it? When we first presented our cultural analysis to a roomful of engineers, economists, and sociologists, we were greeted with a lot of skepticism and critical commentary. How could we prove that culture was really making a difference here? The engineers suggested the real reasons were technical; people did not know how to use weatherizing materials or needed better tests to locate leaks. The economists said that we might not be looking carefully enough at the labor costs of weatherizing and that energy costs were changing so rapidly that people simply could not predict their savings. The sociologists said that our sample size was too small and that we had ignored social class and ethnicity.

The Problem of Explaining Things

I think we were quite right to look for cultural explanations for the peculiar blindness our informants had to the benefits of weatherstripping and caulking the cracks in their siding. There *was* something offensive about weatherization that made people uncomfortable and embarrassed when they spoke about it, as if bringing up the issue was a suggestion that there was something wrong with their house. The house is a centrally important symbolic object for the North American middle class, and it is deeply invested with meaning and emotion. We had fascinating conversations with people about the meaning of "comfort" and listened as people earnestly discussed their decor and the moral implications of different kinds of heat.

But we could also see the validity of some of the points made by our critics. Culture was not the only or the determining factor in people's decisions. For every family in which comfort and meaning made all the difference in choices about the home, there was another family whose decisions were made using a calculator to discover what would save the most money. We even spoke with a couple who had consulted with an economist who did a formal cost-benefit analysis of each alternative energy-conserving system.

The social organization of households also had real effects on the energy decisionmaking we studied. At particular transitional stages in life, when the last child had moved out to go to college, for example, people were much more likely to repair or modify their houses. Couples often did not agree about temperature settings on thermostats, and we frequently found that decisions about home improvements involved a good deal of family politics. Sometimes changing the house had a lot more to do with making the marriage work than it did with saving money or energy. And we also found a significant number of people for whom energy saving was a political issue. Hatred of the nuclear energy industry led some people to cut down their electrical use; others hated being dependent on a huge corporation for their energy.

Because we recognized these diverse motivations and causes, we often found ourselves arguing on different sides of the fence, depending on our audience. We lectured sociologists on the importance of culture and meaning. Our anthropological colleagues were told that if there was no economic benefit, no amount of symbolic persuasion or ideology would get people to conserve energy. The economists heard a lot about households as social units that could not be treated as if they were single individuals with a common utility function.

Our problem wasn't with any of our different models of human behavior. Each worked in some circumstances, with some people, and with some issues. We also didn't have much difficulty matching empirical data to our theories; unlike many of the other social scientists we talked to, we were comfortable with quantitative surveys, personal histories, open-ended interviews, and cost-benefit models. Within its own sphere, in its own universe of argument, using its own tools and data, each mode of explanation made partial sense. The problem was that *together* they made no coherent sense at all. Of course, the three models don't connect with each other because each is founded on different ideas and assumptions about human nature and the motivations of human behavior.

The same problems of interpretation that we encountered in California crop up repeatedly all over the social sciences. They don't appear serious in many small subfields because different kinds of assumptions are never allowed to challenge the dominant ones. People agree to stick to one and push the others to the margin, or they argue about methods, or the validity of science, or other things, instead. But anthropology can't do this, because with its commitment to a holistic study of humanity, anthropology itself is more fundamentally the study of human nature.

The problems of contradictory models for human behavior are not just academic or philosophical. They appear every day in our lives when we try to understand the actions of our fellow beings, and they figure prominently in today's major political debates. Here is an example from an article in the news magazine *The Economist* ("Latin American Finance Survey," 1995).

Academic Barbecue

One of the major reasons the economies of Southeast Asia are growing so fast and those of Latin America are more stagnant is that Asians save so much more of their income. In Singapore, for example, almost 50 percent of gross domestic product is saved and invested every year, whereas in Mexico, the figure is closer to 9 percent. This means much more money is available to finance new businesses, build roads, and keep the economy growing in Asia. Why do Asians save more? *The Economist* is devoted to a free-market economic solution to every problem; its contributors believe the difference in savings rates is simply the result of government overregulation of pension funds and high inflation, which makes it economically irrational for Latin Americans to save. But aren't there also cultural differences that could account for the difference? Give a cultural anthropologist the same question, and you are likely to hear about the difference between a Confucian society and a Catholic one. Ask a political economist and you will get an earful about the more dramatic class differences in Latin America, which leave a majority of the population too poor to eat regularly, much less save for the future. Or you might hear about multinational corporations and the irresponsible Latin American rich who invest their money in Miami instead of their home countries.

The answer to the savings-rate question is vastly important—the economic future for hundreds of millions of people depends on governments finding ways to rapidly increase savings rates. Following the cultural model, do you persuade people to save by using propaganda and appealing to their patriotism or try to change their beliefs? Should you listen to the political economists and change institutions that affect class and power? Or hire some economists to help open the markets and change the costs and benefits of investment?

My point in this book so far has been that none of the actions based on the three perspectives is based on clear facts. Instead, all of them are partially grounded in models of human nature that are matters of faith or conviction. Even the most hard-nosed economists, who present themselves as technicians and empirical scientists, are full of such faith. Here is a U.S. deputy secretary of the Treasury explaining why Mexico recovered so rapidly from the 1994 financial crisis: "There is a natural human tendency, magnified by the political process in every country, to regard good news as permanent and bad news as temporary" (Summers 1995, 46). Now, this may be true of some people some of the time, but is it really hardwired into the human brain? A part of our genetic heritage from *Homo erectus*? Why should this assertion be taken over those of the political economists or the culturalists?

Resolving the Fundamental Issues

In the previous chapters, I have tried to present fair and balanced views of three fundamentally different approaches to human behavior, arguing that they start from different models of human nature. I have always found something good to say about each model, but each chapter has ended on a critical note. All the theorists and theories have something to contribute, but all of them are lacking. I also keep asserting that these deficiencies are more than just intellectual problems. When we jump from just passively studying people to involving ourselves in their lives and trying to help or advise, our practical predictions require a better theory of human motivations. How can we know what will work if we don't have a reliable model of human nature to draw on? These are exactly the questions that preoccupied the theorists of the European Enlightenment (Weyant 1973). But in the eighteenth century, they did not have the tools or knowledge to find the answers, and these days, social scientists seem to have fallen out of the habit of asking such fundamental questions.

Each of the three models of human nature has a history, and each is *internally* fairly consistent. Each makes *some* sense of some things out there in the real world; each seems to have captured a part of the reality of human life. Some of the debates in economic anthropology have brought these models into confrontation, and this allows me to drag the underlying problems into the light. Now we will finally make the three models confront each other in the open. We need to ask whether any of them can be proven wrong and whether we can test them.

One way to think about the relationship between the three models of human behavior is to look at their historical contexts in relation to one another (instead of tracing their individual histories, as I have already done here). Many people have noted that ideas about human nature have a tendency to go through cycles. The archaeologist Andrew Sherratt thinks that social scientists are attracted to utilitarianism and evolutionary ideas of progress in times of economic growth and political optimism. Then they become positive about universal human nature as a force for progress. But when the economy takes a downturn or if there is general pessimism and political strife, theorists turn toward romanticism and think about human beings in particularistic and ethnic terms that deny universals and emphasize differences (1995; see also Kahn 1995, chap. 2). Sherratt, somewhat cynically, thinks that we find the model of human nature that matches the needs of our time. Although this is an intriguing idea, it doesn't solve our problem; it simply adds another layer of complications. Should we just give up hope?

Perhaps a better way to think about the three models is to recognize that in practice we are always mixing them, shuffling through to find the one that best fits or combining them on an ad hoc and case-by-case basis. We look for an assortment of tools to get a job done, and we rarely stop to think whether the tools belong together in a coherent set. In practice, most anthropologists make hybrid models by combining bits and pieces of middle-level theory, rules of thumb, and their own experience. Sometimes these hybrids look like thoroughbreds, but other times they lurch around like Frankenstein monsters. Up to this point in this book I have been looking for relatively pure examples of each of the three models, but let's look at two hybrids now. In the process we can look for some common ground where the three models might meet and share some assumptions.[2] I will conclude by contending that human nature is more complex and variable than any of the three models can account for.

Practice Theory

The term "dialectic" generally means a kind of reciprocal causation between opposing forces or ideas that moves a system forward in time. Faced with the interrelatedness of different aspects of human life, many anthropologists have set up opposing categories and then proposed a dialectical relationship between them. For example, we might have a technological process based in science and a social process based in culture, and then we might inject dynamism by suggesting that they are in dialectical opposition to each other. In this example, social change (population growth) prompts the development of new technologies (the plow), and they in turn cause more social change (political complexity). Can a dialectical theory help us deal with the conflicting models of human nature? Could there be three distinct aspects of human nature that stand in a dialectical relationship with each other?

One example of a synthetic dialectical theory is what has been called *practice theory* (Ortner 1984). The basic elements are laid out in Pierre Bourdieu's *Outline of a Theory of Practice* (1977). His goal was to move away from the dominant British Durkheimian social model of rule-guided behavior and social structure. Instead, practice theorists see everyday life as a form of improvisation, in which people work with rules and norms in a forward-thinking *strategic* way, using their knowledge to pursue their interests. Practice theorists point out that although everyone in a social setting knows the rules for proper behavior and understands what people *should* do, at another level, they break and manipulate rules all the time, strategize to change the rules, or practice deception to make it seem like they are following rules when they are not.[3]

At the same time, practice theorists do not see human beings as free of social restraint. Human ideas and values are formed and shaped by human cultural experience, so people carry around with them a set of assumptions—a sense of how the world works—that is so deeply embedded that they are not aware of it. Bourdieu calls this common sense the *habitus.* Most of the time, in traditional and stable societies, these assumptions and beliefs are never questioned. The *habitus* stays in the background as common and agreed-upon truth that is reaffirmed through ritual but is never questioned in any conscious way. Bourdieu says that in this situation people experience *doxa,* a correspondence between the way they think about their social world and the way that world is actually structured. People never have to pause to think about most experiences because they are experienced as part of the natural order (this should remind you of Durkheim). Most experience "goes without saying because it comes without saying" (Bourdieu 1977, 167). Therefore, when *doxa* exists, there is *no choice,* because people see no options. There is just one way to eat dinner; people don't have to think about how they eat or choose among chopsticks, fingers, and forks because there is just one way to do it. But *doxa* is never perfect, because no unspoken rules or understandings can work in all the messy and contradictory situations that real human life always entails.

The alternatives to *doxa* are the situations where more than one possible rule or meaning exists. *Heterodoxy* means that people recognize and are aware of two or more possible ways of doing things, possible interpretations, or possible courses of action; they may debate their value or choose one interpretation that better fits their own interests. Most of the readers of this book live in a world dominated by heterodoxy, a world where we are used to evaluating different choices and rules and choosing between them (for example, "pro-life" versus "pro-choice"). Public debate in modern society, according to Bourdieu, is heterodox, though much of private life is still dominated by *doxa*.

Bourdieu sees a third possibility, *orthodoxy*, in which powerful people, classes, or interests impose a single choice, often using what Bourdieu calls *symbolic violence* to force people into line. An established church, for example, might define certain thoughts as heretical, a chief may banish a couple who break rules that forbid cross-cousin marriage, or a philosophy might be branded "un-American" or "unpatriotic." The possibility of such action becomes unthinkable and the range of choice is narrowed or eliminated, but not in the same way as in a situation of real *doxa*, because in orthodoxy people remain aware that alternatives exist.

Bourdieu gives anthropologists a way out of the restrictions of thinking about people as naturally social, self-interested, or cultural. He suggests that life is mostly lived in between these three options and that the *social setting* determines the basis of human action. In other words, he is working away from the notion of human nature and toward depicting a world where people are *sometimes* social rule followers, at other times guided by their cultural knowledge. But he never sees them entirely lacking in self-interest, in rational pursuit of their own ends. This is a vitally important step because it makes the basis of human behavior always an *empirical* issue, something to be solved by observing situations in the real world rather than through theorizing or introspective navel gazing.

The issue of rationality in the pursuit of goals comes out most clearly in Bourdieu's critique of economics (1977, 170–197). He begins with the usual Malinowskian attack on "vulgar" economists who think that objects have value in and of themselves. He makes the familiar anthropological point that only society and culture really give value and meaning to things. This means, then, that the economy and society are not separable and are part of each other (embedded). This same insight led Malinowski and Sahlins to reject economics and focus on society, but Bourdieu takes exactly the opposite course. He says, in effect, "Fine, then let's extend economics to all of culture." He did this by inventing the term "cultural capital" to refer to the knowledge and experience that people gain during their lives, which gives them power in daily life, politics, and the economy. Later, he conjured up the related concept of *social capital*, which means the positions, connections, and relationships one has by virtue of birth, marriage, and membership in various organizations or offices.

For Bourdieu, in every society people deploy and use their economic resources (capital and labor) and their cultural and social capital in political struggles to establish and maintain dominance and power. Modern capitalist societies are different from the rest only because of their complex social and economic institutions, which allow people to dominate through control of the economy or through political and social office. You can gain power in France by getting rich, going to college, or being born to an important family. In precapitalist societies, however, domination can only be achieved through face-to-face personal interaction, where people create cultural and social capital themselves. To be a Kwakiutl chief one must inherit some social capital, but one also has to build a great reputation by giving feasts, making exchanges, and building a kinship network.

Bourdieu's ambition is to extend economic concepts like capital and exchange to all of human social life and thereby build an economics that is relevant to all societies past and future. Nonetheless, he ends up promising much more than he delivers, because his economics remains so vague and imprecise. His ideas of cultural and social capital are marvelously stimulating, and in his hands, they become excellent tools for discussing the differences between societies. But he never gives us any indication of how such capital might be measured outside of a modern industrial society.[4] And if we cannot measure cultural and social capital, it is impossible to tell how they are affecting behavior. We end up in a circle: We know people have social capital because of the way they are treated, and we explain people's behavior as a result of the same social capital. Bourdieu's economics is purely *metaphorical.* What he is really saying is that social position and cultural knowledge are *like* capital and that it is useful to think about them as property that can be accumulated, invested, loaned, and spent.

The key strength of practice theory is that it poses the basis of human behavior in particular situations as an *empirical* problem that can be solved through observation, involvement, and research. Bourdieu says culture operates in some things, social life in other things, and rational self-interest in still others. Furthermore there is a dialectical relationship between them, as *doxa* is built and maintained. Here is an alternative to a reductionist approach that wants to boil motives down to a single universal impulse. Instead, Bourdieu thinks that human nature is polymorphous. It depends on the situation and the setting, and that situation is itself a human creation. Another dialectic is therefore that social structure constrains human action, at the same time that human action and politics creates and modifies social structure. This provides a way out of the social and cultural determinism that makes Boasian and structural-functional systems so static.

Although practice theory frames the question of human nature in an important way, it does not explain *when and why* the basis of human nature changes. What is it that makes people act like rational goal seekers sometimes, like rule-minded power mongers at others, and symbol-driven cultural animals the rest of the time? The latest generation of Marxist-inspired political economists have some interesting answers to this question that are worth exploring.

Reworking Marxism (Again)

One of the most interesting attempts to reconcile different models of human nature and social analysis within the framework of Marxist anthropology is Donald Donham's *History, Power, Ideology* (1990). The book draws on Donham's long field experience among the Maale of southern Ethiopia, a farming people who once had their own kings and chiefs but who have recently had to deal with a Marxist revolution, famine, and the collapse of their national government.

Donham's narrative works through Chayanov, formalism, Sahlins's substantivism, and various kinds of Marxism, pointing to the strengths and weaknesses of each. His solution is not to throw them out and start over again but rather to say that perhaps each should be applied to what it does best. Microeconomics works well in the short term, on a small local scale, and does a good job explaining day-to-day decisions. A microeconomic theory of rational choice can tell us why people act particular ways and reach short-term decisions *given an existing social organization and cultural values*. But to understand where those organizations and values come from, we need to go to another level of analysis and use different models of behavior (1990, 39).

As an example, Donham does a neoclassical analysis of Maale household labor in agriculture and shows how it makes sense of their productive strategies, their choice of crops, and the way they work. But this explanation only works as long as we accept that men can exchange their labor with each other but do not sell their labor for wages. We also have to accept that men always control their wives' and children's work. In other words, the neoclassical explanation only works as long as the social rules of labor exchange, age, and gender are given. But how do men control their wives and children, and how could that change? Why can't men sell their labor? Here neoclassical tools fail completely.

Donham argues that beyond the limits of neoclassical rational choice analysis, we have to study "ideology," the systems of meaning and ideas of the natural order that lead people to accept a particular cosmology as natural and given. And we also need to look at social structures, at the groups and organizations like chiefs and clans that exist outside of individual will and for longer than the individual life. For these problems, says Donham, we need Marxian political economy, which can be used to study social units larger than households and time periods longer than a farming year. He illustrates his point with a lucid discussion of power in Maale lineages, the politics of marriage, and the larger-scale ecology of population growth and surplus. In his hands, the classic Marxist concept of the *mode of production* becomes a powerful comparative tool.

But Donham also recognizes the limits of political economy. When it comes to long-term transformations, on national, international, and global scales, both Marx and Adam Smith fail, and we need to turn to "history." The fortunes of the Maale have been affected profoundly over the years by events far beyond their control and even beyond their knowledge, from the Italian conquest of Ethiopia to the Soviet-sponsored Ethiopian revolution of 1975. Although a Marxian analysis is necessary as a point of departure for understanding processes at this level, each situation has its own peculiarities that require an understanding of local, deep culture and history. History cannot be reduced to any simple model of human nature but results from all three models.

Donham's unique solution to the problem posed by the first four chapters of this book is a kind of "Bosnian partition," which seeks to reduce conflict by giving each theory a territory. Microeconomics is an effective microtool for short-term decisions where cultural values and social structure is a given. Marxian anthropology, with a focus on power and social institutions and the role of ideology, is the theory of choice for the medium scale and the longer term. Finally, on the largest scale we need to understand cultures as wholes, as well as global economics and international politics as part of the construction of history (Donham tells us less about this level than the other two).

Donham gives us an excellent way to divide up the "turf" between social sciences. He points a way toward thinking through the problem of why moral and cultural issues become so important at particular times, why daily behavior is so subject to microeconomic rational choice models, and why Marxian analysis works for understanding social structure. In many ways, this is a very firm grounding for economic anthropology, for it tells us to use the conceptual tools appropriate to the problem at hand. He also gives us some ideas for making the three different models work together in a dynamic way in long-term historical research. But in the end, where does Donham stand on human nature? His agenda requires people to be selfish, social, political, and cultural, all at the same time, in different contexts. Could this be possible? Perhaps we need to rethink the way we have framed the issue of human nature, from the ground up.

Rethinking Human Nature

I see no reason to quarrel with all the brilliant social scientists who have argued persuasively for the three different models of human nature. Each one seems to work perfectly well in particular cases, but only in unpredictable ways. The economic theory of the selfish maximizing individual accounts for some behavior, but not all. The sociological theory of normative behavior, of conformity, explains some of what is left over. And an anthropological approach that looks at cognition, semantics, and cultural systems of meaning also makes sense of some behavior, but again not all. The theories appear incompatible, but even if they were compatible, we have no rules (except Donham's) to tell us when to apply which one. Worse, each theory of motive purports to be all-encompassing; they offer themselves as alternatives to each other. We are left with faith or aesthetics to make our choices.

Consider another possibility. What if these three contradictory views of humans as selfish, social, or moral beings are themselves *folk models?* In other words, what if they are the common-sense explanations that people typically offer for their own behavior? "I did it to help others; I did it for myself; I did it because it was right and proper." Each would then be a *rationalization* for behavior, after the fact, as much as a cause of any action. As explanatory tools, the models would then fail for this very reason—because they are not really objective scientific models of human behavior at all. They impose an ethnocentric grid of categories onto a continuum of actual experience and practice, and they do so after the fact.

A more objective and analytical way of looking at human motives might avoid some of the moral and ethnocentric assumptions that seem built into these categories. This would require concentrating on making human nature an empirical problem, one we address directly every time we study human behavior. Our assumptions about human nature are very deeply built into our social theory, so only this kind of empiricism can keep us from seeing everything tinted through the glasses of our choice. Economic anthropology could then more directly *question* human motives instead of *assuming* them.

The folk models of human nature run very deeply in most social science, and it is literally hard to think about how to write ethnography or analyze a situation without them. As a tool for doing this, I find it useful to use a graph that recasts the classical problem of human nature along different dimensions.[5] To avoid posing social, moral, and selfish goals as alternatives, we can instead view them as portions of a wider territory on a scale or along a range. My goal is to show that *all* can be seen as rational, but at *different scales* and in different contexts. Human nature can always be seen as rational; our goal is to empirically find out what makes it so. Furthermore, instead of forcing diverse motives into discrete boxes, we can admit the possibility of mixed and ambiguous or multiple motives.

The graph in Figure 6.1 has two scales. The vertical axis is a time scale, stretching from the immediate present into the infinite future. On the time scale, immediate self-interest, the satisfaction of a need or desire felt at the moment of decision, is at one end of a range of possible self-interests. A person can also be interested in maximizing long-term self-interest, thinking about needs and desires for next week, next year, or a distant retirement. The time scale extends beyond the individual life span into the infinite future be-

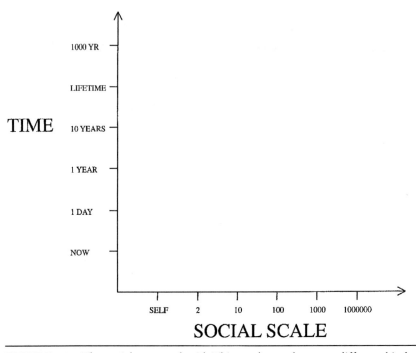

FIGURE 6.1   The social-temporal grid. This can be used to map different kinds of decisionmaking, showing that conventional notions of selfishness and altruism form a continuum.

cause people often take what will happen to them after death into account. Many people believe in an immortal soul and reincarnation, and this certainly influences their decisions in life. In some cultures, the main purpose of life is to provide for well-being after death.[6]

Behavior that is motivated by this infinite time scale is often considered "altruistic" or "moral," because it contemplates the infinite or the supernatural, a time when the individual will be dead and won't benefit from his or her own actions. "Building something for the future" is often seen as a form of altruism. On this scale, however, this kind of moral behavior is just part of a long continuum. The standard anthropological explanation of culturally motivated or "moral" behavior often refers to the infinite end. People are acting rationally in reference to *timeless* concepts of value, that is, eternal moral principles of good and bad, right and wrong. Culture is by definition something that came before the individual and continues on after death. Choices that move beyond the individual life span are therefore inherently cultural.

On this temporal scale, what is rational on an immediate basis may not be rational at all in the long term, and vice versa. If you are on your way home on the bus it may make sense to eat your last candy bar as soon as you want it, but if you are lost in the woods it would be sensible to wait. Eating a huge pile of chocolate truffles might be a rational way to satisfy your immediate craving, but it could be quite irrational if the long-term consequences for your arteries are taken into account. The kind of time scale you use changes as you grow older, and it also depends on your wealth, your status, and your social situation. In most societies, moral persuasion aims at lengthening the time frame, getting us to think about long-term outcomes. Most religions try to pull our values toward the infinite. Learning to delay gratification is a sign of maturity in many cultures, and in the West, we gain status by putting money and effort into things like buildings or books that will last beyond our lives.

The horizontal axis in Figure 6.1 is the social dimension of choice; it appears on the graph in order to acknowledge that people consider the well-being of others in their decisions. The social scale is roughly a measure of the size of the group that a person includes when maximizing, beginning with the self and leading to the infinite, to all humans on the planet.[7] In between are social dyads like friendship, the household, the family network, then on to larger groups like church, community, and nation. As the scale increases, the groups become more abstract and diffuse, though not necessarily less powerful or important. Once again, moral behavior is often construed as belonging at the end of the scale away from the individual. Our families, clans, and nations constantly implore us to think of others instead of ourselves, to think of the good of the group.

When we combine the social and time scales we define a frame for understanding decisions and choice that makes no assumptions about human nature. On the graph, immediate self-interest lies at the intersection, and what is generally conceived of as "altruism" radiates out from it in different directions. "Perfect altruism" could be imagined at the extreme of timeless totality; but surely such behavior is as rare as that which is completely selfish. The point is that all human life occupies the messy difficult gray area in between, and the extremes are no more than debating tools and sacred images. Human nature encompasses the entire territory, and more, if we include antisocial behavior. Humanity is characterized by tremendous plasticity and flexibility, by an ability to adapt behavior to amazingly diverse circumstances. This is why so much of the recent evolutionary genetics of human personality is so unconvincing. Human history and the diversity of culture proves that whatever genetic coding we have for particular behavior is extremely weak. No attempt to find an "altruism gene" can do more than produce headlines, because there is no such thing, or if there is, it has little actual effect on behavior. Of course, there are biological human universals, but most of the things that we all have in common are *abilities* and *potentials* rather than specific traits or characteristics.

The graph in figure 6.1 can also be used as a tool to think about the process of decisionmaking, strategy, and tactics. If we conceive of decision-making as a political process in which the interests of actors and groups differ, we can map the positions in specific decisions taken by different actors. For example, a classic confrontation in households around the world is between adults and children over duties and responsibilities. Adolescents in many societies work within a shorter time perspective than their parents. It therefore makes sense that people often argue over the immediate versus the long-term benefits of a particular strategy, purchase, or decision. Why should people with different time-horizons agree?

Another distinct kind of dispute takes place along the social axis (see Figure 6.2). Who should benefit from a group decision or an individual action? Should our family do what is best for me, for the family, or for our community? Just whose interests should be maximized when we make our decisions? Who is included in the pool of beneficiaries? These issues, which are partially defined through concepts of rights, duties, and justice in every social setting, are essential for understanding the basis of any action. The essential insight offered by using the graph is that any decision or option is based on a prior definition of society that both includes and excludes people.

The graph can also be used as reminder that what people *say* about their motives and what they really *do* are rarely identical. In the real world, most motives are mixed and can be imagined as a range or a circle on the graph instead of a single point. Perhaps successful behavior *always* has multiple motives; it is therefore difficult to interpret after the fact *because it is meant to be that way.* People want their acts to be ambiguous and hard to pin down; they may want to conceal their motives even from themselves. To suppose that this complexity merely conceals or camouflages an underlying selfishness is therefore a basic misconception of reality. The fundamental ambiguity of behavior is quite real; it reflects a compromise between diverse social and temporal priorities.

This exercise with grids makes several points. The first is that motives are continuous variables, not types of behavior or types of people. Motives and choices are never as clearly defined as social theorists want them to be. Selfishness is always relative and may come in many distinct varieties. The second point is that we need to be more explicit when we relate motivations and decisions to the way those decisions are explained, rationalized, and debated. When people claim they are helping others or working for the good of the nation, we should always ask how their explanation is related to the real and expected consequences of their acts. The relationship between motives, actions, and explanation should be a central object in each empirical inquiry, rather than being assumed away or trapped in paradigmatic gridlock.

We can even use the sociotemporal grid to map the ideological traffic flow in economics and anthropology, by showing the assumptions that different

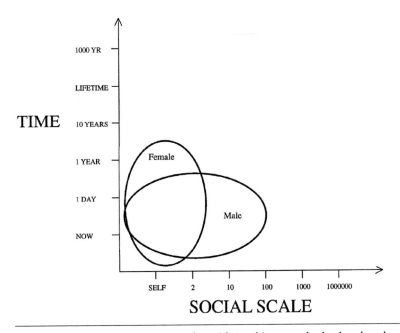

FIGURE 6.2   Social disputes on the grid. In this example, husband and wife disagree on the basis of a major household decision. He thinks the interests of a wider circle of kin should be included, while she is more concerned with the longer-term interests of a small nuclear group.

theorists make about human nature, as in Figure 6.3. Clearly, my own point of view is that the whole area should be considered in any economic theory and that our goals should be to figure out *why* people sometimes act selfishly and other times act "morally" or "altruistically." Economic anthropology, in my view, could then be profitably redefined as the study of the social and cultural basis of rationality and choice. In other words, rationality should be the subject, not the assumption, of economic anthropology.

Questioning human nature might have been a much better way to start our study of household energy consumption in Santa Cruz County. We could have begun by asking people to define the issues for themselves, in order to find out what kinds of social groups they included, how they saw the politics of decisions, and what kinds of time horizons they were using. Then we would have been in a position to see how the various actions people took—buying solar hot-water systems, doing nothing, putting on a sweater and turning down the thermostat—related to their motives, their resources, and their social positions. Ideally, we could then say when people were going to act on a short-time horizon for a small group or for the long term and the benefit of the planet. We knew these issues were important, just as we were aware of

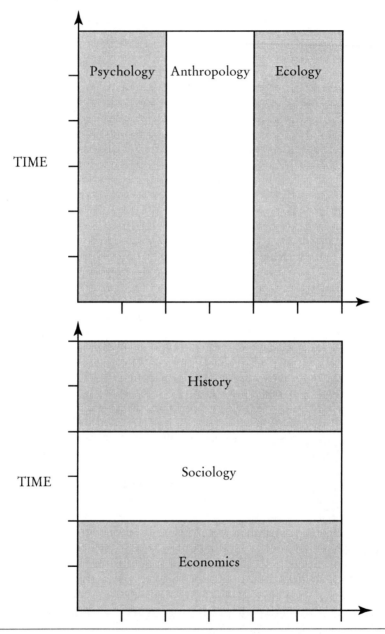

FIGURE 6.3 Mapping disciplines on the grid. The assumptions of different fields are mapped in two ways. Individual scholars could also be placed in the grid.

how the internal politics of families was key to the puzzle, but we were stuck with analytical tools that were based on too many assumptions. Economic anthropology benefits from the broadest possible questions, from the closest possible attention to many different kinds of empirical information.

Conclusions

When I used the first draft of this book in teaching my economic anthropology class at Indiana University, some students were puzzled by the way I ended the book. They said, "You never define economic anthropology!" I was puzzled. I thought I had spent the whole book defining economic anthropology. When we talked it over, though, I began to see why they wanted more resolution than I had offered in my first draft. So much of this book is critical of other people's work and deals with problems, inadequacies, and contradictions. After all this, what hope could I offer that economic anthropology was worth the effort?

Fortunately for my class, the second half of the semester was spent reading recent monographs and ethnographies written by economic anthropologists. It restored their feeling that economic anthropology was something worth doing. We read Daniel Miller's study of consumerism during and after the oil boom in Trinidad (1994), Mary Weismantel's beautiful book on food and household labor among Andean peasants (1988), Diane Wolf's on young women's lives in spinning mills on Java (1992), and Donald Attwood's about the sugar industry in India (1992). This was just a personal selection from the many excellent books we had to choose from. The students found them engrossing and sensitive ethnographies, engaged with problems they could relate to. How do farming families stay together and deal with poverty? Why do some people spend so much money on cars, drink, and partying? How can people organize together and struggle successfully against the rich and powerful? What happens to local cultures faced with global corporations, global telecommunications, and computers in the workplace? How does free trade connect a teenage factory worker in Bali to a mall rat in Ohio? Most of the key problems and issues in the world today are being addressed by economic anthropologists. The work is sophisticated but down-to-earth. The standard of writing is amazingly high. The scholarship is engaged with real people and draws lessons that have real uses, not just for thinking about a past world of tribes and villages but for thinking about a wired future where cyberspace rubs shoulders with millions of destitute ex-farmers. This is work that can really make a difference.

Reading what people actually do with their science is the real proof of its theory. In the light of what I have said in this book, I would argue that recent economic anthropology is powerful and important not because of any particular methodology or devotion to a particular model of human behavior.

Instead, what makes it work so well is that economic anthropologists are, for the most part, more open than other social scientists to *all three* paradigms. They are both eclectic and scientific in the very best sense of both words, willing to use many different tools and test them empirically through careful observation.

I would never claim that economic anthropology is the only science that questions human nature. Certainly sociobiology and human evolution have made some strong claims for understanding the biological basis of human behavior. But economic anthropology has a special place because it is at the very intersection of different philosophical traditions within social science. It has feet in all three camps; and if this sounds like an awkward and difficult position to be in, that is the way I mean it. Being in the middle can make you a target for everyone; without a single identity you may end up being nobody at all. Even so, the rewards may be worth the risks.

Notes

1. Some results of this project are in Wilk and Wilhite 1984 and 1985. For more recent anthropological work on energy use in the home, see Wilhite and Ling (1995), Kempton and Layne (1994), and Kempton, Fevermann, and McGarity (1992).

2. In practice, most anthropologists tend to gravitate toward particular kinds of behavior that are most appropriately understood with the tools they want to use. Therefore, if you have a cultural model of human nature, you are likely to be interested in symbolism, ritual, systems of meaning, and gift economies. Those who hold a social view of human behavior may be fascinated by kinship organization, production, and political change. Rational-choice theorists like market systems, trade and exchange, demography, or some variant of cultural ecology.

3. Richard Jenkins provides an admirably clear and critical discussion of Bourdieu's theory of practice (1992). This book will be an important guide for any student who sets out to struggle with Bourdieu's prose. Elements of practice theory are foreshadowed in Goodenough's critical discussion of social rules (1956) and in much of Barth's discussion of the pragmatic nature of social action (1959, 1967). A wonderful and readable book by political anthropologist Fred Bailey (1969) also anticipates much of practice theory.

4. Bourdieu's *Distinction* (1984) is perhaps his most sociological book. There he does attempt to measure various kinds of social and cultural capital. When I repeated his study in Belize, however, I found most of his measures depended on untested assumptions.

5. Parts of this discussion are taken from a previously published paper (Wilk 1993). It was originally developed for the particular demands of understanding household and family decisionmaking; here I am extending it to encompass all kinds of social behavior in a way that perhaps strains the original intent.

6. Some of my students have proposed that the time scale should be extended backward into the past. It is hard for me to imagine people making decisions in the present in order to maximize some form of well-being in the past. One of my classes argued that sometimes people choose an option for the future because they want to

affect the interpretation of a past event. They might be "good" and unselfish now, in the hope that people will forget past "bad" behavior, for example. This is an interesting point.

7. Again, students have suggested that there could be a negative side end of this scale. As I have sketched it, this scale includes only benefits. Some action is, of course, meant to cause harm. A negative social scale could indicate the size of the group that is hurt by a particular action.

Appendix:
Where to Look for More—
Finding Literature in
Economic Anthropology

Because economic anthropology is published in so many scattered places, students doing research projects often find it hard to start their search. Looking under "economic anthropology" in the average library catalog is likely to turn up only those few books that actually have "economic anthropology" somewhere in their title. This guide is designed to help students begin their searches for sources. It includes a listing of some of the basic books in the field and points to journals that should be searched. It also lists some of the standard textbooks and classic sources for understanding the history of economic anthropology.

Bibliographies

Periodically, people compile bibliographies of works in economic anthropology, but few are published. The best one that is widely available is long out of date, but it is excellent on the literature of the 1960s: H. T. Van Der Pas, *Economic Anthropology 1940–1972: An Annotated Bibliography* (Oosterhout, Netherlands: Anthropological Publications, 1973).

Check also into the *Social Science Citation Index* and the CD-ROM and on-line databases that are available in most libraries. I have found Carl/Uncover particularly useful, for it indexes about 5 million scholarly papers and magazine articles. Reading *Reviews in Anthropology* is an excellent way to keep up with current literature through comprehensive review articles, and the topical papers in *Annual Review of Anthropology* are usually very comprehensive and have extensive bibliographies. The most relevant older entries are William Roseberry's *Political Economy* in 1988 (vol. 17) and Stephen Gudeman's *Anthropological Economics: The Question of Distribution* in 1978 (vol. 7).

Periodicals

I advise students to begin their research by scanning through current journals, looking for a relevant article that will have an up-to-date bibliography. Papers in economic anthropology sometimes appear in the major anthropology journals, including *American Anthropologist, Current Anthropology, American Ethnologist, Ethnology,* and *Journal of Anthropological Research* (previously called the *Southwestern Journal of Anthropology*). Some of the most interesting articles can be found in *Man* (now called the *Journal of the Royal Anthropological Institute*), the *Journal of Peasant Studies, Human Organization,* and for a historical approach, *Comparative Studies in Society and History.* Marxist and critical economic sociology is published most often in *Economy and Society.* Regional and foreign journals should also be checked (I always look at the Scandinavian journals like *Ethnos* and *Folk*), and interesting work often turns up in development studies journals, too (e.g., *Journal of Developing Areas, Journal of Development Studies, Economic Development and Cultural Change*). There are several journals in other fields that publish papers that are useful to economic anthropologists: *Journal of Consumer Research* and *Journal of Economic History* are good examples. Particularly critical papers, often from a Marxian perspective, are published in *Dialectical Anthropology, Critique of Anthropology,* and *Rethinking Marxism.* I find much of the material published in *Gender and Society* and *Signs* to be highly relevant to economic anthropology as well.

Within economics itself there are many journals that publish orthodox neoclassical economics, much of which is incomprehensible to anthropologists. There are, however, many journals of "heterodox" economics that present alternatives that are of great interest to economic anthropology. A good starting point for this literature is *Review of Heterodox Economics,* which is advertised as a "New Publication for Marxist, Institutionalist, Feminist, Post-Keynesian, and Radical Economists." Other journals that have eclectic and interesting approaches to economics include *Capital and Class; Capitalism, Nature, Socialism; Competition and Change: The Journal of Global Business and Political Economy; Economic Geography; Economics and Philosophy; Economics and Politics; Economy and Society; Feminist Economics; Feminist Review; International Contributions to Labour Studies; Review of International Political Economy; International Journal of Political Economy; International Papers in Political Economy; International Review of Applied Economics; Journal of Economic Issues; Journal of Interdisciplinary Economics; Journal of Post-Keynesian Economics; Journal of World-Systems Research* (an electronic journal available at gopher://csf.colorado.edu/wsystems/journals/); *New Political Economy; Research in Political Economy; Review: Journal of the Fernand Braudel Center for the Study of Economics, Historical Systems, and Civilizations; Review of Political Economy; Review of Radical Political Economics; Review of Social Economy; Society and Space; Social Concept; Social Research; Studies in Political Economy; World Development* (extracted from Nilsson 1995).

There are two major publication series in economic anthropology. *Research in Economic Anthropology* (founded by George Dalton, now up to volume 20) is published annually by JAI Press, edited by Barry Isaacs at the University of Cincinnati. The topical coverage tends to be wide and uneven, but the papers are often highly original, and there is a good mix of ethnography and archaeology. The other series is the annual publication of selected papers from the *Society for Economic Anthropology* meetings; these each have a different editor and title and are published by University Press of America. Recent titles include Alice Littlefield and Hill Gates's *Marxist Approaches in Economic Anthropology,* Henry Rutz and Benjamin Orlove's *The Social Economy of*

Consumption, Stuart Plattner's *Markets and Marketing,* and Morgan Maclachlan's *Household Economies and Their Transformations.*

Newsletters can keep you informed of current publications and meetings as well as provide information on scholarships, prizes, and publication opportunities. The newsletter of the Society for Economic Anthropology is basic; student membership in the society costs only $5 a year. It announces the annual Harold Schneider Student Paper Competition, with a prize of $150. Other useful newsletters are published by the Society for the Advancement of Socio-Economics, the Culture and Agriculture group, the Peasant Studies Association, and the Institute for Development Anthropology.

Anthologies

Books of collected papers are often very uneven, and they may be highly technical and specialized. Sometimes it is hard to tell what the papers are really about from the title of the book. But good collections can give an excellent portrait of the "state of the art" at a particular time. Here is a list of general collections of papers on Economic Anthropology that have appeared over the years.

Bohannon, Paul, and George Dalton, eds. 1965. *Markets in Africa: Eight Subsistence Economies in Transition.* Garden City, NY: Anchor Books.

Clammer, John. 1978. *The New Economic Anthropology.* New York: St. Martin's Press.

———. 1987. *Beyond the New Economic Anthropology.* New York: St. Martin's Press.

Dalton, George. 1971. *Economic Development and Social Change.* New York: Natural History Press.

Firth, Raymond. 1967. *Themes in Economic Anthropology.* London: Tavistock.

Firth, Raymond, and Basil S. Yamey. 1964. *Capital, Savings, and Credit in Peasant Societies.* Chicago: Aldine.

Halperin, Rhoda, and James Dow. 1977. *Peasant Livelihood.* New York: St. Martin's Press.

Helms, June. 1965. *Essays in Economic Anthropology.* American Ethnological Society Monographs. Seattle: University of Washington.

LeClair, Edward, and Harold Schneider. 1968. *Economic Anthropology: Readings in Theory and Analysis.* New York: Holt, Rinehart and Winston.

Plattner, Stuart. 1989. *Economic Anthropology.* Stanford: Stanford University Press.

Seddon, David. 1978. *Relations of Production: Marxist Approaches to Economic Anthropology.* London: Cassirer.

Three collections focus particularly on the research methods used in economic anthropology. They are particularly useful for graduate students thinking about fieldwork.

◢◣

Bardhan, Pranad. 1989. *Conversations Between Economists and Anthropologists: Methodological Issues in Measuring Economic Change in Rural India.* Delhi: Oxford University Press.

Gregory, Chris, and J. C. Altman. 1989. *Observing the Economy.* London: Routledge.

Plattner, Stuart. 1975. *Formal Methods in Economic Anthropology.* American Anthropological Association, Monograph 4. Washington, DC.

◢◣

Most recent anthologies in economic anthropology tend to be more specialized in topic, reflecting the diversification of the field. Most of these are excellent places to begin the research for a paper.

◢◣

Appadurai, Arjun. 1986. *The Social Life of Things.* Cambridge: Cambridge University Press.

Barlett, Peggy. 1980. *Agricultural Decision Making.* New York: Academic Press.

Bloch, Maurice. 1975. *Marxist Analyses and Social Anthropology.* London: Tavistock.

Chibnik, Michael. 1987. *Farm Work and Field-Work.* Ithaca: Cornell University Press.

Durrenberger, E. Paul. 1984. *Chayanov, Peasants, and Economic Anthropology.* New York: Academic Press.

Dwyer, Daisy, and Judith Bruce. 1988. *A Home Divided: Women and Income in the Third World.* Stanford: Stanford University Press.

Goody, Esther. 1982. *From Craft to Industry.* Cambridge: Cambridge University Press.

Harris, John. 1982. *Rural Development: Theories of Peasant Economy and Agrarian Change.* London: Hutchinson University Press.

Humphrey, Caroline, and Stephen Hugh-Jones. 1992. *Barter, Exchange, and Value: An Anthropological Approach.* New York: Cambridge University Press.

Leacock, Eleanor, and Helen Safa. 1986. *Women's Work.* Boston: Bergin and Garvey.

Littlefield, Alice, and Hill Gates. 1991. *Marxist Approaches in Economic Anthropology.* Lanham, MD: University Press of America.

McCay, Bonnie, and James Acheson. 1987. *The Question of the Commons.* Tucson: University of Arizona Press.

Moock, Joyce L. 1986. *Understanding Africa's Rural Households and Farming Systems.* Boulder: Westview.

Parry, J., and M. Bloch. 1989. *Money and the Morality of Exchange.* Cambridge: Cambridge University Press.

Salisbury, Richard, and Elisabeth Tooker. 1984. *Affluence and Cultural Survival.* Washington, DC: American Ethnological Society.

Sherry, John. 1995. *Contemporary Marketing and Consumer Behavior: An Anthropological Sourcebook.* Thousand Oaks, CA: Sage Publications.

Smith, Carol. 1976. *Regional Analysis*, vols. 1 and 2. New York: Academic Press.
Wilk, Richard. 1989. *The Household Economy.* Boulder: Westview Press.

Texts

Textbooks in economic anthropology have never been abundant, and they tend to go out of print quickly, so most are no longer available for class use. The definition of a textbook is vague and debatable; in this list I include those that might be suitable as supplementary texts, as well as those explicitly designed for classroom use. The older ones are included for historical purposes only.

Dalton, George. 1967. *Tribal and Peasant Economies.* New York: Natural History Press.
Davis, John. 1992. *Exchange.* Buckingham, England. Open University Press.
Ellis, Frank. 1988. *Peasant Economics.* Cambridge: Cambridge University Press.
Forde, C. Daryll. 1934. *Habitat, Economy, and Society.* New York: E. P. Dutton.
Godelier, Maurice. 1988. *The Mental and the Material.* London: Verso.
Gudeman, Stephen. 1986. *Economics as Culture: Models and Metaphors of Livelihood.* London: Routledge and Kegan Paul.
Halperin, Rhoda. 1988. *Economies Across Cultures.* New York: St. Martin's Press.
Herskovitz, Melville. 1940. *The Economic Life of Primitive Peoples.* New York: Knopf.
_____. 1952. *Economic Anthropology.* New York: Knopf.
Hodges, Richard. 1988. *Primitive and Peasant Markets.* Oxford: Basil Blackwell.
Nash, Manning. 1966. *Primitive and Peasant Economic Systems.* San Francisco: Chandler.
Polanyi, Karl, Conrad Arensberg, and Harry Pearson, eds. 1957. *Trade and Market in the Early Empires.* New York: Free Press.
Sahlins, Marshall. 1968. *Tribesmen.* Englewood Cliffs, NJ: Prentice-Hall.
_____. 1972. *Stone Age Economics.* Chicago: Aldine.
Schneider, Harold. 1974. *Economic Man.* New York: Free Press; reprint, Sheffield, 1989.
Spicer, Edward, ed. 1952. *Human Problems in Technological Change.* New York: Russell Sage.
Wolf, Eric. 1966. *Peasants.* Englewood Cliffs, NJ: Prentice-Hall.

Selected Monographs in Economic Anthropology

I expect that most professors who use this book in an economic anthropology course will want students to read at least one or two ethnographies that take an economic approach or that discuss the economic life of a particular society in some detail. Although there are hundreds of suitable books and new ones appear all the time, I provide a short list of classic books here that I have used successfully, among them those my students have nominated to a "greatest hits" list. I am sure we have missed many great books, but this can at least serve as a starting point. I include books that I do not particularly agree with but that make interesting arguments that provoke good critical thinking. There is some bias toward Latin America, which is my own area of expertise.

∿

Attwood, Donald. 1992. *Raising Cane: The Political Economy of Sugar in Western India.* Boulder: Westview Press.

Barlett, Peggy. 1993. *American Dreams, Rural Realities: Family Farms in Crisis.* Chapel Hill: University of North Carolina Press.

Berry, Sara. 1975. *Cocoa, Custom, and Socio-Economic Change in Rural Western Nigeria.* Oxford: Clarendon Press.

Bohannon, Paul, and Laura Bohannon. 1968. *Tiv Economy.* Evanston, Illinois: Northwestern University Press.

Cancian, Frank. 1992. *The Decline of Community in Zinacantan: Economy, Public Life, and Social Stratification, 1960–1987.* Stanford: Stanford University Press.

Clark, Gracia. 1994. *Onions Are My Husband: Survival and Accumulation by West African Market Women.* Chicago: University of Chicago Press.

Colson, Elizabeth, and Thayer Scudder. 1988. *For Prayer and Profit: The Ritual, Economic, and Social Importance of Beer in Gwembe District, Zambia, 1950–1982.* Stanford: Stanford University Press.

Ehlers, Tracy. 1990. *Silent Looms: Women and Production in a Guatemalan Town.* Boulder: Westview Press.

Firth, Raymond. 1939. *Primitive Polynesian Economy.* London: Routledge and Kegan Paul.

Freeman, James. 1986. *Scarcity and Opportunity in an Indian Village.* Prospect Heights, IL: Waveland Press.

Fricke, Thomas. 1986. *Himalayan Households: Tamang Demography and Domestic Processes.* Ann Arbor, MI: UMI Research.

Greenberg, James. 1981. *Santiago's Sword: Chatino Peasant Religion and Economics.* Berkeley: University of California Press.

Gudeman, Stephen. 1978. *The Demise of a Rural Economy.* London: Routledge and Kegan Paul.

Johnson, Allen. 1971. *Sharecroppers of the Sertao.* Stanford: Stanford University Press.

Miller, Tom. 1986. *The Panama Hat Trail.* New York: Vintage Books.

Nakane, Chie. 1967. *Kinship and Economic Organization in Rural Japan.* London: Athlone Press.

Nash, June. 1979. *We Eat the Mines and the Mines Eat Us.* New York: Columbia University Press.

Netting, Robert M. 1981. *Balancing on an Alp.* Cambridge University Press: Cambridge.

Oboler, Regina. 1985. *Women, Power, and Economic Change: The Nandi of Kenya.* Stanford: Stanford University Press.

Parkin, David. 1994. *Palms, Wine, and Witnesses: Public Spirit and Private Gain in an African Farming Community.* Prospect Heights, IL: Waveland Press.

Pelto, Perti J. 1973. *The Snowmobile Revolution: Technology and Social Change in the Arctic.* Menlo Park, CA: Cummings.

Rosman, Abraham, and Paula Rubel. 1986. *Feasting with Mine Enemy: Rank and Exchange Among Northwest Coast Societies.* Prospect Heights, IL: Waveland Press.

Salisbury, Richard. 1970. *Vunamami: Economic Transformations in a Traditional Society.* Berkeley: University of California Press.

Schneider, Harold. 1970. *The Wahi Wanyaturu: Economics in an African Society.* Chicago: Aldine.

Sheridan, Thomas. 1988. *Where the Dove Calls: The Political Ecology of a Peasant Community in Northwestern Mexico.* Tucson: University of Arizona Press.

Shipton, Parker. 1989. *Bitter Money.* Washington, D.C.: American Anthropological Association.

Strathern, Andrew. 1971. *The Rope of Moka.* Cambridge: Cambridge University Press.

Weiner, Annette. 1976. *Women of Value, Men of Renown.* Austin: University of Texas Press.

Weismantel, Mary. 1988. *Food, Gender, and Poverty in the Ecuadorian Andes.* Philadelphia: University of Pennsylvania Press.

Wolf, Diane. 1992. Factory Daughters. Berkeley: University of California Press.

Bibliography

Acheson, James, ed. 1994. *Anthropology and Institutional Economics.* Lanham, MD: University Press of America.

Albelda, Randy, Christopher Gunn, and William Waller, eds. 1987. *Alternatives to Economic Orthodoxy.* Armonk, NY: M. E. Sharpe.

Althusser, Louis, and Etienne Balibar. 1970. *Reading Capital.* New York: Pantheon.

Amin, Samir. 1976. *Unequal Development.* New York: Monthly Review Press.

Annis, Sheldon. 1987. *God and Production in a Guatemalan Town.* Austin: University of Texas Press.

Arndt, H. W. 1987. *Economic Development: The History of an Idea.* Chicago: University of Chicago Press.

Attwood, Donald. 1992. *Raising Cane: The Political Economy of Sugar in Western India.* Boulder: Westview Press.

Bailey, F. G. 1969. *Stratagems and Spoils.* New York: Schocken.

Baran, Paul. 1957. *The Political Economy of Growth.* New York: Monthly Review Press.

Barlett, Peggy. 1982. *Agricultural Choice and Change.* New Brunswick, NJ: Rutgers University Press.

Barth, Frederik. 1959. Segmentary Opposition and the Theory of Games: A Study of Pathan Organization. *Journal of the Royal Anthropological Institute* 89:5–21.

_____. 1967. On the Study of Social Change. *American Anthropologist* 69:661–669.

Barth, Frederik, ed. 1963. *The Role of the Entrepreneur in Social Change in Norway.* Oslo: Norwegian University Press.

Basch, Linda, Nina Schiller, and Cristina Blanc. 1994. *Nations Unbound.* Langhorne, PA: Gordon and Breach.

Battaglia, Deborah. 1992. The Body in the Gift. *American Ethnologist* 19(1):3–18.

Belk, Russell. 1983. Worldly Possessions: Issues and Criticisms. *Advances in Consumer Research* 10:514–519.

Bendix, Reinhard. 1960. *Max Weber: An Intellectual Portrait.* Garden City, NY: Doubleday.

Benedict, Ruth. 1932. Configurations of Culture in North America. *American Anthropologist* 34:1–27.

_____. [1934] 1949. *Patterns of Culture.* New York: New American Library.

Beneria, Lourdes, and Marta Roldan. 1987. *The Crossroads of Class and Gender: Industrial Homework, Subcontracting, and Household Dynamics in Mexico City.* Chicago: University of Chicago Press.

Bernal, Victoria. 1994. Peasants, Capitalism, and (Ir)rationality. *American Ethnologist* 21(4):792–810.

Binford, Leigh, and Scott Cook. 1991. Petty Production in Third World Capitalism Today. In Alice Littlefield and Hill Gates, eds., *Marxist Approaches in Economic Anthropology* (Lanham, MD: University Press of America), 65–90.

Black, Jan. 1991. *Development in Theory and Practice.* Boulder: Westview.

Blau, Francine, and Marianne Ferber. 1986. *The Economics of Women, Men, and Work.* Englewood Cliffs, NJ: Prentice-Hall.

Bloch, Maurice, ed. 1975. *Marxist Analyses and Social Anthropology.* London: Tavistock.

Boas, Franz. 1940. *Race, Language, and Culture.* New York: Macmillan.

_____. [1932] 1962. *Anthropology and Modern Life.* New York: W. W. Norton.

_____. [1911] 1963. *The Mind of Primitive Man.* Glencoe: Free Press.

Bohannon, Paul, and Laura Bohannon. 1968. *Tiv Economy.* Evanston, IL: Northwestern University Press.

Bohannon, Paul, and George Dalton, eds. 1965. *Markets in Africa: Eight Subsistence Economies in Transition.* Garden City, NY: Anchor Books.

Booth, William. 1993. *Households: On the Moral Architecture of the Economy.* Ithaca: Cornell University Press.

Bourdieu, Pierre. 1977. *Outline of a Theory of Practice.* Cambridge: Cambridge University Press.

_____. 1984. *Distinction: A Social Critique of the Judgment of Taste.* Cambridge: Harvard University Press.

_____. 1988. *Homo Academicus.* Oxford: Polity Press.

_____. 1990. *The Logic of Practice.* Oxford: Polity Press.

Braudel, Fernand. 1982. *The Wheels of Commerce.* New York: Harper and Row.

Buchler, Ira, and Henry Nutini. 1969. *Game Theory in the Behavioral Sciences.* Pittsburgh: University of Pittsburgh Press.

Burling, Robbins. 1962. Maximization Theory and the Study of Economic Anthropology. *American Anthropologist* 64:802–821. Also in Edward LeClair and Harold Schneider, eds., *Economic Anthropology: Readings in Theory and Analysis* (New York: Holt, Rinehart and Winston, 1968).

Cancian, Frank. 1966. Maximization as Norm, Strategy and Theory: A Comment on Programmatic Statements in Economic Anthropology. *American Anthropologist* 68:465–470. Also in Edward LeClair and Harold Schneider, eds., *Economic Anthropology: Readings in Theory and Analysis* (New York: Holt, Rinehart and Winston, 1968).

_____. 1979. *The Innovator's Situation.* Stanford: Stanford University Press.

_____. 1989. Economic Behavior in Peasant Communities. In Stuart Plattner, ed., *Economic Anthropology* (Stanford: Stanford University Press), 127–170.

Cardoso, Fernando, and Enzo Faletto. 1979. *Dependency and Development in Latin America.* Berkeley: University of California Press.

Carrier, James. 1992. Occidentalism: The World Turned Upside Down. *American Ethnologist* 19:195–212.

Cashdan, Elizabeth, ed. 1990. *Risk and Uncertainty in Tribal and Peasant Economies.* Boulder: Westview Press.

Chase-Dunn, Christopher, and Tom Hall. 1991. *Core/Periphery Relations in Precapitalist Worlds.* Boulder: Westview Press.

Chayanov, A. V. 1986. *The Theory of the Peasant Economy,* edited by Daniel Thorner, Basile Kerblay, and R.E.F. Smith. Madison: University of Wisconsin Press.

Chibnik, Michael. 1987. The Economic Effects of Household Demography: A Cross-Cultural Assessment of Chayanov's Theory. In Morgan Mclachlan, ed., *Household Economies and Their Transformations* (Lanham, MD: University Press of America), 74–106.

Clark, Gracia, ed. 1988. *Traders Versus the State.* Boulder: Westview.

Cohen, Marjorie. 1988. *Women's Work, Markets, and Economic Development in Nineteenth-Century Ontario.* Toronto: University of Toronto Press.

Comaroff, Jean. 1985. *Body of Power, Spirit of Resistance.* Chicago: University of Chicago Press.

Comaroff, Jean, and John Comaroff. 1986. Christianity and Colonialism in South Africa. *American Ethnologist* 13(1):1–22.

Cook, Scott. 1966. The Obsolete "Anti-Market" Mentality: A Critique of the Substantive Approach to Economic Anthropology. *American Anthropologist* 68:323–345. Also in Edward LeClair and Harold Schneider, eds. *Economic Anthropology: Readings in Theory and Analysis* (New York: Holt, Rinehart and Winston, 1968).

_____. 1969. The Anti-Market Mentality Re-Examined: A Further Critique of the Substantive Approach to Economic Anthropology. *Southwestern Journal of Anthropology* 25:378–406.

_____. 1973. Economic Anthropology: Problems in Theory, Method, and Analysis. In John Honigman, ed., *Handbook of Social and Cultural Anthropology* (Chicago: Rand McNally), 795–860.

_____. 1984. *Peasant Capitalist Industry: Piecework and Enterprise in Southern Mexican Brickyards.* Lanham, MD: University Press of America.

Coontz, Stephanie. 1992. *The Way We Never Were: American Families and the Nostalgia Trap.* New York: Basic Books.

Coupland, Douglas. 1991. *Generation X.* New York: St. Martin's Press.

Dalton, George. 1969. Theoretical Issues in Economic Anthropology. *Current Anthropology* 10(1):63–102.

_____. 1971. *Economic Anthropology and Development.* New York: Basic Books.

Dalton, George, and Jasper Köcke. 1983. The Work of the Polanyi Group: Past, Present, and Future. In Sutti Ortiz, ed., *Economic Anthropology: Topics and Theories* (Lanham, MD: University Press of America), 21–50.

Davenport, William. 1960. Jamaican Fishing: A Game Theory Analysis. In *Papers on Caribbean Anthropology* (New Haven: Yale University Publications in Anthropology, nos. 57–64), 3–11.

De Janvry, Alain. 1981. *The Agrarian Question and Reformism in Latin America.* Baltimore: Johns Hopkins University Press.

De Waal Malefijt, Annemarie. 1974. *Images of Man.* New York: Knopf.

Deere, Carmen. 1990. *Household and Class Relations: Peasants and Landlords in Northern Peru.* Berkeley: University of California Press.

Donham, Donald. 1990. *History, Power, Ideology: Central Issues in Marxism and Anthropology.* Cambridge: Cambridge University Press.

Douglas, Mary. 1954. The Lele of the Kasai. In C. Daryll Forde, ed., *African Worlds* (London: Oxford University Press).

_____. 1966. *Purity and Danger.* London: Routledge and Kegan Paul.

_____. 1985. *Risk Acceptability According to the Social Sciences.* New York: Russell Sage Foundation.

Downey, Ezekial. 1987. The Futility of Marginal Utility. In Randy Albelda, Christopher Gunn, and William Waller, eds., *Alternatives to Economic Orthodoxy* (Armonk, NY: M. E. Sharpe), 48–59.

Dumont, Louis. 1977. *From Mandeville to Marx.* Chicago: University of Chicago Press.

Durkheim, Emile. [1893] 1933. *The Division of Labor in Society.* Translated by George Simpson. New York: Macmillan.

_____. [1895] 1938. *The Rules of the Sociological Method.* Translated by Sarah Solvay and John Mueller. Chicago: University of Chicago Press.

_____. [1912] 1947. *The Elementary Forms of Religious Life.* New York: Free Press.

_____. [1911] 1953. Value Judgments and Judgments of Reality. In *Sociology and Philosophy.* Translated by D. F. Pocock. Glencoe, IL: Free Press.

_____. [1899] 1958. *Professional Ethics and Civic Morals.* Glencoe. IL: Free Press.

_____. [1925] 1961. *Moral Education: A Study in the Theory and Application of the Sociology of Education.* Glencoe, IL: Free Press.

_____. [1897] 1963. *Suicide: A Study in Sociology.* Translated by John Spaulding and George Simpson. Glencoe, IL: Free Press.

_____. [1898] 1969. Individualism and the Intellectuals. Translated by Steven Lukes. *Political Studies* 17:14–30.

Durrenberger, E. Paul, ed. 1984. *Chayanov, Peasants, and Economic Anthropology.* Orlando, FL: Academic Press.

Durrenberger, E. P., and Nicola Tannenbaum. 1990. *Analytical Perspectives on Shan Agriculture and Village Economics.* New Haven: Yale University Southeast Asia Studies.

Dwyer, Daisy, and Judith Bruce, eds. 1988. *A Home Divided: Women and Income in the Third World.* Stanford: Stanford University Press.

Eatwell, John, Murray Milgate, and Peter Newman, eds. 1990. *Marxian Economics.* The New Palgrave Series. New York: W. W. Norton.

Ellis, Frank. 1988. *Peasant Economics: Farm Households and Agrarian Development.* Cambridge: Cambridge University Press.

Elster, Jon. 1985. *Making Sense of Marx.* New York: Cambridge University Press.

_____. 1986. *An Introduction to Karl Marx.* New York: Cambridge University Press.

_____. 1989. *Nuts and Bolts for the Social Sciences.* Cambridge: Cambridge University Press.

_____. 1990. When Rationality Fails. In Karen Cook and Margaret Levi, eds., *The Limits of Rationality* (Chicago: University of Chicago Press), 19–46.

Engels, Frederick. [1884] 1942. *The Origin of the Family, Private Property, and the State.* New York: International Publishers.

England, Paula. 1993. The Separative Self: Androcentric Bias in Neoclassical Assumptions. In Marianne Ferber and Julie Nelson, eds., *Beyond Economic Man: Feminist Theory and Economics* (Chicago: University of Chicago Press), 37–53.

Ensminger, Jean. 1992. *Making a Market: The Institutional Transformation of an African Society.* Cambridge: Cambridge University Press.

Etzioni, Amitai. 1988. *The Moral Dimension: Toward a New Economics.* London: Collier Macmillan.

Evans-Pritchard, E. E. 1969. *The Nuer.* New York: Oxford University Press.

Fallows, James. 1993. How the World Works. *Atlantic Monthly* 272(6):60–87.

Feathersone, Michael, ed. 1990. *Global Culture: Nationalism, Globalization, and Modernity.* London: Sage Publications.

Ferber, Marianne, and Julie Nelson, eds. 1993. *Beyond Economic Man: Feminist Theory and Economics.* Chicago: University of Chicago Press.

Firth, Raymond. 1967. *Themes in Economic Anthropology.* London: Tavistock.

Firth, Raymond, ed. 1957. *Man and Culture: An Evaluation of the Work of Bronislaw Malinowski.* London: Routledge and Kegan Paul.

Folbre, Nancy. 1993. Socialism, Feminist and Scientific. In Marianne Ferber and Julie Nelson, eds., *Beyond Economic Man: Feminist Theory and Economics* (Chicago: University of Chicago Press), 94–110.

_____. 1994. *Who Pays for the Kids? Gender and the Structure of Constraint.* London: Routledge.

Forde, C. Daryll. 1934. *Habitat, Economy, and Society.* New York: E. P. Dutton.

Fortes, Meyer. 1969. *Kinship and the Social Order: The Legacy of Lewis Henry Morgan.* Chicago: Aldine.

Fortes, Meyer, and E. E. Evans-Pritchard. [1940] 1962. *African Political Systems.* London: Oxford University Press.

Foster, George. 1969. *Applied Anthropology.* Boston: Little, Brown and Company.

Foster, Robert J. 1991. Making National Cultures in the Global Ecumene. *Annual Review of Anthropology* 20:235–260.

Foster-Carter, Aiden. 1978. Can We Articulate "Articulation"? In John Clammer, ed., *The New Economic Anthropology* (New York: St. Martin's Press), 210–249.

Foucault, Michel. 1970. *The Order of Things.* New York: Vintage Books.

_____. 1980. *Power/Knowledge. Selected Interviews and Other Writings.* Edited by Colin Gordon. New York: Pantheon.

Frank, Andre Gunder. 1967. *Capitalism and Underdevelopment in Latin America.* New York: Monthly Review Press.

_____. 1969. *Latin America: Underdevelopment or Revolution.* New York: Monthly Review Press.

Fricke, Thomas. 1986. *Himalayan Households: Tamang Demography and Domestic Processes.* Ann Arbor, MI: UMI Research.

Friedman, Jonathan. 1975. Tribes, States, and Transformations. In Maurice Bloch, ed., *Marxist Analyses and Social Anthropology* (London: Tavistock), 161–202.

_____. 1992. The Past in the Future: History and the Politics of Identity. *American Anthropologist* 94(4):837–859.

_____. 1995. *Cultural Identity and Global Process.* London: Sage Publications.

Friedman, Jonathan, ed. 1994. *Consumption and Identity*. Chur, Switzerland: Harwood.

Geertz, Clifford. 1956. *The Development of the Javanese Economy: A Sociocultural Approach*. Cambridge: MIT Center for International Studies.

_____. 1957. Ritual and Social Change: A Javanese Example. *American Anthropologist* 59:32–54. Reprinted in Geertz, *The Interpretation of Cultures* (New York: Basic Books, 1973).

_____. 1963. *Peddlers and Princes: Social Development and Economic Change in Two Indonesian Towns*. Chicago: University of Chicago Press.

_____. 1973. *The Interpretation of Cultures*. New York: Basic Books.

_____. 1984. Culture and Social Change: The Indonesian Case. *Man.* 19:511–532.

Georgescu-Roegen, Nicholas. 1954. Choice, Expectations and Measurability. *Quarterly Journal of Economics* 69:503–539.

Gereffi, Gary, and Miguel Korzeniewicz, eds. 1994. *Commodity Chains and Global Capitalism*. Westport, CT: Praeger.

Giddens, Anthony. 1979. *Central Problems in Social Theory: Action, Structure, and Contradiction in Social Analysis*. Berkeley: University of California Press.

_____. 1984. *The Constitution of Society*. Cambridge: Polity Press.

Gladwin, Christina. 1979. Cognitive Strategies and Adoption Decisions: A Case Study of an Agronomic Recommendation. *Economic Development and Cultural Change* 28:155–174.

Glance, Natalie, and Benjamin Huberman. 1994. The Dynamics of Social Dilemmas. *Scientific American* 270(3):76–81.

Godelier, Maurice. [1965] 1972. The Object and Method of Economic Anthropology. In Maurice Godelier, *Rationality and Irrationality in Economics* (New York: Monthly Review Press), 249–319.

_____. 1977. "Salt Money" and the Circulation of Commodities Among the Baruya of New Guinea. In Maurice Godelier, *Perspectives in Marxist Anthropology* (Cambridge University Press), 127–151.

_____. 1986. *The Making of Great Men*. Cambridge: Cambridge University Press.

_____. 1988. *The Mental and the Material*. Verso: London.

Godelier, Maurice, ed. 1977. *Perspectives in Marxist Anthropology*. Cambridge: Cambridge University Press.

Goldschmidt, Walter. 1969. Game Theory, Cultural Values, and Brideprice in Africa. In Ira Buchler and Henry Nutini, eds., *Game Theory in the Behavioral Sciences* (Pittsburgh: University of Pittsburgh Press), 61–74.

Goodenough, Ward. 1956. Residence Rules. *Southwestern Journal of Anthropology* 12:22–37.

Goodfellow, David Martin. 1939. *Principles of Economic Sociology: The Economics of Primitive Life as Illustrated from the Bantu Peoples of South and East Africa*. London: G. Routledge and Sons.

Goodnow, Jacqueline, and Jennifer Bowes. 1994. *Men, Women, and Household Work*. Melbourne: Oxford University Press.

Goody, Jack. 1986. *The Logic of Writing and the Organization of Society*. New York: Cambridge University Press.

Grannovetter, Mark. 1985. Economic Action and Social Structure: The Problem of Embeddedness. *American Journal of Sociology* 91:481–510.

Gray, Marion. 1994. The Household as the Economy: The Norms of Gender and Class in Seventeenth-Century German Economic Thought. Indiana University Economic History Workshop, paper 9394–13, Bloomington.

Greenhalgh, Susan. 1990. Towards a Political Economy of Fertility. *Population and Development Review* 16(1):85–105.

_____. 1994. De-Orientalizing the Chinese Family Firm. *American Ethnologist* 21(4):746–775.

Gregory, C. A. 1982. *Gifts and Commodities.* London: Academic Press.

Gudeman, Stephen. 1978. Anthropological Economics: The Question of Distribution. *Annual Review of Anthropology* 7:347–377.

_____. 1986. *Economics as Culture: Models and Metaphors of Livelihood.* London: Routledge and Kegan Paul.

Gudeman, Stephen, and Alberto Rivera. 1990. *Conversations in Colombia: The Domestic Economy in Work and Text.* Cambridge: Cambridge University Press.

Habermas, Jürgen. 1979. *Communication and the Evolution of Society.* Boston: Beacon.

Halperin, Rhoda. 1988. *Economies Across Cultures.* London: Macmillan.

_____. 1989. Ecological vs. Economic Anthropology. In Barry Isaac, ed., *Research in Economic Anthropology* (Greenwich, CT: JAI Press), 13–41.

_____. 1994. *Cultural Economies Past and Present.* Austin: University of Texas Press.

Halperin, Rhoda, and James Dow, eds. 1977. *Peasant Livelihood.* New York: St. Martin's Press.

Hannerz, Ulf. 1990. Cosmopolitans and Locals in World Culture. *Theory, Culture and Society* 7:237–251.

_____. 1992. *Cultural Complexity.* New York: Columbia University Press.

Hardin, Garrett. 1968. The Tragedy of the Commons. *Science* 162:1243–1248.

Harris, Marvin. 1966. The Cultural Ecology of India's Sacred Cattle. *Current Anthropology* 7:51–66.

_____. 1968. *The Rise of Anthropological Theory.* New York: Thomas Crowell.

Harrison, Lawrence. 1985. *Underdevelopment Is a State of Mind.* Lanham, MD: Madison Books.

Hart, Keith. 1983. The Contribution of Marxism to Economic Anthropology. In Sutti Ortiz, ed., *Economic Anthropology: Topics and Theories* (Lanham, MD: University Press of America), 105–146.

Hatch, Elvin. 1973. *Theories of Man and Culture.* New York: Columbia University Press.

_____. 1983. *Culture and Morality: The Relativity of Values in Anthropology.* New York: Columbia University Press.

Heath, Anthony. 1976. *Rational Choice and Social Exchange: A Critique of Exchange Theory.* Cambridge: Cambridge University Press.

Heilbroner, Robert. 1991. Economic Predictions. *New Yorker* July 8, 70–77.

Held, David, and John B. Thompson, eds. 1989. *Social Theory of Modern Societies: Anthony Giddens and His Critics.* Cambridge: Cambridge University Press.

Herskovitz, Melville. 1941. Economics and Anthropology: A Rejoinder. *Journal of Political Economy* 49:269–278. Reprinted in Melville Herskovitz, *Economic Anthropology* (New York: Knopf, 1952).

_____. 1952. *Economic Anthropology.* New York: Knopf.

Hill, Polly. 1982. *Dry Grain Farming Families.* Cambridge: Cambridge University Press.

Hobart, Mark, ed. 1993. *An Anthropological Critique of Development: The Growth of Ignorance.* London: Routledge.

Hobbes, Thomas. 1991. *Leviathan.* Edited by Richard Tuck. Cambridge: Cambridge University Press.

Homans, George. 1958. Social Behavior as Exchange. *American Journal of Sociology* 63:597–606.

Horgan, John. 1995. The New Social Darwinists. *Scientific American* 273(4):174–181.

Houthakker, Hendrik S. 1950. Revealed Preference and the Utility Function. *Economica* 17:33–45.

Hume, David. 1964. The Natural History of Religion. In Richard Woldheim, ed., *Hume on Religion* (New York: World Publishing Company), 31–98.

Ingold, Tim. 1992. Culture and the Perception of the Environment. In Elisabeth Croll and David Parkin, eds., *Bush Base: Forest Farm. Culture, Environment, and Development* (London: Routledge), 39–56.

Isaac, Barry. 1993. Retrospective on the Formalist-Substantivist Debate. In Barry Isaac, ed., *Research in Economic Anthropology* (Greenwich, CT.: JAI Press), 213–234.

Jackson, Michael. 1989. *Paths Toward a Clearing: Radical Empiricism and Ethnographic Inquiry.* Bloomington: Indiana University Press.

Jenkins, Richard. 1992. *Pierre Bourdieu.* London: Routledge.

Jennings, Ann. 1993. Public or Private? Institutional Economics and Feminism. In Marianne Ferber and Julie Nelson, eds., *Beyond Economic Man: Feminist Theory and Economics* (Chicago: University of Chicago Press), 111–130.

Jessop, R. 1990. Mode of Production. In John Eatwell, Murray Milgate, and Peter Newman, eds., *Marxian Economics.* The New Palgrave Series (New York: W. W. Norton), 289–296.

Johnson, Allen. 1971. *Sharecroppers of the Sertao.* Stanford: Stanford University Press.

Kahn, Joel. 1981. Marxist Anthropology and Segmentary Societies: A Review of the Literature. In Joel Kahn and Josep Llobera, eds., *The Anthropology of Pre-Capitalist Societies* (Atlantic Highlands, NJ: Humanities Press), 57–88.

_____. 1990. Towards a History of the Critique of Economism: The Nineteenth-Century German Origins of the Ethnographer's Dilemma. *Man* 25:230–249.

_____. 1995. *Culture, Multiculture, Postculture.* London: Sage Publications.

Kamarck, Andrew. 1983. *Economics and the Real World.* Philadelphia: University of Pennsylvania Press.

Kamenka, Eugene, ed. 1983. *The Portable Karl Marx.* New York: Penguin.

Kaplan, David, and Robert Manners. 1972. *Culture Theory.* Englewood Cliffs, NJ: Prentice-Hall.

Käsler, Dirk. 1988. *Max Weber: An Introduction to His Life and Work.* Cambridge: Polity Press.

Kempton, Willett, and Linda Layne. 1994. The Consumer's Energy Analysis Environment. *Energy Policy* 10:657–665.

Kempton, Willett, Daniel Feuermann, and Arthur McGarity. 1992. "I Always Turn It on Super": User Decisions About When and How to Operate Room Air Conditioners. *Energy and Buildings* 18:177–191.

Knight, Frank. 1941. Anthropology and Economics. *Journal of Political Economy* 49:247–268. Reprinted in Melville Herskovitz, *Economic Anthropology* (New York: Knopf, 1952.)

Kolata, Gina. 1986. Asking Impossible Questions About the Economy and Getting Impossible Answers. *Science* 234:545–546.

Kuttner, Robert. 1985. The Poverty of Economics. *Atlantic Monthly,* February 1985, 74–84. Also in Randy Albeda, Christopher Gunn, and William Waller, eds., *Alternatives to Economic Orthodoxy* (Armonk, NY: M. E. Sharpe, 1987).

Lakoff, George. 1987. *Women, Fire, and Dangerous Things: What Categories Reveal About the Mind.* Chicago: University of Chicago Press.

Lakoff, George, and Mark Johnson. 1980. *Metaphors We Live By.* Chicago: University of Chicago Press.

Landsburg, Steven. 1993. *The Armchair Economist: Economics and Everyday Life.* Glencoe, IL: Free Press.

Latin American Finance Survey: Save, Amigo, Save. 1995. *Economist,* December 9, 1995, 15–18.

Latour, Bruno. 1993. *We Have Never Been Modern.* Cambridge: Harvard University Press.

Leach, Edmund. 1957. The Epistemological Background of Malinowski's Empiricism. In Raymond Firth, ed., *Man and Culture: An Evaluation of the Work of Bronislaw Malinowski* (London: Routledge and Kegan Paul), 119–138.

LeClair, Edward. 1962. Economic Theory and Economic Anthropology. *American Anthropologist* 64:1179–1203. Also in Edward LeClair and Harold Schneider, eds., *Economic Anthropology: Readings in Theory and Analysis* (New York: Holt, Rinehart and Winston, 1968).

LeClair, Edward, and Harold Schneider. 1968. Introduction: The Development of Economic Anthropology. In Edward LeClair and Harold Schneider, eds., *Economic Anthropology* (New York: Holt, Rinehart and Winston), 1–13.

Lehman, D., ed. 1982. *Ecology and Exchange in the Andes.* Cambridge: Cambridge University Press.

Leontieff, Wassily. 1982. Academic Economics. *Science* 217:104–107.

Lévy-Bruhl, Lucien. [1923] 1966. *Primitive Mentality.* Translated by Lilian A. Clare. Boston: Beacon Press.

Lewin, Roger. 1987. *Bones of Contention.* New York: Simon and Schuster.

Littlefield, Alice, and Hill Gates. 1991. *Marxist Approaches in Economic Anthropology.* Lanham, MD: University Press of America.

Loucky, James. 1979. Production and Patterning of Social Relations and Values in Two Guatemalan Villages. *American Ethnologist* 6:702–723.

Lukes, Steven. 1973. *Emile Durkheim: His Life and Work.* New York: Harper and Row.

Lurie, Alison. 1981. *The Language of Clothes.* New York: Random House.

Lutz, Mark, and Kenneth Lux. 1988. *Humanistic Economics.* New York: Bootstrap Press.

Lyotard, Jean-François. 1993. *Libidinal Economy.* Bloomington: Indiana University Press.

Machina, Mark. 1990. Choice Under Uncertainty: Problems Solved and Unsolved. In Karen Cook and Margaret Levi, eds., *The Limits of Rationality* (Chicago: University of Chicago Press), 90–132.

Malinowski, Bronislaw. 1921. The Primitive Economics of the Trobriand Islanders. *Economic Journal* 31:1–16.

_____. 1931. Culture. *Encyclopedia of the Social Sciences.* 4:621–646.

_____. 1944. *A Scientific Theory of Culture.* Chapel Hill: University of North Carolina Press.

_____. [1922] 1961. *Argonauts of the Western Pacific.* New York: Dutton.

_____. 1967. *A Diary in the Strict Sense of the Term.* New York: Harcourt Brace.

Mandel, Ernest. 1990. Karl Marx. In John Eatwell, Murray Milgate, and Peter Newman, eds., *Marxian Economics.* The New Palgrave Series (New York: W. W. Norton), 1–38.

Mansbridge, Jane. 1990. The Rise and Fall of Self-Interest in the Explanation of Political Life. In Jane Mansbridge, ed., *Beyond Self-Interest* (Chicago: University of Chicago Press), 3–22.

Margolis, Howard. 1982. *Selfishness, Altruism, and Rationality.* Cambridge: Cambridge University Press.

Martin, Emily. 1987. *The Woman in the Body: A Cultural Analysis of Reproduction.* Boston: Beacon Press.

Marx, Karl. 1904. *The Critique of Political Economy.* Translated by I. N. Stone. Chicago: International Library.

_____. 1975. *Early Writings: Karl Marx.* Translated by Martin Nicolaus. New York: Vintage.

_____. 1983. *The Portable Karl Marx.* Edited by Eugene Kamenka. New York: Viking Penguin.

Mayhew, Anne. 1980. Atomistic and Cultural Analyses in Economic Anthropology: An Old Argument Repeated. In John Adams, ed., *Institutional Economics: Contributions to the Development of Holistic Economics* (Boston: Martinus Nijhoff). 72–81.

McCloskey, Donald. 1985. *The Rhetoric of Economics.* Madison: University of Wisconsin Press.

_____. 1990. *If You're So Smart: The Narrative of Economic Expertise.* Chicago: University of Chicago Press.

_____. 1993. Some Consequences of a Conjective Economics. In Marianne Ferber and Julie Nelson, eds., *Beyond Economic Man: Feminist Theory and Economics* (Chicago: University of Chicago Press), 69–93.

_____. 1994. Bourgeois Virtue. *American Scholar* 63(2): 177–192.

McGraw, Thomas. 1992. The Trouble with Adam Smith. *American Scholar* 61:353–373.

Mead, Margaret, ed. 1955. *Cultural Patterns and Technical Change.* New York: UNESCO.

Medick, Hans, and David Sabean. 1984. Interest and Emotion in Family and Kinship Studies: A Critique of Social History and Anthropology. In Hans Medick and David Sabean, eds., *Interest and Emotion* (Cambridge: Cambridge University Press), 9–27.

Meillassoux, Claude. 1972. From Reproduction to Production: A Marxist Approach to Economic Anthropology. *Economy and Society* 1 (1):93–105.

_____. 1981. *Maidens, Meal, and Money.* Cambridge: Cambridge University Press.

Miller, Daniel. 1994. *Modernity: An Ethnographic Approach.* London: Berg Publishers.

Mintz, Sidney. 1974. *Caribbean Transformations.* Chicago: Aldine.

_____. 1985. *Sweetness and Power: The Place of Sugar in Modern History.* New York: Penguin.

Moberg, Mark. 1992. *Citrus, Strategy, and Class: The Politics of Development in Southern Belize.* Iowa City: University of Iowa Press.

Molyneux, Maxine. 1977. Androcentrism in Marxist Anthropology. *Critique of Anthropology* 3:55–81.

Moore, Omar Khayam. 1957. Divination: A New Perspective. *American Anthropologist* 59:316–327.

Morley, David, and Kevin Robins. 1995. *Spaces of Identity: Global Media, Electronic Landscapes, and Cultural Boundaries.* London: Routledge.

Murdock, George P. 1961. *Outline of Cultural Materials.* New Haven: Human Relations Area Files, Inc.

Murphy, Robert F., and Julian H. Steward. 1956. Tappers and Trappers: Parallel Process in Acculturation. *Economic Development and Social Change* 4:335–353.

Myers, Milton. 1983. *The Soul of Modern Economic Man.* Chicago: University of Chicago Press.

Myrdal, Gunnar. 1957. *Rich Lands and Poor.* New York: Harpers.

Nash, June. 1979. *We Eat the Mines and the Mines Eat Us.* New York: Columbia University Press.

Nash, Manning. 1958. *Machine Age Maya.* Glencoe, IL: Free Press. (1967 edition by University of Chicago Press.)

Nelson, Julie. 1992. Gender, Metaphor, and the Definition of Economics. *Economics and Philosophy* 8(1):103–125.

Netting, Robert. 1965. A Trial Model of Cultural Ecology. *Anthropological Quarterly* 38:81–96.

_____. 1977. *Cultural Ecology.* Menlo Park, CA: Cummings Publishing Company (1986 edition by Waveland Press.)

_____. 1993. *Smallholders, Householders: Farm Families and the Ecology of Intensive, Sustainable Agriculture.* Stanford: Stanford University Press.

Nilsson, Eric. 1995. "Thanks, Journal Info." E-mail posted to listserve group femecon-l@bucknell.edu, on June 26, 1995. Author's address is enilsson@wiley.csusb.edu.

Nisbet, Robert. 1966. *The Sociological Tradition.* New York: Basic Books.

North, Douglass. 1990. *Institutions, Institutional Change, and Economic Performance.* Cambridge: Cambridge University Press.

_____. 1993. Economic Performance Through Time. Nobel Prize lecture, circulated as manuscript.

Olmstead, Jennifer. 1995. "Economics Jokes." E-mail posted to listserve group femecon-l@bucknell.edu, on February 13, 1995. Forwarder's address is olmstead-j@crob.flint.umich.edu.

Ong, Aihwa. 1987. *Spirits of Resistance and Capitalist Discipline: Factory Women in Malaysia.* Albany: State University of New York Press.

Ong, Walter J. 1982. *Orality and Literacy: The Technologizing of the Word.* New York: Methuen.

Oppong, C., ed. 1983. *Female and Male in West Africa.* London: George Allen and Unwin.

Orlove, Benjamin. 1980. Ecological Anthropology. *Annual Review of Anthropology* 9:235–275.

Ortner, Sherry. 1984. Theory in Anthropology Since the Sixties. *Comparative Studies in Society and History* 26:126–166.

Parsons, Talcott. 1963. Introduction to *Max Weber, The Sociology of Religion.* Translated by Ephraim Fischoff. Boston: Beacon Press.

Peacock, James. 1986. *The Anthropological Lens.* Cambridge: Cambridge University Press.

Plattner, Stuart, ed. 1975. *Formal Methods in Economic Anthropology.* Washington, DC: American Anthropological Association, Monograph 4.

Polanyi, Karl. 1944. *The Great Transformation.* New York: Rinehart.

_____. 1957. The Economy as Instituted Process. In Karl Polanyi, Conrad Arensberg, and Harry Pearson, eds., *Trade and Market in the Early Empires* (New York: Free Press), 243–270.

Polanyi, Karl, Conrad Arensburg, and Harry Pearson, eds. 1957. *Trade and Market in the Early Empires.* New York: Free Press.

Popkin, Samuel. 1979. *The Rational Peasant: The Political Economy of Rural Society in Vietnam.* Berkeley: University of California Press.

Pospisil, Leopold. 1963. *Kapauku Papuan Economy.* New Haven: Yale University Publications in Anthropology, No. 67.

Prattis, J. Iain. 1973. Competing Paradigms and False Polemics in Economic Anthropology. *Anthropological Quarterly* 46(4):278–296.

_____. 1978. Alternative Views of Economy in Economic Anthropology. In John Clammer, ed., *The New Economic Anthropology* (New York: St. Martin's Press).

Prattis, J. Iain, ed. 1973. The State of the Arts in Economic Anthropology: Reflections on a Theme. Special issue of *Canadian Review of Sociology and Anthropology* 10(3).

Priban, Karl. 1983. *A History of Economic Reasoning.* Baltimore: Johns Hopkins University Press.

Quinn, Naomi. 1978. Do Mfantse Fish Sellers Estimate Probabilities in Their Heads? *American Ethnologist* 5:206–226.

Radcliffe-Brown, A. R. [1922] 1948. *The Andaman Islanders.* New York: Free Press.

_____. 1965. *Structure and Function in Primitive Societies.* New York: Free Press.

Rappoport, Roy. 1968. *Pigs for the Ancestors.* New Haven: Yale University Press.

Rebel, Hermann. 1991. Reimagining the *Oikos:* Austrian Cameralism in Its Social Formation. In Jay O'Brien and William Roseberry, eds., *Golden Ages, Dark Ages:*

Imagining the Past in Anthropology and History (Berkeley: University of California Press). 48–80.

Redclift, Nanneke, and Enzo Mingione, eds. 1985. *Beyond Employment: Household, Gender, and Subsistence.* New York: Basil Blackwell.

Redfield, Robert. 1947. The Folk Society. *American Journal of Sociology* 52:292–308.

Rey, Pierre-Philippe. 1975. The Lineage Mode of Production. *Critique of Anthropology* 3:27–79.

Richman, Michael. 1982. *Reading Georges Bataille: Beyond the Gift.* Baltimore: Johns Hopkins University Press.

Rius. 1976. *Marx for Beginners.* New York: Pantheon.

Robben, Antonius. 1989. *Sons of the Sea Goddess: Economic Practice and Discursive Conflict in Brazil.* New York: Columbia University Press.

Rocha, Jorge. n.d. Rationality, Culture, and Decision Making. Paper, Department of Anthropology, University of Florida, Gainesville.

Rodney, Walter. 1972. *How Europe Underdeveloped Africa.* London: Bogle-L'Ouverture.

Rosaldo, Michelle. 1980a. The Use and Abuse of Anthropology. *Signs* 5:391–417.

_____. 1980b. *Knowledge and Power: Ilongot Notions of Self and Social Life.* New York: Cambridge University Press.

Rosaldo, Renato. 1993. *Culture and Truth.* Boston: Beacon Press.

Roseberry, William. 1988. Political Economy. *Annual Review of Anthropology* 17:161–185.

_____. 1989. *Anthropologies and Histories.* New Brunswick: Rutgers University Press.

Rosenberg, Alexander. 1992. *Economics—Mathematical Politics or Science of Diminishing Returns?* Chicago: University of Chicago Press.

Rostow, Walt W. 1960. *The Stages of Economic Growth.* Cambridge: Cambridge University Press.

Rothstein, Frances, and Michael Blim, eds. 1991. *Anthropology and the Global Factory: Studies of the New Industrialization in the Late Twentieth Century.* New York: Bergin and Garvey.

Sahlins, Marshall. 1957. Land Use and the Extended Family in Moala, Fiji. *American Anthropologist* 59:449–462.

_____. 1960. Political Power and the Economy in Primitive Society. In Gertrude Dole and Robert Carneiro, eds., *Essays in the Science of Culture in Honor of Leslie White* (New York: Thomas Crowell Company), 390–415.

_____. 1965. On the Sociology of Primitive Exchange. In Michael Banton, ed., *The Relevance of Models for Social Anthropology,* ASA Monograph No. 1 (London: Tavistock), 139–227.

_____. 1972. *Stone Age Economics.* Chicago: Aldine.

_____. 1976. *Culture and Practical Reason.* Chicago: University of Chicago Press.

Sahlins, Marshall, and Elman Service. 1960. *Evolution and Culture.* Ann Arbor: University of Michigan Press.

Said, Edward. 1978. *Orientalism.* Harmondsworth, England: Penguin.

Salaff, Janet. 1981. *Working Daughters of Hong Kong: Filial Piety or Power in the Family?* Cambridge: Cambridge University Press.

Salisbury, Richard. 1973. Economic Anthropology. *Annual Review of Anthropology* 2:85–94.

Samuelson, Paul. 1948. *Economics.* New York: McGraw-Hill.

Schiebinger, Londa. 1993. *Nature's Body: Gender in the Making of Modern Science.* Boston: Beacon Press.

Schiffer, Michael B. 1976. *Behavioral Archaeology.* New York: Academic Press.

Schneider, Harold. 1974. *Economic Man.* New York: Free Press.

Scott, James. 1976. *The Moral Economy of the Peasant: Rebellion and Subsistence in Southeast Asia.* New Haven: Yale University Press.

———. 1985. *Weapons of the Weak: Everyday Forms of Peasant Resistance.* New Haven: Yale University Press.

———. 1990. *Domination and the Arts of Resistance.* New Haven: Yale University Press.

Sen, Amartya. 1990. Rational Fools: A Critique of the Behavioral Foundations of Economic Theory. In Jane Mansbridge, ed., *Beyond Self-Interest* (Chicago: University of Chicago Press), 25–43.

Shanin, Teodor, ed. 1990. *Defining Peasants: Essays Concerning Rural Societies.* Oxford: Basil Blackwell.

Sherratt, Andrew. 1995. Reviving the Grand Narrative: Archaeology and Long-Term Change. *Journal of European Archaeology* 3(2):1–32.

Shipton, Parker. 1989. *Bitter Money.* Washington, DC: American Anthropological Association.

Simon, Herbert. 1957. A Behavioral Model of Rational Choice. In Herbert Simon, ed., *Models of Man: Rational and Social* (New York: John Wiley), 99–118.

———. 1987. Rationality in Psychology and Economics. In Robin Hogarth and Melvin Reder, eds., *Rational Choice* (Chicago: University of Chicago Press), 25–40.

Smith, Adam. [1776] 1937. *The Wealth of Nations.* Edited by Edwin Cannan. New York: Modern Library.

———. [1759] 1966. *The Theory of Moral Sentiments.* New York: Augustus M. Kelley.

Smith, Carol. 1983. Regional Analysis in World-System Perspective: A Critique of Three Structural Theories of Uneven Development. In Sutti Ortiz, ed., *Economic Anthropology: Topics and Theories* (Lanham, MD: University Press of America), 307–360.

———. 1984. Forms of Production in Practice: Fresh Approaches to Simple Commodity Production. *Journal of Peasant Studies* 11(4):201–221.

Spicer, Edward, ed. 1952. *Human Problems in Technological Change: A Casebook.* New York: Russell Sage.

Spiro, Melford. 1966. Buddhism and Economic Action in Burma. *American Anthropologist* 68:1163–1173.

Steward, Julian. 1955. *Theory of Culture Change.* Urbana: University of Illinois Press.

Steward, Julian, Robert Manners, Eric Wolf, Elena Padilla, Sidney Mintz, and Raymond Scheele. 1956. *The People of Puerto Rico.* Urbana: University of Illinois Press.

Stigler, George, and Gary S. Becker. 1977. De Gustibus Non Est Disputandum. *American Economic Review* 67(2):76–90.

Stocking, George. 1968. *Race, Culture, and Evolution.* New York: Free Press.

Strathern, Marilyn. 1988. *The Gender of the Gift.* Berkeley: University of California Press.

Summers, Lawrence. 1995. Ten Lessons to Learn. *Economist,* December 23, 1995, 46–54.

Tambiah, Stanley. 1990. *Magic, Science, Religion, and the Scope of Rationality.* Cambridge: Cambridge University Press.

Tax, Sol. 1953. *Penny Capitalism: A Guatemalan Indian Economy.* Smithsonian Institution, Institute of Social Anthropology, Publication 16. Washington, DC.

Terray, Emmanuel. 1972. *Marxism and "Primitive" Societies.* Monthly Review Press: New York.

Tomlinson, John. 1991. *Cultural Imperialism.* Baltimore: Johns Hopkins University Press.

Trouillot, Michel-Rolph. 1988. *Peasants and Capital: Dominica in the World Economy.* Baltimore: Johns Hopkins University Press.

Turner, Victor. 1964. Symbols in Ndembu Ritual. In Max Gluckman, ed., *Closed Systems and Open Minds* (Chicago: Aldine), 15–31.

Tversky, Amos. 1969. Intransitivity of Preferences. *Psychological Review* 76:105–110.

_____. 1981. The Framing of Decisions and the Rationality of Choice. *Science* 211:453–458.

Van Der Pas, H. T. 1973. *Economic Anthropology, 1940–1972: An Annotated Bibliography.* Oosterhout, Netherlands: Anthropological Publications.

Voget, Fred. 1975. *A History of Ethnology.* New York: Holt, Rinehart and Winston.

Wagley, Charles. 1941. *Economics of a Guatemalan Village.* Memoirs of the American Anthropological Association, Number 58. Menasha, Wisconsin.

Waller, William, and Ann Jennings. 1991. A Feminist Institutionalist Reconsideration of Karl Polanyi. *Journal of Economic Issues* 25(2):485–497.

Wallerstein, Immanuel. 1976. *The Modern World System.* New York: Academic Press.

Waud, Roger. 1983. *Microeconomics,* 2d ed. New York: Harper and Row.

Weber, Max. 1946. *Max Weber: Essays in Sociology.* Edited by H. H. Gerth and C. W. Mills. New York: Oxford University Press.

_____. 1958. *The Protestant Ethic and the Spirit of Capitalism.* Translated by Talcott Parsons. New York: Charles Scribner.

_____. 1968. *Economy and Society.* New York: Bedminster Press.

Weiner, Annette B. 1992. *Inalienable Possessions: The Paradox of Keeping-While-Giving.* Berkeley: University of California Press.

Weismantel, Mary. 1988. *Food, Gender, and Poverty in the Ecuadorian Andes.* Philadelphia: University of Pennsylvania Press.

Werbner, Pnina. 1989. *The Migration Process: Capital, Gifts, and Offerings Among British Pakistanis.* Oxford: Berg Publishers.

_____. 1990. Economic Rationality and Hierarchical Gift Economies: Value and Ranking Among British Pakistanis. *Man* 25:266–285.

Weyant, Robert G. 1973. Helvetius and Jefferson: Studies on Human Nature and Government in the Eighteenth Century. *Journal of the History of the Behavioral Sciences* 9:29–41.

White, Jenny. 1994. *Money Makes Us Relatives.* Austin: University of Texas Press.

Whorf, Benajamin. 1956. *Language, Thought, and Reality: Selected Writings of Benjamin Lee Whorf.* Edited by John Carroll. New York: John Wiley.

Wilhite, Harold, and Rich Ling. 1995. Measured Energy Savings from a More Informative Energy Bill. *Energy and Buildings* 22:145–155.

Williams, Raymond. 1980. *Problems in Materialism and Culture.* London: Verso.

_____. 1985. *Keywords: A Vocabulary of Culture and Society.* New York: Oxford University Press.

Wilk, Richard. 1985. The Ancient Maya and the Political Present. *Journal of Anthropological Research* 41(3):307–326.

_____. 1991. *Household Ecology.* Tucson: University of Arizona Press.

_____. 1993. Towards a Unified Anthropological Theory of Decision Making. In Barry Isaac, ed., *Research in Economic Anthropology* (Greenwich, CT: JAI Press), 191–212.

_____. 1995. Learning to Be Local in Belize: Global Systems of Common Difference. In Daniel Miller, ed., *Worlds Apart: Modernity Through the Prism of the Local* (London: Routledge), 110–134.

Wilk, Richard, ed. 1989. *The Household Economy: Reconsidering the Domestic Mode of Production.* Boulder: Westview Press.

Wilk, Richard, and Harold Wilhite. 1984. Household Energy Decision Making in Santa Cruz County, California. In Bonnie Morrison and Willett Kempton, eds., *Families and Energy: Coping with Uncertainty* (East Lansing: Michigan State University, College of Human Ecology), 449–459.

_____. 1985. Why Don't People Weatherstrip Their Homes? An Ethnographic Solution. *Energy* 10(5):621–631.

Wilson, Edward O. 1980. *Sociobiology.* Cambridge: Belknap Press of Harvard University.

Winokur, Jon, ed. 1987. *The Portable Curmudgeon.* New York: NAL Books.

Wolf, Diane. 1992. *Factory Daughters.* Berkeley: University of California Press.

Wolf, Eric. 1966. *Peasants.* Englewood Cliffs, NJ: Prentice Hall

_____. 1969. *Peasant Wars of the Twentieth Century.* New York: Harper and Row.

_____. 1982. *Europe and the People Without History.* Berkeley: University of California Press.

Wolf, Margery. 1986. *Revolution Postponed: Women in Contemporary China.* Stanford: Stanford University Press.

About the Book and Author

This text is the first synthesis of modern economic anthropology for advanced un-
dergraduates and beginning graduate students. It goes to the heart of an emerging
subdiscipline and identifies the fundamental practical and theoretical problems that
give economic anthropology its unique strengths and vision.

Tracing the history of the dialogue between anthropology and economics, Richard
Wilk identifies three recurring arguments about human nature and the moral basis of
human action. Modern economic anthropology, he says, emerges from the controversies and tensions between these radically different propositions about the essence
of humanity. More than any other anthropological subdiscipline, economic anthropology constantly questions and debates the practical motives of people as they go
about their daily lives.

Wilk moves economic anthropology beyond the narrow concerns of earlier debates and places the field directly at the center of current issues in the social sciences.
He focuses on the unique strengths of economic anthropology as a meeting place for
symbolic and materialist approaches and as a means of understanding humanity as
both practical and cultural. In doing so he argues for the wider relevance of economic
anthropology to applied anthropology and identifies other avenues for interaction
with economics, sociology, and other social and natural sciences.

This short text is designed to be used with monographs or collections as a core
reading for economic anthropology courses. It will complement other texts in general sociocultural anthropology courses and in graduate core courses, and it will be a
useful supplement in teaching ecological and applied anthropology.

Richard R. Wilk is professor of anthropology at Indiana University.

Index